We never played frisbee and I am excited for those cookies. Good luck with everything, your a very talented & special individual
—Travis Allen

Good luck!
Alex S...

Good luck in the future Kaitlin Callahan

Mandy,
Best of luck with everything. Even though I know you don't need it.
Congratulations,
Eric Pacifici

Thanks so much for all the tours this year! :) You did a great job! Good luck in the future!
Ashley Wetterodt

♡ —David Topping

Congrats + good luck with everything!
~Geena~

Mandy,
Congratulations♡! I hope you fulfill all of your future dreams! God Bless
♡ Amanda Jandahl

Good Luck
with everything!
—Katie Stubler

Can we flute jam sometime? Please & thanks
—Kristina

Congrats!
Kallista~

Good Luck!
+ congrats.
Angela

Good luck w/ everything hope all goes well. B

Hey! Good

Bree

Congrats!
Good Luck with your future —Kristen Logan

Brown and Golden Memories

Western Michigan University's First Century

This painting of Dwight Waldo hangs in the Waldo Library and was restored by Mike McNun in May of 1990.

Brown and Golden Memories

Western Michigan University's First Century

By Larry B. Massie

WESTERN MICHIGAN UNIVERSITY

Centennial
1903-2003 Celebration

Western Michigan University

Kalamazoo, Michigan

2003

Brown and Golden Memories
Western Michigan University's First Century
By Larry B. Massie

Graphic design by Tammy M. Boneburg, Office of University Relations, Western Michigan University
Photo Direction: Larry B. Massie and Tammy M. Boneburg
Production by David H. Smith, Shannon Sovia and Kristy Feldpausch
Edited by Maria A. Perez-Stable
Proofreading by Jessica English, Ruth Heinig, Cheryl Roland and Tonya Hernandez

Western Michigan University
Office of University Relations
1903 W Michigan Ave
Kalamazoo MI 49008
Phone: (269) 387-8400
Fax: (269) 387-8422

Printed in the United States of America
ISBN 1-58044-078-9
First Printing   5,000, hard cover

Dedication

To the strivers, who rose above
their economic birthrights
to win education at Western,
and then the world was theirs

Table of Contents

Foreword

Centenarians can appear wobbly and weak, but as Western Michigan University celebrates its 100th birthday, it is vigorous and energetic as never before. The signs of its health can be seen and felt all across campus: unprecedented enrollment levels, an engaged and capable faculty and staff, and a beautiful, vastly expanded campus.

In all its constant progress, the university has deliberately built on the strengths of its past. It has carefully preserved its tradition of teaching its students well and with dedication while adding, in recent decades, a strong research orientation. It lovingly maintains the campus that many alumni remember from thirty or fifty years ago, but it also added to the historic buildings many modern research and teaching facilities. It made great efforts to beautify the entire campus, creating a place where teachers and learners enjoy coming to work. And the school has succeeded in keeping strong the bonds that tie its many graduates to their alma mater and to the happily remembered days of their student years in Kalamazoo.

Western Michigan University means many things to many people. For our alumni there are the affectionate memories of the friends of their youth, perhaps of meeting one's spouse; of special professors and staff members who left a mark; of sports triumphs; of the long-gone Knollwood Tavern; of preparation for life and profession; of passing exams; and finally, of the glorious moment of commencement. For faculty and staff there are the myriad recollections of our students—bright ones, dear ones, troubled ones—and of our colleagues—brilliant ones, beloved ones, irksome ones— with whom we spent our rich professional lives. And all who are part of the century-long history of WMU have seen it in happy and sad days: going through years of expansion and recession, seeing its members go to and return from wars, or watching both angry student protests and happy student reunions.

Larry Massie, the eminent Michigan historian, has given us this informative, colorful history of our institution. It is a most readable, sweeping account of our past, that every Bronco—past and present—will want to own. It is chockfull of fascinating facts and certain to induce nostalgia among us older ones.

As I read the book, I let pass before my inner eyes the Western presidents, all but two of whom I knew personally; the many students I have taught and counseled on this campus; the touchingly loyal alumni I met all over the country; the untold donors and friends who so generously supported us; the superb faculty and staff who built this university and made it great. All of them I remember with gratitude and the utmost fondness. Their prized contributions and achievements are chronicled and celebrated in this wonderful book.

Actor Tim Allen received an honorary doctor of fine arts degree as well as the Distinguished Alumni Award from President Haenicke in June of 1998.

Diether H. Haenicke
WMU President 1985-1998

Preface

Near the foot of Oakland Drive, at the intersection of Eddie's Lane (named for a beloved campus bus driver) rests a 32-ton granite and gneiss monolith. Eons before, a mile-high glacier had scooped that big rock from the far north, dropping it near Cooper. As a youth, Dwight Waldo had clambered over the boulder. As a man guiding Western through its fledgling decades, Waldo had repeatedly expressed a desire that the stone be moved to campus. In 1944, five years after Waldo's ashes had been laid to rest in the cornerstone of Western's original structure, now known as East Hall, the alumni club funded trucking of Waldo's rock to the site where once stood the antebellum Eames Mill, The Playhouse of fond memories to generations of Western thespians. The alumni dedicated the boulder as a permanent memorial to Waldo and as a "mark of loyalty" to the college. How many of the thousands of motorists who stream by each day know the story of Waldo's big rock?

Sangren, Seibert, Hoekje, McCracken, Miller—names enshrined in brick and mortar once were flesh and blood—Dunbar, Knauss, Siedschlag, Sprau, Kohrman. How many of the students passing through those buildings know of the sacrifice, dedication, loyalty and skill of those Western legends?

Yes, Western has a proud heritage and it is a story worth the knowing. Colorful traditions and vibrant memories crowd its century-long annals, a tapestry of cupola kisses and campus schools, trolley rides and daisy chains, homecoming bonfires and hoe-down days, sock-hops and J-hops, freshman beanies and Arbor Day outings, Hilltoppers and Valleyites.

I often think of the wonderful scholar-teachers who helped mold my mind, taught me to think better, evaluate sources and communicate as I pursued three degrees from Western in the 1970s—Ernst Breisach, Al Castel, Alan Brown, Lew Carlson, Peter Schmitt, John Houdek, Dale Pattison, Paul Maier, Nick Hamner, Graham Hawks, Ross Gregory, Wayne Mann, Tom Straw, Bob Sundick and Ed Heinig, to name just a few. And after they taught me, they became my friends.

Armed with my WMU education, I entered my chosen field and in the process frequently rubbed elbows with graduates of more prestigious institutions. Well, I remain proud of

Larry Massie's daughters Maureen (on right) and Autumn make themselves comfortable on President Waldo's favorite boulder.

the university education I received at Western and am convinced that past and future graduates of Western need take a back seat to those of no other school in the nation.

It is my hope that the pages of this book will help alumni, students, faculty, staff and the Kalamazoo community gain an enhanced appreciation and sense of pride for Western Michigan University's first century of quality, accomplishments and heritage.

I am deeply indebted to many others who assisted in the preparation of this book. I often found myself walking in the footprints of James Knauss in his two histories of Western, Leo Stine in *Western—A Twentieth Century History* and Avis Sebaly's fine dissertation written in 1950. I am thankful for the work done by Hal L. Ray and Thomas C. Slaughter in their two histories of Western athletics. Of particular value was the major collection of oral histories housed in the University Archives which Alan Brown, Lew Carlson, Tom Coyne and others had the foresight to record in preparation for this book.

This history would not have been possible without the overwhelming support of Sharon Carlson, director of the WMU Archives and Regional History Collections, and her helpful staff. Alan Brown, John Houdek, Charles Heller, Sharon Carlson, Tom Coyne, Ruth Heinig, Cheryl Roland, Diether Haenicke and Jamie Jeremy read all or parts of my manuscript and made valuable suggestions. However, I take full responsibility for any errors or misconceptions that remain.

My special thanks go to those who entrusted me with this important project: the Ad Hoc Centennial Committee, Ed and Ruth Heinig, Matt Kurz and his staff, Sue Beougher, Jessica English, Jeanne Baron, Cheryl Roland, Dave Smith, and especially Tammy Boneburg. Last but not least, I thank my wife and workmate, Priscilla, who put up with me as I again faced the travail of the blank page.

Larry B. Massie
Allegan Forest, Michigan

Chapter 1

The View From Prospect Hill

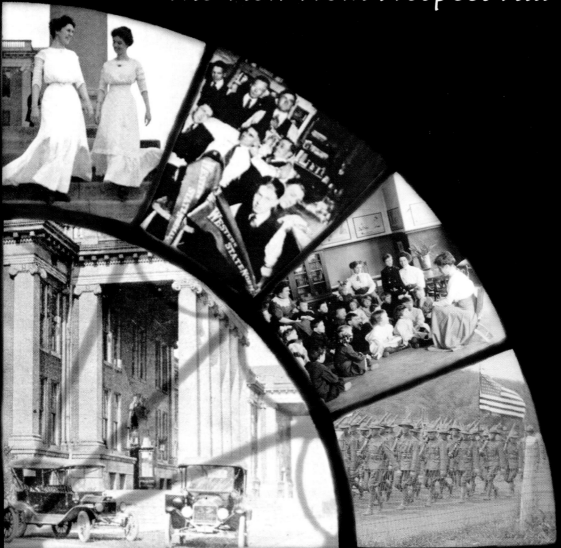

Old Henry Vandercook posed proud as a peacock for the portrait to hang in the lobby of the men's dormitory the college named in his honor in 1940. Thirty-five years before, at the dedication of the original structure on the campus, now known as East Hall, "The Father of Western" had delivered a stirring blow-by-blow account of his fight to ram through the state legislature the bill that created the school. Understandably, during that speech Vandercook had failed to mention that he originally advocated the site of the normal be Grand Rapids, the city that had elected him state representative in 1900 and 1902, and where he had resided since 1891, plying his twin trades of tombstone manufacturer and lawyer.

This turn-of-the-century postcard pictures Ramona Park in Grand Rapids.

Grand Rapids might indeed have won the hotly contested campaign in 1903, which pitted 28 Michigan communities eager to secure the new teacher training institution known as a normal. That is, had that city not offered as the site a tract adjacent to the Ramona Amusement Park, which lured recreationists to pitch pennies, toss darts, hurl baseballs for prizes and enjoy other "games of chance." Worse yet, the legislators learned the park featured "girlie shows" to entice straw-hatted oglers for a glimpse of "stockinged ankles." The Ramona Park vicinity, where the morals of young school teachers risked becoming tainted, was clearly not acceptable.

This portrait of Henry Vandercook, "Father of Western," hung in Vandercook Hall for decades.

Kalamazoo, however, had come up with no less than 24 sites for the new normal, and the tract atop the steep ridge known as Prospect Hill with its existing educational heritage seemed destined. Anson Van Buren, a student attending the University of Michigan branch in Kalamazoo's Bronson Park in 1843, remembered Prospect Hill as his "Acropolis." He and fellow students strolled its wooded heights during leisure hours, conversing of their futures following graduation, practicing Greek and Roman orations and picnicking beneath the great burr-oaks that crowned its summit.

The park-like hill remained a favorite place for contemplation, picnics and celebrations throughout the nineteenth century. In 1855, Schoolcraft resident A.S. Dyckman recorded in his diary that on August 1, Kalamazoo's black citizens gathered atop the hill for a "great celebration of the emancipation of the West Indies." They considered the anniversary of that 1833 event a Fourth-of-July-type holiday.

By the 1880s, George Colt had acquired the hill, planted its sides with grape vines and pear trees and operated the "Prospect Hill Vineyards." Kalamazoo youngsters continued to value the hill's steep sides as prime winter sledding courses. In the springtime, local boys sometimes mounted a small cannon in the woods Colt left near the summit and blasted

This steel engraving of the original Michigan Asylum for the Insane was published in 1862, three years after it opened.

away at the enormous flocks of passenger pigeons that darkened the sky.

By the turn of the twentieth century, the passenger pigeons were forever gone, largely victims of hunters' greed. Colt's enterprise, too, had failed and he was forced to mortgage his hill to a Massachusetts lender. Neglected pear trees and tangled grape vines covered most of the steep sides and top of Prospect Hill. A twenty-foot high ridge called a "hog back" ran across its summit. Numerous foot paths carved by generations of strollers angled through the

Prospect Hill and vicinity appeared in an 1874 birdseye view of Kalamazoo.

Judging from the appearance of another birdseye view published in 1883, Prospect Hill had lost its oak trees by then.

shin tangle springing from its sandy soil. At its north end gaped a commercial sand pit. Kalamazoo's once pristine Prospect Hill had become an eyesore.

The city, itself, however, had burgeoned since Van Buren described Prospect Hill in its glory days. Founded in 1831 by Titus Bronson, an eccentric Yankee who had named the town after himself, the community's viability soon became tied to its periodic success in landing government institutions— county, state and federal. The first such political plum came the year of its founding when Bronson won designation as Kalamazoo County's seat over rivals Comstock and Schoolcraft. Three years later, the removal of the federal land office from White Pigeon to Bronson brought boom times as hundreds of frontier land seekers crowded its streets. To its founder's chagrin, political enemies renamed the town Kalamazoo in 1836, and he soon moved west in disgust. Two years later, the first state award came with the establishment of a branch of the University of Michigan in a two-story structure in Bronson Park.

The effects of the financial panic of 1837 brought nearly a decade of hard times to the Michigan frontier. But Kalamazoo's fortune brightened in 1846 with the arrival of the Michigan Central Railroad, a state and federally funded project that linked the city with Detroit and eastern markets.

South Burdick St.
Kalamazoo, Mich.

This circa 1909 postcard depicts a busy South Burdick Street.

Epaphroditus Ransom from Kalamazoo won election as governor in 1847. Thanks to his influence and that of Charles Stuart, local lawyer and member of the location committee, as well as the community's subscribing $1,500 and a plat of land for the project, Kalamazoo won designation in 1850 as the site of the state's first asylum for the insane. Nine years later, that model institution formally opened on a 160-acre tract on the southwest side of Prospect Hill. At the turn of the century, more than 3,000 patients would reside in the Kalamazoo State Hospital. Hundreds of staff members and lucrative local contracts for supplies and services had fully demonstrated the economic value of the presence of a major state facility. By that time, Kalamazoo had become a burgeoning metropolis. Its population increased 62 percent during the first decade of the twentieth century to nearly 40,000 in 1910. It had become the paper maker to the nation as well as home to a diversity of thriving manufacturers who crafted products ranging from cigars and corsets to stoves and buggies. Local celery growers proudly promoted their commodity nationwide, "Fresh as the Dew from Kalamazoo!"

The turn of the century also brought another opportunity for the "Celery City" to secure a prime state facility—a new teacher training school. Since territorial days, Michigan had been a pioneer in educational reform. The constitution of 1835 included provisions that made Michigan school systems models for many other states. Isaac Crary and John D. Pierce of Marshall adapted a progressive Prussian system of state instruction to provide for district schools, and a university with eight branches intended to serve as preparatory schools for the University of Michigan and to train teachers. The branches proved too expensive to maintain, and the state dropped support in the 1840s. Ultimately, local high schools took their place, and the Kalamazoo School Case of 1872 established the right of a community to tax its residents for a high school as well as grade schools.

In 1849, the Michigan State Normal School in Ypsilanti (later renamed Eastern Michigan University) opened as the first institution for the training of teachers west of the Alleghenies. Six years later, Michigan founded the nation's first agricultural college in East Lansing. The University of Michigan established America's first professorship in the science and art of teaching in 1879. Increasing demand for professionally educated teachers spurred the state legislature to create a second normal school at Mount Pleasant in 1895 and a third at Marquette four years later. If residents of the scattered logging towns of northern Michigan and the Upper Peninsula's mining communities deserved normals, did not western Michigan, where 17 counties contained a quarter of the state's population, also merit a local teacher training school?

State Senator William D. Kelly, a real estate developer from Muskegon, thought so, and he could conceive of no better location for the new normal than his own port city. Accordingly, on January 10, 1901, he introduced a bill into the Senate that provided for the "location, establishment and conduct of a state normal and manual training school at Muskegon." Eleven days later, Luke Luggers, a representative from Ottawa County and former longtime school teacher, introduced a similar bill in the House calling only for the location of the school in the "western part of the state." Whereupon, Representative Albert E. Sharpe from East Tawas, north of the Thumb on Lake Huron, jumped on the bandwagon by submitting a bill to place the normal in his hometown.

Over the succeeding five months, wrangling in committees and in the Senate and House resulted in a bill that stipulated only that the new normal be located somewhere in the state. Both the Senate and House passed the diluted bill and it was presented to Governor Aaron Bliss on May 20, 1901. Bliss, a wealthy lumberman from Saginaw, felt the time not propitious for the establishment of another normal. With numerous colleges throughout Michigan developing their own teacher training curricula and anxious for students, he saw no need for additional expense to the state. Furthermore, he did not like the pork barrel nature of the bill. He said,""It will hardly be denied that local

Western's 1931 *Brown and Gold* was dedicated to Henry Vandercook and included this "authentic sketch of Mr. Vandercook in his legislative days."

influences and local desire for the possession of a state institution had also much to do with it." Bliss's veto killed the bill.

But the seeds had been sown and on January 16, 1903, Vandercook introduced a new bill in the House for the creation of a normal school in western Michigan. Five days later, Kelly reintroduced his bill in the Senate

This rare view of Kalamazoo, looking east from Prospect Hill, circa 1890, was preserved as a stereoscope card.

without stipulating Muskegon as the site. Then came another five months of political infighting at the committee level and on the floor of the House and Senate. Vandercook and Kelly fought effectively in their respective arenas and on May 7, 1903, the bill creating a normal in western Michigan went to Bliss. Twenty days later, he signed Public Act No. 196 into law.

The pinch-penny state legislature voted an appropriation of a mere $37,001 to fund the bill. It allocated $25,000 for construction of a suitable building, $5,000 to equip it, $7,000 for the entire first year's salaries and one dollar for acquisition of a tract of land of at least 20 acres. Obviously, the legislature intended the bulk of the financing to come from the pockets of residents of the community chosen as the site. The bill also authorized the State Board of Education to decide on the appropriate location. No less than 28 communities threw their hats in the ring. They included: Three Oaks, Niles, Cassopolis, Dowagiac, Centreville, Three Rivers, Decatur, Galesburg, Vicksburg, Battle Creek, Allegan, Hastings, Charlotte, Holland, Zeeland, Grand Rapids,

Muskegon, Whitehall, Manistee, Pentwater, Benzonia, Traverse City, Charlevoix, Ludington, Howard City, Alto, Petoskey and, of course, Kalamazoo.

The Celery City acted quickly. On May 21, six days before Bliss signed the bill, *Kalamazoo Evening Telegraph* editor Edward Dingley, who, incidentally, had been chairman of the House Ways and Means Committee that would have decided the location of the normal in the failed 1901 bill, advocated in his columns "the formulation of plans to raise money in order that the city would be in a position to obtain the new normal school." On June 3, the Press Club, a booster organization composed of civic and business leaders that evolved into the Kalamazoo Chamber of Commerce, held a meeting to launch a fund drive. A club spokesman declared, "A little ginger in the make-up of every citizen just now will go a long ways toward securing the school."

Following that initial meeting, Mayor Samuel Folz and President of the School Board Nathaniel H. Stewart spearheaded the drive, as the committee hurriedly secured options on 24 tracts of land in and near the city and prepared for the arrival on June 28 of the members of the State Board of Education charged with determining the site of the Normal. Four of those members showed up two days early. Surprised, but up to the challenge, the executive committee of the Press Club squired the educators around the community to inspect the various tracts available. In the event none of those appealed, the committee assured the members "any twenty acres within a radius of five miles of Kalamazoo would be given for the asking." Having been "driven and dined, talked and walked; and impressed with the unrivaled advantages of Kalamazoo," the members boarded the train. Undoubtedly, Mayor Folz's final promise also left a strong impression: "Anything you want is yours, gentlemen. If we haven't shown you what you want, indicate it and it is yours."

The Kalamazoo committee later upped the ante by offering $40,000 cash for building and developing the campus. In addition, the city pledged to grade the streets and lay cement sidewalks adjoining the site, install gas, electricity, sewer and water hookups free, allow use of a public school building until the state could construct a training school and even pay half of the initial salaries of the Normal's faculty.

Despite those inducements, Kalamazoo did not have the game in the bag yet. Members of the State Board of Education continued to visit other communities vying for the Normal. On July 9, a member toured nearby Galesburg.

The State Board of Education met on August 28. Following several hours of debate, the board proceeded to vote for the site of the new normal. Kalamazoo, Allegan and Hastings emerged as the leading contenders. But 14 rounds of balloting brought no results. Because Kalamazoo "seemed to have the fewest objections to it," on the 15th vote the board unanimously selected it, providing the city would agree to certain conditions that were

basically the same as had already been offered by the local booster group.

The next day, three members of the state board traveled to Kalamazoo to present the proposition to the Press Club committee. Meanwhile, resentment over the decision surfaced in a number of the rival communities. "It is money that gets the school," grumbled the editor of the *Niles Daily Star*. In reference to celery's folk medicine reputation as a nerve rejuvenator, the editor of the *Allegan Press* gibed, "One hundred thousand dollars is a pretty big price to pay for the western Michigan normal school, but Kalamazoo has plenty of celery and therefore an abundance of nerve."

Incensed that Muskegon had lost out, Senator Kelly called on Bliss "to stop any further steps being taken until some understanding can be reached that will at least carry out the intention of the legislature." He also asked for "the resignation of the State Board of Education members involved in the decision." Kelly's protests came to naught.

Only one nagging item lay in the way of Kalamazoo's complete triumph—local voter approval of $70,000 of bonded indebtedness. The tight-fisted fiscal tradition that would earn Kalamazoo its title as "The Debt Free City" during the Great Depression of the 1930s was already well established. But a massive promotional campaign by the Press Club and rare non-partisan support by the Democrat-oriented *Gazette* and the Republican *Telegraph* trumpeted the advantages of the new school with its projected 1,000-student enrollment. Both newspapers made special appeals urging women to vote. Although they had yet to win complete suffrage, the state constitution gave female taxpayers the right to vote on bond issues. The special election held on October 19 brought an unusually large turnout of 999 voters, including 330 women. The bond issue passed by nearly a nine-to-one majority.

School Board President Stewart crowed that Kalamazoo had shown "she is fully

Prospect Hill, the future site of Western, looked like this, circa 1900.

imbued with the spirit that makes a city great and influential in the commonwealth. Workingmen went to the polls and voted 'yes' that their children may enjoy better privileges than were ever offered their parents."

While Kalamazoo was clearly eager to begin work on the project, the state board had yet to decide on the precise site of the Normal. During a return visit to Kalamazoo on November 14, members of the board reviewed the 24 sites, this time without accompaniment and the wining and dining, and pared the total down to four possible tracts. Unable to decide among those "too many good ones," the board sought assistance from the Olmsted Brothers of Brookline, Massachusetts, the nationally renowned firm of landscape architects responsible for New York City's Central Park and the grounds of the 1893 World's Columbian Exposition in Chicago. The Olmsteds inspected the final four sites and submitted a report to the board. Based on that recommendation, the state board decided on the property known as Prospect Hill.

The Olmsteds saw great potential in the overgrown tract of 20 acres of rutted blow sand and scrubby oaks that ran 1,000 feet along Davis Street to the east and bordered on the irregular contours of Asylum Avenue (renamed Oakland Drive around 1912 partly through the efforts of an erstwhile real estate developer) to the west. They submitted a detailed landscape plan. But the state board soon discovered that to implement the plan would cost considerably more than the $7,500 appropriated by the legislature. So the Olmsteds trimmed their grandiose plan into a more modest version.

When Kalamazoo representatives sought to acquire clear title to the 20 acres, money also posed a problem. Prospect Hill actually consisted of two separately owned parcels and, despite its unkempt appearance, those owners were holding out for the highest amount. Negotiations dragged on for over three months. Stewart journeyed to Massachusetts to appeal to one owner. In an era when prime Kalamazoo lots brought $200 to $300 and surrounding farm land could be purchased for

$25 to $30 an acre, the city ended up paying $24,000 for the run-down 20-acre tract. On March 24, 1904, Stewart presented warranty deeds for the two parcels of land to the state board on behalf of the citizens of Kalamazoo. The board accepted with thanks and a consideration of 50 cents for each deed.

The delay in selecting and acquiring clear title to Prospect Hill impinged on the planned construction schedule. The act creating the Normal had stipulated that the school be ready for occupancy by September 1, 1904. However, not until April 16 were the bids for erection of the structure designed by E.W. Arnold of Battle Creek opened. The local firm of George Rickman and Sons won the contract with a bid of $53,500, only $295 less than that of a Chicago company. Albert J. White, a prominent black construction contractor from Kalamazoo, would supervise the masonry work. The contract to grade and landscape the grounds went to W.A. Drake of Kalamazoo on May 13, 1904. Three days later, almost a full year after Bliss had signed the bill, workmen using horse-drawn scrapers and hand shovels began leveling the summit of Prospect Hill. Drake's laborers drew $2 for their 10-hour work day—their equine work mates earned $3 per team.

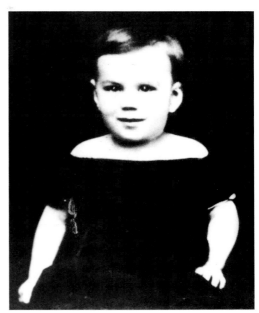

Young Dwight Waldo, about 1865

Skilled Kalamazoo contractor Albert J. White supervised the masonry construction of Western's first structure, now East Hall.

Although the physical development of Western State Normal lagged, the state board intended that the June 27, 1904, formal opening date be met. On April 1, it appointed Dwight Bryant Waldo principal of the incipient institution. The selection of the 39-year-old administrator would prove of paramount importance in the evolution of the school.

Born in Arcade, New York, on June 13, 1864, Waldo spent his first nine years in that Wyoming County village. His paternal grandparents, H. Nelson and Polly Upum Waldo, had been active in the Underground Railroad. His father, Simeon S. Waldo, earned a reputation as "one of the leading Republicans of his section." In 1873, the Waldos, like so many of the other western New Yorkers who pioneered in Michigan, moved to the Allegan County community of Plainwell, where Simeon opened a grocery store. Young Waldo labored in his father's store part-time until he graduated from Plainwell High School in 1879. He went to work full-time for his father for two years before attending the Michigan Agricultural College in East Lansing from 1881 to 1883. He then enrolled in Albion College, where he graduated in 1887. He

Waldo's first daughters, Elizabeth and Barbara, posed for the cameras, about 1915.

taught as an instructor at Albion, spent a year of graduate studies in history and political science at Harvard and received his master's degree from Albion College in 1890. After a year teaching history at Beloit College in Wisconsin, he returned to Albion as professor of politics and economics.

But history remained his true love. In 1898, when he learned that the legislature was about to establish a new normal in Marquette, Waldo discussed with a colleague at Albion, Richard Clyde Ford, the possibility that the new school might need a professor of history. Ford agreed to broach the matter with State Superintendent of Schools Jason E. Hammond. When he got to Lansing, Ford decided, instead, to formally submit his friend's name as a candidate for the head of the new school.

Despite his lack of administrative experience, Waldo evidently impressed the state board with his zeal. On June 23, 1899, the board appointed him principal of the nascent Northern Michigan Normal School. Waldo and his wife and former classmate at Albion, Minnie, soon found themselves on the cold shores of Lake Superior.

In Marquette, Waldo demonstrated skill in building a teacher's college from the ground up. With no physical campus yet constructed, the first classes were held on the second floor of city hall. By October 1902, Waldo had dedicated the second of the school's original sandstone structures. In addition to administrative duties, he taught classes in pedagogy. His wife became the institution's first librarian.

Tragically, Minnie died of cancer on January 30, 1903. Waldo returned her remains for burial in her hometown of Vicksburg. In September 1904, he married Lillian Trudgeon from Vulcan in Dickinson County. Eighteen years younger than Waldo, she had been the honor graduate of the class of 1904 at Northern Michigan Normal.

In April 1904, in recognition of his success in pioneering Northern Michigan Normal, the State Board of Education named Waldo principal of the incipient Western State Normal. Family tradition maintains that he was more than pleased to leave the chilly Upper Peninsula for Kalamazoo, despite

Dwight Waldo in 1906

Court House, Kalamazoo, Mich.

A cramped corner in the Kalamazoo County Court House served as Western's original administration center.

having to face the prospects of again launching a college without buildings, teachers and adequate funding. His starting salary would be the same as at Northern, $2,500 a year.

As principal of a school that existed only on paper, Waldo initially concerned himself with securing faculty. And since his leadership was still required in Marquette, he needed an administrative assistant in Kalamazoo. He persuaded Josephine Wing, an efficient young woman serving as assistant postmistress in Vicksburg, to accept the position, despite a decrease in salary. She would start in May, pay her own expenses and serve as registrar, publicity director, librarian and editor of the first *Western Bulletin*, as well as dean of men and women the first year. In her remaining time she canvassed community members willing to rent spare rooms to students. Her office and Waldo's would be in a cramped corner of the county school commissioner's office in the courthouse adjacent Bronson Park. Wing's $500 yearly salary, as well as the funds slated to pay the first faculty members, would not be available until July 1, 1904. She managed to talk a Vicksburg bank into a loan

to help the school cover expenses.

In recruiting Wing and other early staff members, Waldo demonstrated a persuasive, almost mesmerizing ability. He convinced candidates of the history-making role they would play in building the institution. Because more than half the grade schools in southwestern Michigan were one- or two-room country schools, Waldo decided to launch a "rural

Josephine Wing was 26 when Waldo hired her. Years later, her granddaughter, Maury E. Parfet (Reed) became a WMU trustee (See page 203).

Rural Department Head Ernest Burnham, right, posed with brother Smith Burnham, a history professor, about 1919.

children of the farms, hamlets and villages."

Then Waldo led him to Prospect Hill. As the two scrambled up its steep vine-choked side, pausing to catch their breath while admiring the beautiful Kalamazoo River Valley stretched below, Waldo continued his sales pitch. Burnham would participate in "what was to be the most exhilarating adventure in public education yet to be experienced by mere man."

school department" oriented toward the needs of rural educators. He chose Ernest Burnham, an old friend and fellow Albion College graduate, to head that unique experiment. Then employed as the Calhoun County school commissioner in Marshall, Burnham received a telephone call from Waldo one Saturday morning in April 1904, commanding him to take the Michigan Central Railroad to Kalamazoo at once. Waldo met him at the railroad station, conveyed him to the Burdick Hotel on Michigan Avenue and harangued him in a hypnotic voice "about the kingdoms of the world of education and with special reference to a glowing future for the dear

Two weeks later, Burnham agreed to leave his desirable position in Marshall and cast his lot with the normal school at a $300-per-year cut in pay. During a long and prestigious career at Western, he would count among his accomplishments the organization of the first department of rural education in any state-supported teacher education institution in the United States.

By June 27, 1904, the opening of the first summer session at the Normal, Waldo had secured ten additional instructors. With the foundations yet to be laid for the Normal building, the institution held classes in the old Kalamazoo High School on Vine Street. A total of 117 students from 13 counties enrolled for that initial session, choosing from a catalog prepared by Wing that listed twelve rudimentary departments, ultimately offering a total of 78 courses.

The curricula included several general teacher education degrees. Students who had graduated from the eighth grade could finish the rural school course in seven semesters. Those who held high school diplomas could, in two years, graduate with

From left to right, Waldo, his right-hand man, chemistry professor William McCracken and English professor George Sprau showed little humor in this circa 1909 photograph.

The old Vine Street School was the site of Western's first summer session in 1904.

the highest degree—a "Life Certificate," which entitled them to teach indefinitely in Michigan.

Despite the temporary classroom, the classes that started as early as 7:00 a.m. and the mandatory chapel services each day, many of Western's pioneer students remembered an enjoyable summer. The first social event of the Normal came on the opening night of the session. The program included short speeches by dignitaries and music provided by local talent, capped off with a "barrel of lemonade." Throughout the session seven prominent outside speakers lectured on various aspects of education. Waldo also arranged for a free exhibit of paintings, "the finest ever brought to Kalamazoo," by the Thurber Art Gallery of Chicago.

During that first term, Waldo established patterns characteristic of his efforts to gain recognition for the school during its early years of development. He would continue to bring

Students, then as now, enjoyed learning in an outdoor setting, as seen in this photo of a 1908 sketching class.

In the fall of 1904, 107 students attended Western's first regular semester, with classes held in this old Kalamazoo College building on Lovell Street.

in esteemed speakers and outside exhibits for the cultural enlightenment of students and faculty and to encourage faculty members to make themselves available as free speakers to audiences in Kalamazoo and the surrounding communities. The more gifted faculty would speak at special student assemblies. Western's first summer session closed on August 5, 1904,

One of Western's first black students, Myrtie Sheppard, pursued a degree in the Rural Department in 1910.

with a lecture by local physician Caspar K. La Huis about his trip to Palestine.

Another 107 eager students arrived for the opening of Western's first regular semester on Monday, September 26, 1904. Male students donned mandatory coats and ties for classroom attendance, while coeds trailed their fashionably long skirts along the city's dusty and manure-laden streets. With the Vine Street School in session and the Normal building still little more than a hole in the ground, Waldo secured alternate classroom space. A dilapidated Italianate brick structure abandoned by Kalamazoo College, north of Prospect Hill between Lovell and South Streets, served as an expedient.

The first semester included training school classes during which Normal students honed their teaching skills under the watchful eyes of four "critic teachers." Those classes were scattered around the community at available sites, including the People's Church, the Methodist Church and the YMCA. Not until 1909 would the training school reside in its own facilities on campus. The Normal High School (later State High then University High) began three years later, when the eighth grade graduating class asked to continue its studies under the Normal teachers.

Despite the rather confusing nature of administering a normal without a campus, Waldo made surprising progress during that first year. By October 1904, the nucleus of the library had been established. The first shipment of books consisted entirely of psychology, educational and reference works. By June 30, 1905, some 1,300 volumes stood in solemn order on makeshift shelves.

The faculty, including Principal Waldo, who taught European and American history, organized a club that met at intervals to sip tea, deliver lectures and discuss current affairs. A faculty committee offered a prize of $5 to the student who could write the best school song to the tune of *The Heidelberg Stein Song*. Gerald Whitney and Bernice Crandall split

William Spaulding, top left, coached his 1909 football team to an undefeated season.

the prize, enough to pay for a week's room and board for each of them, with an entry that began:

> Hail to our jolly student life,
> Hail with a right good cheer,
> Hail to our hopeful daily strife,
> To conquer without a fear.

Waldo charged another faculty committee with the responsibility for naming the school colors on November 28, 1904. Conflicting testimony exists concerning the actual origin of the colors, however. Waldo's secretary, Wing, remembered commenting to Waldo after they had occupied the first building during the late summer of 1905, that since the brown-eyed Susans were in bloom, their colors would be appropriate. But on April 25, 1905, some four months before, the Kalamazoo' *Telegraph* had noted that "the students in the Normal training department are making pennants of brown and gold, the Normal school colors."

About the same time as the adoption of the school colors, another group of students created the original school "yell":

> Hy-lo-zo
> Hy-lo-zo
> Western Normal Kalamazoo

The colors and the yell were prerequisites for an athletic program for the school. The first fall semester, a pair of students who had played football in high school attempted to organize a gridiron team for Western State Normal. Fifteen of the 20 males enrolled

Chuck Weldon, a Western football player in 1914, displayed the effects of scrimmaging before the advent of face guards.

turned out for practice, but most found the sport, played without helmets and little

Spaulding, in the derby, posed with his baseball team, about 1909.

padding, too rough and they quit. By the following semester the school's original basketball team competed against local church teams, losing most of its games.

By the fall of 1905, the school's enrollment had risen to 185 and the first Western State Normal football team took the field against local high school elevens. Coach John McManis achieved a perfect record—all losses. The following year, the "Hillsmen" (Western's nickname before Hilltoppers and later Broncos) tackled other college teams, including arch rival Kalamazoo College. Prior to 1907, without the benefit of a trained coach, students also developed rudimentary baseball, track and women's basketball teams.

In 1907, Waldo hired the school's first regular coach, William H. Spaulding. He had just graduated from Wabash College where he had been a hard-hitting halfback on a championship team. That first year, Spaulding's team won the state normal championship, and by 1909, Western's eleven boasted an unbeaten, untied season. Spaulding organized the school's first official intercollegiate baseball team in 1911, followed by the basketball team in 1914.

Prior to 1916, varsity athletes sported an "N" for Normal on their sweaters rather than a "W." Before he left in 1922 to become head football coach at Minnesota, Spaulding laid a solid foundation for the future greatness of intercollegiate sports at Western.

In the meantime, Western Normal had held its first commencement exercises on June 22, 1905. During ceremonies held at the new Vine Street School, eight women and one man received teaching degrees. That pioneer class—Archibald Polley, Hebe Hunt, Vivian Simmons, Josephine La Duke, Ione Peacock, Shirley Braden, Ada Seabury, Mabel Pomeroy and Sarah Turner—dutifully listened to a University of Chicago professor's commencement address on "The Larger Selfishness."

Finally, in September 1905, precisely one year later than initially mandated, the administration building (later renamed East Hall) stood complete. An amalgam of classical architectural styles, its handsome façade would inspire the Kalamazoo community for a century and, hopefully, more. The structure featured a Greek, temple-like portico supported by six massive pillars. A Romanesque

Workmen were putting the finishing touches on Western's first structure in the summer of 1905.

arch surrounded the main entrance, and an observation tower crowned the two-story brick and cement temple of learning. Its 136-foot-by-95-foot circumference housed administrative offices, 12 classrooms, a 400-seat auditorium and physics and chemistry laboratories. Esther Braley, the school's first librarian, converted two classrooms on the northeast corner of the building into a library and reading room.

Dignitaries gathered on November 23, 1905, for the formal dedication. Kalamazoo citizens turned out en masse to tour the imposing structure. Kalamazoo School Superintendent Stewart, State Superintendent of Public Education Kelly, State Representative Vandercook and other prominent officials delivered stirring orations, not neglecting to mention their respective roles in creating the institution. Governor Fred Warner also spoke. Western's first historian, James O. Knauss,

termed the occasion "one of the most notable events in the history of Kalamazoo."

As Kalamazoo residents inspected the grounds of the campus that day, they might have commented on the absence of concrete walks. But there was a logical reason for their delayed construction. Waldo had sagely accepted the advice of the Olmsted firm. Rather than lay out preconceived walks, he would let students tramp paths across the campus. Those most direct routes would then be paved.

It did not take long for class rivalry to emerge. The mortar between the bricks of the Normal's first structure had hardly dried when the Class of '06 hoisted its class flag atop the cupola and guarded the pennant all night against raids by the Class of '07.

One Saturday morning not long after the occupation of the administration building, Waldo called out Ernest Burnham, Leslie

Western's original set of wooden stairs can be seen in this 1914 photograph.

Wood, Thomas J. Riley, John T. McManis and other faculty members who were handy with tools for a work session. It seems that the school had enough funds to purchase a supply of pine planks, but not enough to hire carpenters to construct a set of stairs up the steep slope from Davis Street to the entrance of the new structure. So, under the supervision of the school janitor, the faculty shoveled, sawed and sweated, and before long the school's original stairway stood complete.

Those primitive and steep stairs soon became a sentimental landmark, one commemorated by a student bard in 1914:

> *When we stand at the top of the old*
> *pine stair*
> *That reaches to the Normal on the hill,*
> *How our hearts are filled with yearning,*
> *Fellowship within us burning,*
> *For the souls that hear a voice they can—*
> *not still;*
> *While we listen to the tramp*
> *of the feet upon the plank,*
> *climb, climb, climb,*
> *To the dim-discovered land of*
> *somewhere...*

Some 1906 class members staged a stunt photograph while displaying the 1905 class pennant they had liberated.

Waldo, atop the ladder, worked alongside his faculty and staff to construct Western's first set of wooden stairs that led up Prospect Hill.

One sweltering June day in 1907, Waldo treated a visiting state legislative committee to a hearty lunch at a downtown Kalamazoo hotel and then led them to the foot of Prospect Hill. Halfway up the steep wooden stairs, Waldo paused so that one portly legislator could catch his breath. During the rest of the climb, Waldo, in his usual persuasive tone, bemoaned the lack of a better way for his young female students, with their perceived inherent internal weaknesses, to reach the Normal. The object lesson worked just as he had planned. The legislature soon reallocated $3,500 originally budgeted for a ventilation system to fund a double-track railroad running from the northeast corner of the hilltop to the bottom.

In June 1908, the trolley became a reality. Operated by a stationary electric motor situated in a small brick building at the top and assisted by the funicular action

A full load of passengers creaked up Prospect Hill in this 1908 view of the trolley.

Western's railroad looked like this in 1910.

of one car's descent while the other rose, the cars ascended to the top in a little over a minute and made approximately 50 trips an hour. The first conductor, William Champion operated the controls at the top of the hill and made sure that no more than the limit of 16 passengers boarded each of the cars. But he could not tolerate the constant whir of the cable drums winding and unwinding and soon quit. Alfred Colvin succeeded him, and over the subsequent four decades, he became a campus institution. By 1917, he transported an average of 3,000 passengers up and down the hill daily. Students inevitably overcrowded the bottom car in their haste to get to class on time, but gruff Colvin refused to raise the car until enough had dismounted. The ride was free except to green freshmen bilked by upper classmates into buying "trolley ride tickets." Western's nationally famous electric-cable railway carried millions of passengers until it

was closed down in 1949, a victim of lack of funds for repairs. The tracks were torn up in the spring of 1951 and the cars sold for scrap.

Western's miniature railroad began

Mathematics professor J.B. Faught and English professor Bertrand Jones posed before one of the trolley cars about 1914.

operating just in time to convey hundreds of Kalamazooans to the campus for the formal dedication of two new buildings in 1908. Waldo had campaigned hard for additional funds and the legislature rewarded his persistence with an appropriation of $72,000 for additional construction—a gymnasium and a classroom building linking that structure with the original administration building on the north.

The new gymnasium featured such avant-garde luxuries as showers, a swimming pool and a baseball batting cage. Contemporaries described it as "one of the best planned and best equipped structures of its kind to be found in the normal schools and colleges of the Northwest Territory."

A member of the class of 1908 wrote a poem describing her feelings for the school she had grown to cherish:

> How dear to our hearts
> are the scenes of the Normal,
> When fond recollections presents
> them to view.
> The assembly, the art room,
> the brand new gymnasium,
> And every loved spot surely
> all of us knew,
> The grand Normal pond,
> and the onion patch by it,
> The trees and leaves
> all the best ones can tell,
> The hall of our pleasures,
> the office so nigh it,
> And even the good fountain,
> for there wasn't a well,
> The dear old Normal,
> the iron clad Normal,
> The Western State Normal,
> we all loved so well.

By 1909, when this picture was taken, a gymnasium and classrooms had been added to the Administration Building.

Women students donned similar uniforms for physical education classes, as seen in the photograph taken about 1915.

The legislature continued its generosity by appropriating $60,000 for construction of a training school building. Ida Densmore, director of the Training School, toured some of the nation's outstanding existing facilities and contributed to its design. Built north of the administration building with a harmonizing architectural style, the 118-foot-by-100-foot building featured classrooms arranged around a majestic two-story central rotunda. The rotunda, into which all the classroom doors opened, offered a memorable setting for hundreds of student parties and programs over the succeeding decades.

It was standing room only in the reading room of Western's first library, circa 1906.

The Training School moved from the basement of the Vine Street School to its new building in the fall term of 1909. Within the first year of the structure's occupancy, the Normal faculty began holding monthly dinners in the basement. A close-knit group in the early days, faculty members enjoyed numerous social occasions together. They attended assemblies and dances in the Normal gymnasium, where a corner of the big room was converted into a makeshift faculty lounge. Dances traditionally began with a grand march led by the biology instructor, Leroy Harvey, and women's physical education instructor Mattie Lee Jones.

Marion Sherwood, who taught manual arts for 18 years beginning in 1911, never forgot the time Waldo remarked to him with great feeling in his voice while watching a faculty square dance in the Training School rotunda, "Isn't that a wonderful group of people?" Waldo clearly cared for his faculty. Yet he maintained a paternalistic relationship.

Originally he did not allow distinctions in the rank of faculty that might interfere with his freehanded determination of their salaries. With no set rankings, he merely called individuals into his office and told them how much they would be paid the forthcoming year. Nevertheless, he did consistently cam-

Ida Densmore, Director of the Western State Normal Training School in 1911

The Training School Building, constructed in 1909, mirrored the architecture of the other two original structures.

outlying agricultural regions began May 24, 1907, when Burnham launched an annual Rural Progress Day. Over the succeeding decade, the occasion evolved from a simple evening lecture attended by a few hundred people to a day-long conference with multiple sessions.

Each spring, a thousand or more farmers, rural teachers, county normal students (as many as 50 Michigan counties operated their own normals to train rural teachers) and others packed the gymnasium to listen to nationally prominent speakers such as South Haven-born horticulturalist Liberty Hyde Bailey. In 1913, Burnham shifted Rural Progress Day from May to March. It continued to offer a vital link with rural southwestern Michigan under Burnham's administration and that of his successor, William McKinley Robinson, until 1940. Burnham also maintained close contact with local Granges, farm

paign for more personnel funding from the legislature, citing the high cost of living prevalent in Kalamazoo during the first two decades of the twentieth century.

Prior to the 1920s, faculty members enjoyed no separate offices. They utilized empty classrooms to prepare lectures, grade papers, and so on. Monthly faculty meetings were held in Waldo's office, where each instructor brought in a chair and sat in a semi-circle around Waldo's big rolltop desk.

A major social and educational event that furthered the Normal's rapport with the

Training School kindergarteners enjoyed a story in 1911.

Ernest Burnham, seated on the left, posed with the Rural Education juniors in 1913.

bureaus, cooperatives and other rural organizations, and he gave hundreds of speeches to southwest Michigan audiences that helped keep Western's name in the forefront. Waldo recognized Burnham's zeal and energy when he commented, "The Lord only made one like Ernest Burnham and when he did he threw away the cast."

The activities of the music department also furthered camaraderie between town and gown. Martha Sherwood, the first director of the Training School, organized a children's chorus prior to 1905. In January 1905, Florence Marsh arrived on campus to head the music department. The following month she created the school's first orchestra. In October 1905, she organized the Choral Union, composed of Normal students and Kalamazoo citizens. Beginning with its first public concert in 1906, the Choral Union offered Kalamazoo music lovers a wide variety of classical and popular concerts. In 1908

and 1909, the Choral Union augmented its company with professional artists from Chicago, drawing audiences of 900. In 1906, Marsh also organized a Conservatory of Music composed largely of community members.

With his appointment as director of Western's music department in the summer of 1913, professor Harper Maybee launched an energetic campaign to make Kalamazoo even more receptive to music's allure. Born in Monroe County in 1875, Maybee graduated from the Michigan Normal College at

The Western State Normal School Orchestra in 1913

Harper Maybee posed with music majors in 1914.

Ypsilanti in 1898. For 12 years beginning in 1901, he served as director of Central State Normal's music department. With an evangelistic fervor, he continued to build on the city/Normal cooperative efforts begun by Marsh. In December 1913, Maybee staged a rendition of Handel's *Messiah* in the Normal gymnasium, which featured a 220-voice choir of students and community members accompanied by Charles Fischer's ("the man with the million-dollar smile") popular Kalamazoo orchestra and professional Chicago soloists.

In addition to his campus endeavors, Maybee became director of the Kalamazoo Musical Society, a civic organization that had been sponsoring an annual May Festival for a number of years. He also reinvigorated the Kalamazoo Choral Union, which set as its twin goals to bring some of the world's greatest artists to Kalamazoo and to provide a 300-voice chorus of Kalamazoo and Normal artists. By 1915, the Choral Union had begun

funding appearances by internationally famous musicians—a tradition that would be continued decades later by Irving Gilmore and ultimately the Gilmore International Keyboard Festival. Prior to 1920, Kalamazoo audiences were treated to performances by Walter Damrosch, Leopold Stokowsky, Alma Gluck and other star performers of the times.

Two literary societies had been formed prior to the establishment of Western's speech department (known as the Department of Expression until 1918) under the direction of Mary Master in 1906. The Riley Literary Society for men and the Amphictyon Society for women date from the fall of 1904. The Normal Literary Society, open to both sexes, began in 1906. The three organizations sometimes invited the public to the debates, essay and poetry readings, and other performances they staged. In 1907, the societies launched an annual oratory contest, which continued for the succeeding ten years.

Music professor Harper Maybee, front, directed the Normal Chorus in a 1913 production of Handel's *Messiah*.

The Normal's initial theatrical efforts date from December 11, 1906, with a Christmas program featuring two comedies. In 1908, Department of Expression students performed a dramatized version of Sir James Barrie's *The Little Minister* as the first formal event held in the new Normal gymnasium. By then, the staging of at least two plays each year had become a tradition. Elva Forncrook succeeded Master as department head in 1911, and she soon organized several dramatic clubs. In 1915, they united to form the Dramatic Association. The following year, the association presented another of Barrie's plays, *The Admirable Crichton*, at the Academy of Music in downtown Kalamazoo.

Amphictyon Society members dressed in costume for the play *Cranford* in 1905.

Along with rural conferences, musical concerts, debates and plays, coach Spaulding's athletic teams increasingly supplied entertainment to school and community alike. But one major problem limited the development of strong athletic traditions—the Normal had no football or baseball field. Its teams played home games at the Kalamazoo Public School's Woodward Avenue field. Despite having no home facilities, Spaulding's athletes gave the student body plenty to cheer about. His

football teams won the normal school championship and city championship (they played high school teams in the early days) for three consecutive seasons beginning in 1907. In 1912, Western's baseball team also won the normal championship.

On October 10, 1913, Spaulding's eleven pummeled the Albion College team 20 to three. Western's student body celebrated the victory by staging a gigantic snake dance that wound its way down Oakland Drive and Michigan Avenue to culminate in a rowdy raid into the Elite Theatre on South Burdick Street. Kalamazooans complained loudly to Waldo about the unseemly spectacle of his coeds cavorting in the streets. When he called a mass meeting of his female students, they offered as an alibi that they had been driven to the exuberant display because of the lack of social activities on campus. The outcome was the formation of The Women's League, a prominent social organization first directed by education instructor Lavina Spindler.

Waldo had convinced the legislature to appropriate $5,000 for the acquisition of land

Theatre students, then part of the Department of Expression, performed the Irish play *Cathlene Ni Houlihan* in 1912.

Western students donned elaborate costumes for an outdoor play in 1908.

for an athletic field in 1909, but that amount proved inadequate. In 1913, after two years of negotiating, he secured an option to purchase 14 acres of swampy terrain west of the campus, adjacent the Michigan Central Railroad tracks. Waldo raised the remainder of the $12,000 price by launching the school's initial community and alumni fund drive and by borrowing money from local banks. Faculty members obligingly cosigned those notes.

Faculty involvement in the creation of the first athletic field did not end there. The tract comprised a brushy swamp through which Arcadia Creek meandered. At the west end lay a three-acre mill pond, dammed in the 1840s to provide water power via a mill race for the Eames Mill, located near the present-day intersection of Stadium Drive and Oakland Drive. The pond also served as a source of ice harvested in the winter by the Root Ice Company. Waldo declared a school holiday and the male students and faculty reported to the site with shovels and pick axes. Sometimes wading in mud up to their knees, they proceeded to rechannel Arcadia Creek to the opposite side of the tracks, drain the pond and

tile the swamp. The Hillsmen baseball team played the first games on their new diamond in the spring of 1914, and the Western eleven kicked off from their own gridiron that fall.

Pride in their new facilities, in conjunction with Spaulding's fine coaching and a student enrollment that had grown to 784 by the fall of 1914, helped usher in Western's first golden age of athletics. The 1915 baseball team went unbeaten. For four seasons beginning in 1914, Western's eleven lost only five games. However, one game that the Hillsmen lost in 1916 made the record books. The hard-fought match against the Notre Dame freshman team stood at seven to seven late in the fourth quarter, thanks largely to the skilled broken-field running of the Irish's George Gipp from Laurium in the Upper Peninsula. Notre Dame was stymied on their 38-yard line, and the quarterback called for Gipp to punt. Instead, he launched a drop kick that sped through the air like a line drive in baseball to split the uprights. To Western's chagrin, that 62-yard drop kick won the game. Gipp's feat remains the second-longest drop kick in football history.

Until his death from pneumonia in 1920, Gipp enjoyed a spectacular football career under coach Knute Rockne. Ronald Reagan played the role of Gipp in the movie *Knute Rockne—All American.* The scene in which Rockne, played by Patrick O'Brien, inspired his team during a halftime speech to "win one for the Gipper," although apocryphal, has become a cinema classic.

During another 1916 season game, Western's first black athlete, the legendary Sam Dunlap, would be sidelined not through sickness but because of racism. His teammates, like Gipp's, sought to win the game in his honor.

Waldo, who idolized Abraham Lincoln, was far ahead of most college presidents of his day in condemning racial unfairness. He had been following the exploits of Dunlap, who at Benton Harbor High School won selection as an all-state halfback for three consecutive years. Originally scheduled to be recruited by the University of Michigan, Dunlap was rejected by Georgia-born coach Fielding Yost, who never allowed a black athlete to play for him. Whereupon, Waldo sent Spaulding on a recruiting mission to Benton Harbor. Dunlap chose Western over the Michigan Agriculture College in East Lansing that was also wooing the athlete.

Dunlap recalled his relationship with Waldo in a 1958 interview: "He seemed just to open his arms to receive me like my own father would. I was never treated

Students and faculty rechanneled Arcadia Creek to construct Western's first athletic field in 1914.

better, or had any closer conversations with my father than I did with Mr. Waldo. Whenever I was in trouble, or he was worried how I was getting along, he would call me into his office and we would sit down and take time to talk over whatever problem I had, or any suggestion that he had to give me in order to get along as he thought I ought to."

Some of the faculty members, however, were not so accepting of a black student on campus. Worried about his possible relationship with white coeds, they spied on him.

This photograph of a track meet, about 1919, captures the look of Western's first athletic field.

The entire student body, faculty and staff attended assemblies in East Hall, about 1914.

Sam Dunlap, the legendary Western athlete, posed in 1917.

displayed his exceptional ability to kick and punt. The six-foot-two-inch, 192-pound halfback could "run like the wind and stop on a dime."

Dunlap saw limited action during Western's first two games of 1915, but during the third contest against Alma, he ran for a total of 430 yards to score four touchdowns and threw a 35-yard touchdown pass as well. The final score was 79-0.

The last game scheduled for the season was against Indiana's Culver Military Academy, a popular annual rivalry with a big crowd expected. But about a week before the game a Culver official notified Waldo that the team would not play against a "colored man." Waldo assembled his faculty on Sunday afternoon and asked their advice. The next morning he called Dunlap into his office and said, "We had a meeting, Sam, and the faculty decided that whatever you said about playing them—that's just what we would do. If you wanted to go ahead, we'd go ahead, if you say no we would cancel the game. But I want to assure you of one thing: This situation will never happen again, because we will cancel all athletic relations with them in the future." Dunlap replied, "Go ahead and play it." Before the game his teammates assured him, "We'll beat them for you, Sam." Dunlap sat on the bench and watched his teammates trounce Culver 83-14.

Dunlap left Western during World War I to join the army. He returned after the Armistice, winning a total of eleven letters in football, baseball and track. Rockne said that if he had played for a bigger school he would have been a certain All-American. Following graduation, Dunlap coached at West Virginia State College for three years before entering industry. In 1951, he returned to the campus he had loved so well to accept a job as custodian in the faculty housing complex.

During Dunlap's college days and well into the Depression, athletic scholarships had yet to make their appearance at Western.

Waldo called him into his office one day, told him of their concerns and announced, "I want to say that there isn't a thing they can point their finger at and I want to congratulate you."

Dunlap also ran into some prejudice during his first pre-season conditioning session held at Crooked Lake. When an athlete from Kentucky approached Spaulding and said he would not play on a team with a black member, Spaulding replied, "All right, tonight when the train comes through we'll send you back home," and that ended that player's Western career. At Crooked Lake, Dunlap

The lunchroom, operated by Grace Moore in the basement of the Training School building, is shown in this 1916 view.

Needy athletes might, however, find part-time employment on campus, but they were far from easy jobs. Dunlap never forgot getting up at four or five on bitterly cold mornings to shovel snow for 15 cents an hour.

Yet, small as that sum seems by contemporary standards, it went a long way prior to World War I. S. Forrest Bowers, who enrolled as a student in 1913, kept a running record of his expenditures. In the fall of 1913 they included tuition of $10, room and board $3.50 per week, a new algebra text book at $1.27, a downtown dinner 20 cents, streetcar fare five cents, haircut 25 cents and a movie at the Fuller Theatre 25 cents. Despite those prices, many a Western student was hard-pressed to make ends meet. Some took their sole meal of the day at the People's Church, which offered inexpensive dishes.

In 1910, Grace Moore opened a lunch room in the basement of the Training School where she served at a minimal cost soups, cocoa, sandwiches and fruit, prepared at her home and transported by horse-drawn hack up the hill. But for many students, getting sustenance remained a major challenge of college life. While there were no dormitories to provide meals, those living in surrounding rooming houses, particularly at the foot of the hill on Davis Street, often had limited cooking privileges. On Friday nights they headed back, en masse, to rural homes to replenish their larders, returning Sunday evening by train with bags of potatoes, fresh vegetables, canned goods lovingly prepared by proud mothers, and hams and other foods from the farm. Others, too poor to afford train tickets, hitchhiked. But hitchhiking in the early days over Michigan's notoriously miserable, unpaved roads posed its own problems. Automobile traffic was definitely light.

Probably the first horseless carriage to

The view from Prospect Hill, about 1910

make its appearance on campus belonged to Dr. Alvin Rockwell who conveyed his daughter, Ethel Rockwell, a physical education teacher from 1904 to 1907, up the hill. Sometime after Spaulding's arrival in 1907, he acquired a Model T Ford and graciously carried other faculty up muddy Asylum Avenue to campus. One time the vehicle was so loaded that Marion Sherwood, the manual arts instructor, rode on the hood. In the fall of

The Science Building, shown under construction, was completed in 1915.

1913, social science professor T. Paul Hickey wheeled a new Cadillac his mother had given him around campus. Soon, a flivver owned by John B. Fox, head of the Department of Physics, and a Model T pickup Waldo had bought for school use, made pedestrians a little more wary.

The year 1913 also proved a banner one for Western's physical development when Waldo won the campaign he had waged since 1909 for funds for a science building. Newly elected, progressive Governor Woodbridge Ferris had influenced the legislature to appropriate $75,000 for its construction and another $10,000 for equipment, as well as an additional $40,000 for building a central heating plant. Waldo, who had remarked to more than one colleague, "There is no good Democrat, but a dead Democrat," had swallowed his pride to back Ferris in the 1912 election, perhaps, in part, because of his work in founding Ferris Institute in Big Rapids. Ferris rewarded Waldo's loyalty by supporting the appropriations. That fall, work began on the science building, located west of the gymnasium. By the spring of 1915, the 148-foot by 80-foot, three-story, brick structure stood complete. Later called West Hall, the new science building initially housed the departments of geography, psychology, biology, chemistry and physics.

Western paused briefly to celebrate the tenth anniversary of its opening on January 27, 1914. The program featured the Choral Union's rendition of songs from Handel's *Messiah,* Russian and Swedish dance performances, vocal solos from the opera *Carmen,* various exhibits from the art and manual training departments and refreshments served in the Training School rotunda. A souvenir pamphlet prepared for the event proudly described the advances of the previous decade. The physical plant had grown from nothing to six buildings, including those under construction. The cramped library, still in the administration building, bulged with 11,000 volumes.

Quality reproductions of 173 famous paintings adorned campus walls. The faculty now numbered 60, including some who would leave an indelible mark on the institution, such as English professor George Sprau, who arrived in 1909, and newly hired Department of Mathematics head John Everett. Student enrollment had climbed to 654 for the winter semester of 1914. Over the previous ten years, 1,500 students had graduated from Western Normal.

During commencement week of the summer session, in 1914, the Normal held another Decennial Celebration marking the completion of its tenth year. The event included the dedication of the new athletic field, an outdoor pageant commemorating the evolution of education in Michigan, numerous concerts and probably the first alumni reunion party. A special *Decennial Number of the Kalamazoo Normal Record* glowingly described the development of numerous campus clubs and organizations, including the Equal

Western's library stacks looked like this around 1910.

Western's entire male faculty members posed around 1914.

Suffrage Association begun in 1911. The publication noted the basement lunch room, which was operated by about 20 student workers and catered to 200 to 250 patrons daily. A Normal Co-Operative Store, established in 1912 to sell textbooks, paper, pencils and other supplies at a small profit margin, had sales of more than $9,000 the previous year. Kalamazoo benefactress Blanche Hull had donated $200 in 1913, as the seed money for a Western Normal Loan Fund to benefit needy students. Two years later, the fund totaled over $1,100, with money lent at 5% interest by a faculty committee that determined the worthiness of applicants.

Even as Western celebrated the progress of its initial ten years, on June 28, 1914, an assassin murdered Archduke Francis Ferdinand and his wife at Sarajevo. A month later, a war began that would escalate into a world crisis.

The 1911 *Kalamazoo Normal Record* carried an advertisement for Western's original pennant, which featured an "N." It was manufactured by the local Henderson-Ames Company.

Chapter 2

It Stands Upon a Hill, Four-Square to All

Ⅰn the fall of 1916, many a Western booster lustily sang *The Squad*, written by Kalamazooan Burton Fischer in honor of the Hillsmen's gridiron prowess. Others across the nation sang political campaign ballads such as *We Take Our Hats Off to You—Mr. Wilson*, celebrating the president who had kept his countrymen out of the Great European War. Woodrow Wilson won reelection thanks, in part, to that widely held perception. But German submarine warfare and Allied propaganda inexorably drew America into the conflict. On April 2, 1917, Wilson announced a call to arms, and the United States entered World War I four days later.

This postcard view depicts Main Street (now Michigan Avenue) at night about 1917.

Kalamazoo responded as it had in previous wars—with overwhelming enthusiasm. Cheering crowds and marching bands serenaded early volunteers departing the Michigan Central Depot. More than 2,200 men from Kalamazoo County would ultimately serve in uniform. Western's campus seethed with that same patriotic fervor. Within a week of the declaration of war, some 50 Western students began drilling with Colonel Joseph Westnedge's local National Guard unit.

In 1916, Waldo had hired a recent Kalamazoo College graduate, Ralph Ralston, to edit the new student newspaper, *The Western Normal Herald,* and perform general publicity work. Waldo gave his young editor a lesson in fund raising to pay for publication of the first issue. He telephoned various merchants and businessmen, told them about the project and then said, "I've got you down for a space for advertising and it will cost you so much a week, is that all right?" Waldo used a similar technique a decade later in raising money to rebuild the Presbyterian Church that had

burned down. He found out from a banker friend how much a number of well-to-do church members earned a year and asked them to tithe accordingly. In any event, Ralston hammered away on the typewriter at his desk in a corner of Waldo's office until the war began, when he enlisted in the navy along with physics professor Paul Rood. Ralston never returned to campus, but Rood did to become a venerable figure until his retirement in 1964. More than 418 other faculty, graduates, students and Normal High School students served their country in uniform during the war. Beginning with Donald Miller, 12 made the supreme sacrifice.

Few espoused more patriotism than Waldo, and he wanted his campus in the thick of war work. He campaigned for over a year to secure Student Army Training Corps (SATC) status for Western. Eventually he went to Washington and, with the backing of the Kalamazoo community, achieved his goal in June 1918.

Then came the task of recruiting. Waldo and many of his faculty traveled across the state to high schools, wooing prospective military training students. Dr. William Brown, who had joined the Department of English faculty in 1917, remembered journeying to the Upper Peninsula to recruit. Eventually, 370 SATC trainees arrived in Kalamazoo on September 3, 1918, well ahead of the completion of the two-story wooden barracks carpenters hammered away at adjacent the Michigan Central Railroad tracks. The "boys" found quarters in the basement of the science building, around the pool in the gymnasium basement and anywhere else on campus a cot could be placed.

At the end of the first week, the recruits were formally inducted into the U.S. Army during a ceremony held on the playgrounds south of the training school. A crowd of 1,500 attended the event. After the students took the oath of allegiance, Waldo delivered a stirring address representative of his oratorical style:

> *Despite all the horrors of the past four years, these are the best days the world has ever known. For these are days when young people are facing real problems and are deciding for the right even though it may mean the supreme sacrifice. You men will go forth to free the peoples of the world. You will help to free Belgium. You will help to free France. You will stand shoulder to shoulder with the valiant armies of Great Britain. You will stand side by side with the Italians. You will do your part to help free Serbia, Romania and Poland, and you will help set Russia up where she should be.*
>
> *We want you to live clean lives. We want you to study hard, to drill well. We are going to help you to do your level best to prepare yourselves to free these countries.*
>
> *Never were there days like these in all the world. We men of the faculty envy you. There have been many heartaches because we could not do real war work. But now we feel that we have some real war work to do. We are going to do our best to carry out everything the government expects us to do to prepare you for your work ...*

Student Army Training Corps recruits learned to march in step at Western's Athletic Field in 1918.

Built as a barracks for SATC recruits in 1918, the structure, shown here in the 1930s, was pressed into service as a classroom for several decades.

By October 20, the barracks stood complete. No sooner had the troops moved in and begun college course work and military training classes, than the Spanish influenza pandemic hit Kalamazoo. Millions died worldwide, but thanks to the efforts of Drs. William Upjohn and Leslie DeWitt, who served as post surgeons, only two SATC students succumbed to the disease. However, several other Western students, leaders of campus organizations, lost their lives to influenza.

The army converted the basement of the training school building into the mess hall, and three times a day, the recruits marched to "chow," and in the evening they marched to study period. Judging from a surviving menu dated November 10, 1918, the food was definitely above regular army standards: breakfast—apples, rolled oats, scrambled eggs, potatoes, hot biscuits and coffee; dinner— cream of tomato soup, celery, sirloin steak, fried potatoes, asparagus tips, salad, apple pie with ice cream and coffee; supper—cold meats, salad, hot Parker House rolls and coffee. As in other army camps, unlucky trainees pulled K.P. duty, the bane of military garrison life.

Divided into companies A and B under the command of Lieutenant R.G. Walters, the men studied military science under three other lieutenants and traditional college subjects taught by Normal instructors. The regular army officers and sergeants worked the recruits hard. Reveille came at 6:10 a.m. and taps at 9:30 p.m. In between were five assemblies, six hours of classes and various drills. In their limited spare time, the trainees participated in campus extracurricular activities. Harper Maybee secured 83 extra men in his choir, 61 in the glee club, 13 in the band and 17 in the orchestra. Enough SATC students swelled the football team to give Coach Spaulding another winning season.

Two tough regular army lieutenants commanding the companies gave Waldo one of the trials of his life. The president had always prohibited smoking on campus, even by his professors. English professor William Brown never forgot how "these two hard-boiled lieutenants cussed all the time and always had a cigarette hanging out of their mouths. I can see poor Mr. Waldo now when one of them would dash into the office and I'd be waiting in the hall maybe to talk to him

Western students studying agriculture launched a U.S. War Garden Project in 1918.

about something, and one of those fellows would go in with a cigarette hanging out of his mouth and lay Mr. Waldo out and tell him 'you do this' and 'you do that.' He wasn't used to being told like that and poor Mr. Waldo how he suffered through that thing."

The lieutenants ultimately forced Waldo to allow smoking on campus, but only by the military. Military experts had projected the war would continue until 1920, but the Armistice came suddenly on November 11, 1918. None of Western's SATC recruits got the chance to prove their mettle in battle. On the evening of

The general office of the Administration Building (East Hall) featured two secretaries around the WW I era.

December 13, 1918, faculty members attended a "delightful banquet in the mess hall where, with toasts and song," they bade farewell to the SATC, and none more thankfully than Waldo. A week later, they were formally discharged.

In the meantime, the Kalamazoo home front had also served well the nation's war needs. Kalamazooans endured wheatless and meatless days, grew victory gardens and bought more than $11 million worth of bonds during five Liberty Loan drives. Propaganda became an important element of this first modern war, and the Kalamazoo Protective League encouraged "right thinking" by sponsoring "patriotic mass meetings" where celebrities like Clarence Darrow delivered speeches and Camp Custer's Crack Band performed stirring martial airs.

The campus home front proved no less dedicated. A week after the United States entered the war, the Western Normal Food Commission was formed to investigate local agricultural conditions and formulate plans to assist farmers. As a result, the Western Normal Food Brigade came into existence on April 16, 1917, with an enrollment of 132 students, to help area farmers produce crops for the war effort. Another 150 coeds rushed to join the

Cookery department students experimented with recipes to develop substitutes for the wheat needed for the war effort.

Red Cross, enrolling in hospital sewing classes where they sewed and knitted thousands of sweaters, hats, wristlets and bandages.

Grace Moore instructed more than 100 coeds in the art of canning fruits and vegetables. Students of the cookery department tested scores of recipes to replace the use of wheat for the war effort and published a pamphlet, "Wheat Substitutes," filled with recipes for cornmeal bread, potato bread, barley biscuits, corn peanut cookies and liberty bread. The Agriculture Department under Susie Ellett taught seed testing and gardening as applied to the war effort.

The Training School children demonstrated their patriotism as well. In October 1917, they paid for the erection of their own steel flag pole just southwest of the training building, where the "beautiful emblem waved daily over our campus and city as an inspiration and a call for service." Even the Normal kindergartners joined the effort. The children sewed, pressed clothes and made artifacts to earn $36 to adopt an orphaned French child for a year.

In early 1918, Waldo called a student assembly to solicit pledges for support of the YMCA's efforts among servicemen. After "brief, snappy talks" by Waldo and history professor Paul Hickey, the student body went "over the top" with a pledge of $3,300 in a 15-minute period. The 1919 *Brown and Gold* summed up Western's campus support of the war: "We will do our bit. At the Western State Normal one learns to love loyalty, enthusiasm, co-operation and liberty for all."

When the war ended in November 1918, the Training School students launched another fund drive to help feed starving German children. Within a few months, they collected $450 to nourish their former enemies. The patriotic spirit aroused by the war would continue into the 1920s. The entire student body and most faculty marched through the streets of Kalamazoo each November 11 as part of the Armistice Day Parade. Helen Master, who joined the Department of English in 1921 recalled, in 1950, the last such parade:

In order to identify ourselves in the parade, it was arranged that we each wear a sort of sailor style tam, made of brown crepe paper with a band and streamers of stiffer gold paper. These had been made for the whole school by the sewing classes, so that we would be uniform. Some of us looked vaguely simple in such a style, but we all wore them. They were brown and gold and there was no question as to our identity. There was no question as to our identity then or later, because it rained. Nothing daunted, we marched on, while the brown ran into the gold, the gold down our necks, and the combined drip onto our coats with a staunch and true stain that no dry cleaner in Kalamazoo could do anything about. Many the new fall coat that went into the furnace the next day, useless now but to add a little heat. Yet the hottest heat came in the story of one of the faculty women who had marched and been ruined. As she mounted her home step, bedraggled, discouraged and sneezing, she observed her next door neighbor, a faculty member at Western who had been one of the parade planning committee, come from his dry house, in his warm, dry carpet slippers, and in his warm, dry shirt sleeves to pick up his warm, dry evening paper! After that there were no more Armistice Day parades.

Kalamazoo and the campus alike had greeted the returning doughboys with bands, parades and cheering crowds. But the veterans encountered a rapidly changing society. Disillusioned by the horrors and ultimate failure of the "war to end all wars," America longed to return to prewar "normalcy" but never could. The war had marred the nation's innocence, and the era of the 1920s reflected the abandoned hopes and morals of a "lost generation." As expatriate American authors wrote novels of bitterness, American women exercised their newly won equality by de-emphasizing their femininity. The boyish "flapper" look—an unaccentuated figure, and bobbed hair—replaced the voluptuous curves of the Gibson Girl's hourglass figure and luxuriant tresses.

Training School students, shown here in 1924, presented annual Christmas pageants in the rotunda.

Students enjoyed a dance class around 1920.

Needless to say, Western's campus was not in the forefront of those changes in mores and garb. Among Waldo's dictums was an unwritten law that forebade faculty or students from bobbing their hair. In a much later era, long hair came to symbolize rebellion, but in the 1920s short bobbed hair signified a certain wildness in character. One of the faculty women went ahead and got her hair bobbed, but took the precaution of wearing a wig on campus. Longtime geography professor Lucia Harrison recalled, in a 1958 interview, an incident from the early 1920s: "An excellent, very attractive student stopped by one day at the close of the class and asked if she could show me something. She removed her hat; her naturally curly hair had been bobbed. 'How beautiful,' was my immediate reaction to it and she joyfully exclaimed, 'Then you don't think I've done something wrong?' I inquired whether she had signed a contract. When she replied in the negative, I suggested it might be advisable for her to be hatless when she was interviewed by any superintendent so that he would know he was getting a bobbed-haired teacher." A few days later the Placement Office reprimanded Harrison for condoning a practice it had sought to discourage.

School dances held in the gaily decorated gymnasium in the 1920s featured Kalamazoo's famous Fischer's Orchestra playing the sedate waltzes and two-steps favored by Waldo. Students attempting the Charleston or other popular dances drew warnings by faculty to practice more modest dance steps. Attendance by all faculty, as chaperones, was mandatory. Three faculty women who failed to appear at a school dance earned a sharp reprimand from Waldo the following morning. Attending downtown movies or picnics on Sunday also remained taboo in the early 1920s.

Smoking on campus, which had been anathema since the school's founding, remained so in the 1920s. The only exception, apparently, was an old Dutch gardener named John Van Elk. Waldo allowed him to smoke his pipe while working. Professor Theodore Henry, pacing back and forth just off campus between classes while solemnly puffing a cigar, was a cherished memory of many students and faculty alike. Henry, an inveterate smoker, allegedly left his unfinished stogie on a post just off school property and retrieved it for his next smoking break. Coeds who dared light up a cigarette in downtown gathering places long remembered the fear that Dean of Women

Bertha Davis might catch them. Yet, apparently, the school permitted other forms of tobacco consumption. John Gill, who graduated from Western in 1924 and later returned as football coach, recalled a certain science teacher who chewed tobacco and spit in the sink during his lectures.

Students who thought they could get away with shenanigans off campus were also sadly mistaken. Faculty Visiting Committees sometimes startled students with inspection tours of their rooms in local boarding houses. As Helen Master, who served on several such search parties in the 1920s, remembered: "The members of the faculty paired off, male and female, and what the male didn't discover about how students lived, the female did; that was the idea!"

Or worse yet, Waldo might make a personal off-campus appearance at one of the boarding houses. One oft-told story had Waldo receiving a phone call from an irate neighbor complaining about a loud student party. Waldo telephoned one of the culprits and identified himself. The student, thinking it was a trick, said, "You're Mr. Waldo—I'm sure you are." When Waldo insisted on who he was, the student invited him to "come over." Five minutes later came a knock on the door and to the miscreant's mortification, there stood Waldo. The party promptly ended.

Waldo did not restrict such personal appearances to students. A faculty member who was habitually late for class found, to his consternation, the president sitting in the front row of his classroom one morning.

A boarding house, remembered by Eunice Kraft, who joined the language department in 1920, as "Mrs. Wood's," housed both male and female Western students, in discrete privacy

Western students made merry at a mock wedding held in a local student's home. The merriness would have ended abruptly had Waldo appeared at the door.

A view of the campus across Oakland Drive in the early 1920s

from each other, of course. The women even ate their meals at separate tables from the men. The only mingling occurred in the parlor during after-dinner socializing around a decrepit upright piano.

Two leading boarding houses catered to Western's faculty and were operated by the Hill and Cummings families. Both were distinguished by the quality and quantity of the food served. Kraft remembered, in particular, Sunday afternoon dinners at the Cummings house. The 24 lodgers would dress in their Sunday-best suits and taffeta dresses, to sit down to a splendid repast of chicken or turkey, incomparable potato salad and mincemeat pie made of succulent roast beef bits spread with homemade strawberry jam. But no matter how gay the repartee at those Sunday socials, the faculty were careful to heed Waldo's stern warning not to engage in gossip about campus matters.

The 1920s were also remembered as a watershed decade, a tremendous growing and maturing period for Western. Having tasted college life, many of the former SATC students returned to help swell the campus population to over 1,000 during the summer term of 1919. By the fall term of 1928, the enrollment exceeded 2,200. Burgeoning enrollment sometimes brought registration problems. Dr. William Brown never forgot the near catastrophe during the registration period at the start of the fall semester of 1922. To get into a class at that time, a student had to acquire a certain starred slip—first come, first served. Someone got the bright idea of laying out the coveted slips along the elevated running track hanging from the ceiling of the gymnasium. Then came a mad rush by students, with hundreds crowding the narrow confines of the straining and creaking track. Fearing danger of the track collapsing under the weight, someone ran for Dr. William McCracken, chemistry professor and acting president while Waldo took a one-year leave of absence to improve the operation of Bellingham Normal School in western Washington. But having stood in line waiting for a chance at one of the starred slips for more than hour, few of the students were willing to give up. Eventually, McCracken had to remove some physically to avert the danger.

The increase in the student body brought additional faculty members. Waldo personally did the hiring and he enjoyed competing with other colleges to get the best professors available. Personal recommendations by his network of friends in academia counted heavily, but Waldo never hired without personally interviewing candidates and, if possible, their spouses as well. He considered himself an excellent judge of character and felt a sense of failure from the few misjudgments he made. Sometimes, however, his interviews were rather informal.

J. Towner Smith, a star 440-yard runner at Western in the 1920s who returned to coach track and eventually serve as dean of men, recalled how Waldo hired economics professor Floyd Moore in 1919:

> Moore was over in some college in Minnesota and he had written to Waldo that he would like to come to Kalamazoo and join the faculty here. He had his degree, and he had been holding a job in this college and Waldo thought, well, sounds like a pretty good prospect, made an appointment with him for a Saturday to come over here from Minnesota and he would interview him. Well, I guess the train that he came on got in about noon and he walked from downtown up to the campus, and he asked where Waldo was. "Well," they said, "we don't know right now. He is not in his office, but there is a baseball game on this afternoon and he will be there." And Floyd Moore went down to the baseball game and they pointed out Waldo. He

> went over and introduced himself to Waldo and Waldo said, "Well, sit down," and they started talking about baseball and about the fellows who were playing and this and that. After an hour, all they had talked about was this baseball game. Moore said, "Dr. Waldo, I have to catch the train back to Minnesota. I came over to be interviewed about a job." And Waldo looked at him and said, "About a job, well, you are hired."

Moore retired from Western 40 years later.

Waldo could hire and he could also fire. He enjoyed telling his faculty about the time a certain male instructor behaved in an unruly way downtown, thus injuring the prestige of the college. When the president called him to

The series of photographs on this page and the following page, taken in the early 1920s, captured Western students at the various hands-on activities that comprised such an important part of education then and now. Students are shown constructing model homes and making bricks (above).

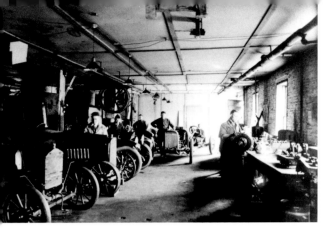

These photographs (above and below), taken in the early 1920s captured Western students at a number of hands-on activities that were considered then, as now, an important part of their education. Students are shown repairing automobiles, learning blacksmithing skills, at work in chemistry labs and sketching a rather Rubenesque model.

tion, and Waldo had eradicated a problem.

But the real testimonial to Waldo's success in hiring lies within the roster of faculty who joined Western in the decade following World War I, men and women who left their mark on the campus through their skilled teaching and dedication. The year 1919 brought Smith Burnham to the Department of History, Floyd Moore to economics, Herbert (Buck) Read to physical education, Fred Huff and Elmer Weaver to manual arts and Blanche Draper as editor of the *Herald*. In 1920, Burnham's daughter Margaret (later MacMillan) began teaching history in the Normal High School and Eunice Kraft started her long career in Latin. Helen Master came to the Department of English in 1921, as did Nancy Scott, and D.C. Shilling to the Department of History. The following year brought Hugh Ackley and Grover Bartoo to the Department of Mathematics, Ruth Van Horn and Louis Foley to English, Manley Ellis to education and Robert R. Russel, who would remain involved with Western as a centenarian, to history. Ethel

task, he defended himself by saying that Waldo had no right to criticize his off-campus activities as long as his behavior on campus was appropriate. Waldo replied: "All right, from this minute consider yourself as permanently off the campus."

Impudence was one thing, but for faculty who simply did not perform to the level of Waldo's expectations, he was usually kinder. William McKinley Robinson, who arrived on campus in 1927 and eventually succeeded Burnham as head of the Department of Rural Education, recalled that Waldo never told them they were failing, but would try to land them a better job via his network of friends on other campuses. The faculty member would leave Western thanking Waldo for his promo-

Western's entire faculty gathered for a group photograph in 1921. Where's Waldo?

Hale, whom Russel would marry two years later, also joined the staff of the Training School in 1922. In 1923, Isabel Crane began teaching in the Department of Physical Education; George Hilliard, Ray Pellet and Paul Sangren started in the Department of Education; Leslie Kenoyer in biology; Louise Struble in art; Walter Terpenning in sociology and Louise Walker in English. Elmer Wilds came to the Department of Education in 1924, and the following year Howard Bigelow arrived to teach economics, and Frederick Rogers to teach education. In 1926, Western's first historian, James Knauss, started in the Department of History and Don Pullen in manual arts. The year 1928 proved a banner one, with the hiring of Homer Carter in education, Mitchell Gary and John Gill in physical education, Leonard Kercher and Charles Starring in sociology and Lydia Siedschlag in the Training School.

Dedicated, loyal, hard-working and at the top of their profession, Waldo's faculty produced—in part, because he had high expectations of them, and not just on the campus. He encouraged them to participate actively in Kalamazoo's cultural life by providing numerous lectures on almost any conceivable topic, *pro bono*, and to serve in civic affairs. At one time, three faculty members sat on the board of the Kalamazoo Chamber of Commerce.

Waldo set the example by his active participation in the Rotary Club, by heading up the Community

Blanche Draper, pictured in 1946, was co-publicity director of Western Michigan College for more than 27 years.

The dilapidated old Eames Mill at the intersection of Oakland Drive and Michigan Avenue was utilized for manual training classes in the WW I era and later as a theatrical playhouse.

The interior of the Eames Mill contained a machine shop for student use.

his faculty to show up for periodic weekend work details unrelated to their academic load. He knew human nature well enough to know how odious some of that extracurricular work must have been and he retained a well-developed sense of humor. Cornelius MacDonald, who graduated from Western in 1923 to begin a long career with his alma mater as an administrator, recalled the time Waldo called in Ernest Burnham and William McCracken and asked if they were free the coming Saturday morning. Both quickly explained how very busy they were that day with committee meetings, appointments, and so on. Waldo replied, "Well, that is a shame. You see I've got four tickets to the Notre Dame game and thought maybe you'd like to go."

As Western's student body and faculty grew during the post-war decade, the campus burgeoned from its original 20 acres with a 13-acre athletic field, to nearly 57 acres. In 1916, the school purchased a nearly two-acre plat of land south of the campus, formerly the site of the Fletcher Sanitarium. The following year, the school bought a triangular piece of land northeast of the athletic field, at the intersection of Oakland Drive and Michigan Avenue. The old Eames Mill there, dating back to the 1840s, was remodeled to house the Department of Industrial Arts. Another 15-acre tract south and southeast of the athletic field acquired in 1920 and 1923, gave Western possession of all

Chest and other fund-raising activity and by serving as Kalamazoo police commissioner. Involvement in politics, on the other hand, remained strictly taboo, although monetary support was sometimes sought. In 1919, Waldo requested his faculty to contribute toward purchasing a large advertisement in the *Kalamazoo Gazette* backing Mary Ensfield, a candidate for Kalamazoo School Commission. She had taught in Western's rural department for two years. She won handily.

And even into the 1920s, Waldo expected

The Manual Training Building was completed in 1921.

the land between Oakland Drive and the Michigan Central Railroad tracks north of the Kalamazoo State Hospital grounds.

In 1915, the legislature had appropriated an impressive sum of $480,000 to be paid in six annual installments to build an auditorium and conservatory, a library building, an addition to the gymnasium and a manual training building. But the needs of the war intervened and by 1921, the only structure completed was a 216-foot-by-80-foot single-story brick and concrete manual training building located northeast of the athletic field. Wartime inflation in the value of building materials made it impossible to construct the other planned structures with the funds allocated.

In 1921, Waldo decided to again campaign for more building funds. Newly hired manual arts instructor Fred Huff recalled his role in the project:

[Waldo] called me into his office, pointed to the stacks of books and said, "We need more room. I am going to Lansing Monday and ask for money to build three new buildings. This pile concerns a new men's gymnasium. This pile is for a new library." [The third was for an auditorium]. Small notes were sticking out of the books saying

this and that. Reverse this floor plan, change the stairs, put in a fourteen-lap track, omit the gym basement, put more book stacks, etc., etc. I picked up the books Friday afternoon, went downtown and bought a big roll of tracing paper, saw the city's largest architect, went home and set up a large drawing board, hung a drop lamp over it and went to work. My wife called friends in Battle Creek we had invited over for Sunday dinner and called that off and they took offense and never saw us again. I started late Friday afternoon and I drew the last line Monday at 5:00 a.m. I took the tracings downtown and at 7:00 a.m. I laid the three rolls of blueprints on Mr. Waldo's desk. At 7:30 our phone rang and Mr. Waldo's secretary Lloyd Jessen said, "Fred, Mr. Waldo is ready to go to Lansing and needs his blueprints or whatever you call them. Where are they?" I said "I put them on his desk in his office at seven o'clock this morning." Lloyd's voice was very faint but it sounded like "Oh, Lord, we never looked there." That evening Mr. Waldo called me to say "Well I got two of the three, the library and the gym."

Once the pride of the campus, the new library (now North Hall) was built in 1923-1925.

Work began on the library building (now called North Hall) in May 1923, and the two-story brick structure was formally dedicated on June 22, 1925. In addition to the steel-shelved stacks where 24,000 volumes from the old library in the administration building found new quarters, the building contained staff work rooms, classrooms, lecture rooms and a majestic two-story-high main reading room, 148 feet long by 38 feet wide, capable of accommodating 300 researchers. Albert M. Todd, the Kalamazoo "mint king," decorated the reading room with examples from his notable art collection.

Laborers broke ground for the men's gymnasium on June 4, 1924. One year later, renowned coaches, including Alonzo Stagg of the University of Chicago and Fielding Yost of the University of Michigan, attended the dedication ceremonies. A huge cheer reverberated from the 3,000-seat bleachers when Spaulding, Western's first athletic director who had left to become head coach at the University of Minnesota in 1922, took the podium. A state-of-the-art facility in 1925, it was the largest gymnasium in any American teacher's training institution. The two-story-high, 188-foot-by-86-foot structure with a basement and sub-basement housed a regulation basketball court with three cross courts, a dirt floor area for training in field events, a 14-lap cork running track, offices, classrooms, locker rooms, showers, and alleys for archery and golf. With the completion of this facility, the original Normal gymnasium received designation as the women's gymnasium.

The Grand Reading Room of the new library featured art work donated by Kalamazoo "mint king" Albert M. Todd.

The new men's gymnasium, shown here under construction in 1924, was considered one of the finest facilities of its type in America.

The new gymnasium was Waldo's pride and joy. He had personally persuaded Governor Alexander Groesbeck to add an additional $50,000 to the original appropriation to render it the finest of its type. Herbert (Buck) Read, Western's illustrious basketball coach from 1922 to 1949, never forgot the time, shortly after the dedication of the gymnasium, when as Waldo was about to enter the building "he saw a great splotch of tobacco juice on the steps leading into the main door." Waldo did not rest until he had found the culprit who had so foully given a second dedication to the building and promptly expelled him. Unhappily for Read, it turned out to be one of his basketball players.

The building that Waldo campaigned for in 1921 and did not get, the auditorium, would not become a reality until completion of Miller Auditorium in 1967. But Western's drama students, known as the Players, under director Laura Shaw, did not allow the lack of a suitable venue to limit their activities. They presented popular plays including *The Big Idea* and *Peg O' My Heart* during the early 1920s in Kalamazoo's Fuller Theatre. Then in 1922, when the Department of Manual Arts moved from the Eames Mill to its new building, the Players convinced Waldo to let them convert the run-down old structure into the playhouse.

They raised money, built a stage, made curtains, arranged lighting effects, secured old chairs and painted them and "completely transformed the building into one of the finest little theatres in the county."

The playhouse opened on May 10, 1922,

In 1926, Laura V. Shaw directed Western's drama program and taught speech classes.

WSN Dramatic Association members cavorted in a pageant, *The Progress of Education in Michigan*, performed in 1919.

An aerial view of the campus in 1925

During the 1920s, this bus conveyed Western practice teachers to the Portage School Building seen in the background.

with three one-act plays was "an unqualified success." In 1923, the midwinter play, *Beyond the Horizon,* drew rave reviews, as did the *Western Normal Review* staged in May. The following year, a week before the scheduled performance of the midwinter play, *The Romantic Age,* a coterie of Lansing bureaucrats toured the campus and inspected the playhouse. A few days before opening night, a telegraph arrived announcing the playhouse was condemned. Disheartened but not defeated, the Players returned to using other Kalamazoo venues, but continued to utilize the

The interior of the Playhouse, which opened in 1922

playhouse as a theatrical clubhouse and for rehearsals until the structure was finally razed in 1942.

Other popular entertainments of the 1920s included recitals by major American poets, sponsored by Western's senior class. In 1924, Lew Sarett, who had grown up in Benton Harbor, read his verse at the Kalamazoo Central Auditorium. Carl Sandburg, then living in Harbert, played the banjo and chanted his poetry, including "The Sins of Kalamazoo," in 1925. The following year, Vachel Lindsay, the tramp poet, regaled the audience with his rendition of "The Congo," "Kalamazoo" and other alliterative poems.

Western's practice teaching network grew to encompass additional facilities during the 1920s. Portage Township erected a five-teacher school building six miles south of Kalamazoo that became an integral part of Western's teacher training system. In 1924, the Richland Township school and a new school in Paw Paw were also affiliated with Western. Also that year, a model Hurd School, five miles west of the campus, replaced the old Michigan Avenue one-room school used for practice teaching.

A number of college-owned buses conveyed education students back and forth to those various schools.

Western's faculty, who journeyed near and far to teach extension classes—as continuing education was originally termed—faced a different set of obstacles in the 1920s. From 1905, when the extension department began, through the 1920s, trains and "interurban" coaches provided practically the sole means of travel to extension classes. Historian Knauss recorded the travails of extension travel in a 1943 article. During the early 1920s, "One instructor, who had a class in Traverse City, left at four o'clock on Friday afternoon and came back on the one-thirty train on Sunday morning." Another routinely left at 5:30 a.m. on Tuesday for Saginaw, changed trains in Battle Creek and Flint and arrived in Saginaw in time to teach a two-hour class starting at 4:00 p.m. and another one in Bay City in the evening. Whereupon, he caught a "sleeper" train and reached Kalamazoo in time for his 8:00 a.m. class on campus.

Monteith Junction near Martin was the scene of three Western professors' snowbound adventure.

Waldo and Frank Ellsworth, director of the Training School, posed proudly with Western's new buses, purchased in the late 1920s.

Around 1920, John Hoekje, director of extension since 1917, English professor George Sprau and education professor Theodore Henry boarded an interurban for the one-hour trip to their extension classes in Grand Rapids. A blizzard struck and they found themselves snowbound for 30 hours in Monteith Junction near Martin. They and about 25 others huddled in a little unheated baggage room and subsisted on frozen milk. The situation worsened when Henry, the inveterate smoker who blew his clouds of smoke just off campus, ran out of cigars. All survived to tell the story, *ad infinitum*, according to Knauss. The advent of more faculty-owned automobiles in the middle and late 1920s made extension travel faster, but the educators lost the bonus of relaxation during train trips.

The 1920s brought more and more traffic chugging up Oakland Drive to the campus. That road had been paved with bricks in the summer of 1919, with streetcar tracks laid along its west side. During rush hours, a streetcar passed every six minutes and every 12 minutes the remainder of the day. Buses ultimately brought about the demise of the streetcar system in Kalamazoo, and the tracks were torn up in 1934.

In the 1920s, parking on campus was haphazard at best.

As ownership of automobiles by faculty increased, parking problems emerged on campus. Knauss recalled that when he started teaching at Western in 1926, drivers backed their cars close to the basement windows of the administration building and "the resulting noise and escaping fumes from the exhaust pipes made the life of the conscientious teachers in the basement a nightmare." A main campus thoroughfare traversed the children's playground on the south side of the Training School, and drivers zoomed through the unfenced area endangering the youngsters. Eventually, the playground was fenced and a pedestrian bridge constructed to link the Training School and the Administration Building.

But for the Western students of the 1920s, ownership of an automobile, even one of Henry Ford's "Tin Lizzies" which sold new for as little as $280, lay well beyond their reach. Walking remained the dominant mode of transportation. Kalamazoo native Leo "Tiny" Redmond, who attended Western in the early 1920s, recalled trudging across town to work an eight-hour shift in a paper mill each night after a full day of classes and football practice. In his spare time he served as president of his senior class. The six-foot-one-inch Redmond weighed over 300 pounds and was "quick as a

Students from the 1920s posed for a snapshot on the elevated walkway connecting the Training School and the Administration Building, dubbed the "Bridge of Sighs."

Three-hundred-pound "Tiny" Redmond starred on the unbeaten 1922 Western eleven.

cat." He played center and served as captain of the unbeaten and never-scored-upon 1922 football squad.

Thanks initially to the hardened veterans returning from the trenches to attend Western, the post-World War I decade produced some of the school's finest athletic teams. In 1920, the basketball team won the state championship while defeating Michigan State 27-14 and beating Notre Dame twice. Later, Herbert "Buck" Read's adoption of the fast break around 1930 would make Western's hoopsters practically unstoppable. The baseball team won the Michigan Collegiate Conference championship four consecutive years beginning in 1927.

Western's track teams in the early 1920s included such standouts as shot put and discus

"Juddy" Hyames played shortstop for Western in 1915 and served as baseball coach from 1922-1936 and athletic director from 1935-1949.

John Hoekje, back left, coached this 1926 tennis squad.

Charlie Maher, Western's catcher from 1922-1924, coached the baseball team for 30 years, beginning in 1937.

thrower Hilliard Hulscher and runner Towner Smith. Each year from 1923 to 1925, the cross country team placed first in the state intercollegiate meet.

Tennis had been played informally at the Normal by students and faculty on the courts constructed at the foot of the hill as early as the spring of 1905, and it was first officially recognized as a school sport in 1923. Hoekje played tennis and managed the teams in the early and middle 1920s. The sport received continuing support when he became registrar in 1921 and took on more administrative duties and power. Cornelius MacDonald, who had been hired by Hoekje in 1923 as a receiving clerk and would become comptroller of the college in 1948, remembered his boss as a "tireless worker and very efficient." One of Hoekje's many duties under Waldo was to personally supervise all student loans. In 1963, MacDonald told Dr. Alan Brown, the University's first archivist, an oft-quoted story about Hoekje's proverbial Dutch frugality when dispensing loans:

Eddie Gaines, left, and Mason Evans ran as part of Western's record-breaking 1928 two-mile relay team.

A fellow went in and said "Mr. Hoekje, I want to borrow ten dollars." Mr. Hoekje, as you know, was deaf and said, "What did you say?" The fellow said, "Mr. Hoekje, I wonder if I could borrow twenty dollars?" Mr. Hoekje said, "I heard you the first time."

Everyone who attended or taught at Western, it seems, remembered the ubiquitous Hoekje. By the middle 1920s, each Tuesday morning began with a mandatory assembly in the women's gym. Charles A. Smith, a Western student in the late 1920s who joined the Department of English faculty in 1935, recalled with his usual humor one particular assembly:

The dean of men, Ray C. Pellet, and the dean of women, Bertha S. Davis, handed us attendance slips as we filed in. We handed these back, filled out, as we left. If you missed an assembly, your name was posted and you had a session with your dean in which there was a complete absence of jollies. The faculty sat in rows of folding chairs on the stage. During the assembly hour the faculty and the students stared at each other with some amusement and speculation on both sides. Sometimes there was more occasion for amusement than at other times. One morning, a very large and rangy hound slipped through the deans at the entrance doors, ambled past the front rows of students, who did what they could to make him feel welcome, and up onto the stage. He went from faculty member to faculty member, coming back again and again to sniff at the guest speaker, who sat out in front of the faculty between President Waldo and Mr. Hoekje, our registrar. The guest speaker kept pushing him away, but the dog got the idea this was some sort of game and began to put everything he had into it. The students

were beginning to get rather enthusiastic about the situation, and even some of the faculty weren't viewing it with as much regret as they probably should have. It was obviously up to Mr. Hoekje to do something about it, and he did. He scooped the hound up in his arms and started off the stage toward the door with him. It was a long walk. The dog was big and lanky and heavy, and it was all Mr. Hoekje could do to hang onto him. And somehow the dog got twisted around in Mr. Hoekje's arms and began to lick his face with great loving lollops of the tongue. There was nothing the registrar could do but hang on and keep going. The whole student body broke out in thunderous applause. The two finally got to the door and went through it out of sight. A moment later we heard a howl of anguish from the dog.

In addition to serving as registrar, dog catcher and general henchman to Waldo, Hoekje continued to run the extension department. In 1925, he published a *Normal School Bulletin* "Speakers Available" that

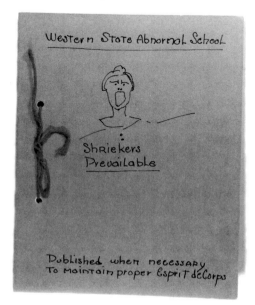

In 1925, the "Shriekers Prevailable" parody of the *Normal School Bulletin* made an effort to get a fair shake for faculty women.

Members of Western's band in 1920 were proud to wear their pants—the new matching pants purchased through student donations.

included the photographs of 21 faculty members and the titles of 51 speeches they offered to audiences across the state. Hoekje had not included a single female faculty member in the pamphlet. Thoroughly irritated, the faculty women chose a facetious rebuttal. Under the leadership of Edna Liek of the Department of Education, and with cartoons rendered by Lydia Siedschlag of the Training School office and art instructor Elaine Stevenson, they produced a mimeographed parody, the "Western State Abnormal School Bullet—Shriekers Prevailable." Twenty-one female faculty members contributed humorous versions of speeches included in the genuine bulletin. Dr. Elmer Wild's "Eight Cylinder Life" became Bernice Hesselink's "Six Cylinder Love;" Manley Ellis's "Choosing a Vocation"

became Anna Evans's "Losing a Vacation;" and Walter Terpenning's travelogue "To Russia and Return" appeared as Elizabeth Zimmerman's "To Paw Paw and Return." Waldo, in particular, who always enjoyed a good joke, was elated with the "Bullet." Hoekje surrendered, and the next edition of the *Bulletin* issued that fall included six female speakers.

The Roaring Twenties seem to have been a time of great frivolity on campus. A well-remembered stunt occurred as part of the annual football banquet of 1920. One of Maybee's new students, Christopher Overly, was an expert violinist. Maybee hatched a scheme to disguise his student as Fritz Kreisler, the famous Austrian violin virtuoso who was then touring America and who had actually appeared at the Kalamazoo Armory three years

Elisabeth Zimmerman in 1927 taught Latin and German.

in the basement, a telegram arrived stating that Kreisler would be happy to appear at the banquet. The excited crowd could hardly believe their ears—the famous Kreisler would play at the Normal! When they were seated in the basement, Overly entered with fur cap, coat and violin. After rendering several pieces, he was accorded a huge ovation. When he left, baseball coach Judson "Juddy" Hyames rose to say that "the appearance of the great man was an inspiration and a challenge to all assembled there." So successful was Maybee's hoax, for which he had taken the precaution of obtaining Waldo's blessing, that he had a difficult time convincing several faculty members the next day that they had not heard the real Kreisler.

before, and have him play at the banquet. Theatre students made up Overly with a moustache and darkened complexion, while downtown clothier Samuel Folz lent a fur cap and coat with a fur collar similar to Kreisler's trademark outfit.

As the students and faculty milled around in the rotunda of the Training School awaiting the announcement that the banquet was ready

Charles Starring, a Western sophomore when the Kreisler prank was played, remembered the 1920-21 student year as "a time of renaissance, of burgeoning organizations, of anxiety for new responsibilities." That fall, a coterie of students, including Starring, organized the Booster Club to improve school spirit at athletic games and, as noted in the *Herald*, to "get behind all activities with a force which will put them over the top with a triumph exceeding the most glorious achievements of the school heretofore." One of the booster's first projects was a trouser fund drive. A Western marching band had sprung into existence in 1915 but had languished during the war. Revived in 1920, the band sported dashing jackets but lacked pants—matching pants, that is. During a school assembly on December 1, 1920, the Western student body rose in cheering unison to the challenge that "a band with a 100 percent rating in ability and spirit should be 100 percent uniformed." The Booster

Western's marching band drummed up student spirit for the 1922 gridiron match against Waldo's alma mater, Albion College.

Western rooters decorated the interurban train for the 1922 ride to Albion. Western beat its arch rival 20-9.

Committee soon raised $200 and by January 5, 1921, the *Herald* announced the trouser fund drive had reached its goal, "and now may the Western Normal Band appear in all its glory. For the new uniforms are complete. The trousers are here!"

The Booster Club chose four of its members as the first student staff of the *Herald* in January, 1920. A few years later, students took more control of the journal. By the fall term of 1921, the Booster Club had also created a Student Association and a Student Council. On November 9, 1921, the Western student body, 935 pupils strong, elected Rolland Maybee the first president of the Student Association.

The legislative arm of the Student Association, the Student Council, voted to collect 25 cents from each student who enrolled the following semester and ultimately, with the sanction of the State Board of Education, that amount was incorporated into the student activities fee. In the fall of 1921, the council sponsored a contest for the words and music of a school song. The winning entry began:

The girl with brown bewild'ring eyes
Terrifically laden
With golden lightning of the skies,
O she's a Western Normal maiden;
With eyes of brown and heart of gold—
A Western Normal maiden.

But those lyrics failed to gain acceptance among the student body and did not replace the traditional pieces that appeared in *Songs W* published in 1921, including Warren E. Johnson's *Western Normal Pep Song*:

Western State, our hearts go out to you,
All our teams are fighters thru and thru,
Watch them go down the field making
opponents yield a vict'ry for Western State,
Rah, rah, rah...

Western's Fight Song by William Bakeman

Hail! Hail! for Western Normal School.
We have the pep and the fight and vim
in all our games we go out to win
either in football, baseball or track
Western's the spirit that most schools lack,
Rah!

Alma Mater, Brown and Gold by Wilma G. Mayer

Hail! To the Brown and Gold,
We're for you as of old!
Dearer by far than all the rest,
We praise you as the best,
We'll give our strength to you,
Fight for you and be true,
Here's to you, our Alma Mater,
Brown and Gold!

Adelaide Hart's *Brown and Gold*, remained popular through the 1930s.

Brown and Gold we sing to you
And in our hearts your standards hold.
We pray that fortune's smile may favor you.
And in her mantle you enfold
Hail, Oh, Western Western
Back of you We're standing firm
Our Watchword ever Loyalty.

Yes, Brown and Gold the tried and true
We'll doff our hats to you.
Western, we're proud of you...

Waldo permitted the creation of a Student Association and a Student Council, but he still held the line against the formation of campus fraternities and sororities because he disapproved of the social stratification usually associated with them. He did, however, allow organizations relating to improvement in some pursuit, such as debating. Some rudimentary organizations had occasionally engaged in debate, such as the Riley Literary Society for men founded by mathematics professor Thomas J. Riley in 1904, and the Amphictyon for women started by Mary Lowell of the Department of English. But the first formed for the exclusive purpose of debate came in 1913, when history professor Paul Hickey sponsored the Hickey Debating Club for men.

Members of the Erosophian Society, a debate and speech club, adopted a serious pose in 1915.

In 1919, Western's students were ready for work in a nature study garden they planted alongside Oakland Drive.

In 1916, Lousene Rousseau of the speech department developed one for women called the Senate.

In 1919, the Hickey Debating Club changed its name to the Forum and began debating the Senate. In the initial match, "Should the United States Enter the League of Nations," the men proved victorious. The debate in 1920, "Resolved that the Soviet Government should be recognized by the United States," saw the women best the men. Stung by that loss, the Forum developed a schism and the Tribunal emerged, becoming Theta Chi Delta in 1930. Three years later, the Forum became Phi Sigma Rho. The Senate would eventually evolve into the women's social organization Alpha Chi Omega. The oldest of the honorary Greek letter societies on campus, the co-educational science organization Kappa Rho Sigma, began in 1920. Tau Kappa Alpha and Kappa Delta Pi, national honorary societies, date from 1927.

Faculty members sometimes sponsored less formal gatherings for students. Dr. William R. Brown, who taught in the Department of English for 40 years beginning 1917, recalled his and his wife's efforts:

During the first world war, they wouldn't let us heat the building at night; they had to turn off the heat as early as possible. That was the beginning of Mrs. Brown and myself having mobs of students in our house, which I want to say has been the greatest joy of our lives.

Well, we opened our house, a little house down there on Locust Street, and some undertaker or other would send up a carload of chairs and we had the meetings of this society. And I remember those bitter cold nights and the kids would come, and a lot of them would sit on the floor before the fire. And I suppose Mrs. Brown and I got the idea from that and on up through the thirties and the [radio] opera broadcasts, after we moved out to the house on Oakland Drive. We had a bigger house, and we have enjoyed so much having the students come. Then we had English clubs and we had book review clubs—boys who since have become quite good teachers and that we are very proud of, were in a club of ours for four or five years. Then we had a club of girls. We had fifteen or twenty come to the broadcasts and then my wife would make a big lot of doughnuts and goulash and to this day when I meet students of those years, they never ask me how I am? They say, "Does Mrs. Brown still make goulash?" That's the thing they remember."

The faculty also began organizing clubs for their own enjoyment and edification during the post-war decade. A faculty club begun in the early days to share papers on current topics of interest had disbanded by the start of the war. In late 1918, a Language Club and a Faculty Science Club sprang into being. The latter, developed by geography professor Leslie H. Wood and nine other professors, held its first meeting at Wood's home just two days after the Armistice. Intended to foster "scholarship and the research spirit" on campus, the club, throughout the 1920s, delved into such diverse subjects as radio communication, astronomical explorations, sand dunes, dinosaurs and remaking the map of Baffin Island.

Another organization, intended to help faculty wives get better acquainted with each other, began in 1913 as the Faculty Dames. By the 1920s, the club had taken on the responsibility to acquaint wives of new faculty of their duty to uphold Western's reputation for dignity and proper etiquette, especially off campus. Eloise Seibert recalled her initial experience with Faculty Dames when she moved to Kalamazoo with her husband Russell, a newly hired history professor:

> *You see, shortly after new members arrived they were called on by a couple of lovely established Dames—mine were Helen Hoekje and Emma Brown. Helen wore a lavender hat—I'll never forget her. In the nicest, friendliest way*

Daring students earned extra money washing East Hall windows during the summer of 1922.

during our conversation, it was subtly hinted that when faculty women attended the Dames Tea on the third Thursday of each month, hat, gloves and heels were worn. Also, when we went downtown we were likewise attired. As a sweet young thing, I secretly wanted to do my part. I was glad, really, that they cared enough about me and the status of the college to give me the rules straight; but after they left I was scared stiff. Sometime later one of the new gals forgot her hat— or maybe she was testing the rule— anyway the omission was quietly brought to her attention. We had a tradition to uphold and you can't imagine how pretty and proper we all looked at our lovely teas.

In early 1928, Waldo decided he needed a small formal organization within the faculty to advise him on campus matters. He appointed a committee to determine its structure, functions and name. It met over a period of several months while investigating similar organizations at other colleges. On April 17, 1928, came the creation of the Faculty Council, composed of 12 faculty members elected by their colleagues, with the president and registrar as ex-offico members.

The development of such clubs and organizations in the 1920s should not imply that faculty had a lot of extra time on their hands. On the contrary, Waldo continued to keep them plenty busy with extracurricular duties. The task of selling tickets in the community to the various concerts and lectures sponsored by the school fell to the faculty. That included the week-long Redpath Chautauqua that set up its huge tent on the tennis courts at the foot of the hill adjacent to Davis Street from 1916 to 1926. The highlight of the summer, the Kalamazoo Chautauqua, featured Shakespearean players, bands, equestrian acts, concerts, and celebrated orators such as William Jennings Bryan, who spoke with such enthusiasm that he needed to cool his forehead with a big block of ice at his side. Until it succumbed to the competition of motion pictures and radio in the middle 1920s, the Chautauqua served as a sort of cultural circus that provided midwestern communities with extraordinary entertainment.

At the opening of football season, faculty members were "sent out in all directions to post big signs" advertising the school's gridiron schedule. Faculty attendance at athletic events was practically mandatory. Even during practice sessions, Waldo expected at least six or eight professors to show their support from the sidelines. To make sure their interest was genuine, he quizzed his teachers during staff meetings about game events, student athletes' names, where they were from and what their fathers did for a living.

Some faculty members also found themselves scheduled for work details on Saturdays at the college farm, four miles south of the campus. The original 100-acre farm was acquired in 1925 and an

The Redpath Chautauqua pitched its tent on Western's tennis courts adjacent to Davis Street from 1916-1926.

The interior of the Chautauqua's big tent circa 1917

Football games at Western's gridiron drew big crowds during the 1920s.

adjacent 50 acres three years later (the land was later sold at a big profit). In 1927, Waldo canceled classes on Arbor Day so students and faculty alike could troop to the 50-acre preserve donated by Caroline Kleinstuck to the State Board of Education five years before. They spent the day planting 10,000 pine saplings.

As the 1920s drew to a close, Western took stock of its robust development during the decade. Enrollment had surpassed 2,300 during the fall semester of 1927. By 1929, 201 faculty members taught approximately 500 subjects in 21 departments. Western began offering a four-year curriculum leading to a bachelor's degree in education in 1919. In 1927, the state legislature renamed the school Western State Teachers College, and by 1929, Western offered additional bachelor's degrees in arts and science. Tuition remained $5 per semester, with a student activities fee of $7.50 that included tickets to all games. "Students who must earn their way through

Waldo, faculty and students planted 10,000 pine saplings at Kleinstuck Preserve on Arbor Day 1927.

Western's band led the entire student body in a march to Kleinstuck Preserve in April 1927.

college," a promotional brochure published in 1929 promised, "are welcome. There are no social classes on the Hilltop. Ambition and sincerity and hard work are the passwords to recognition." More than 12,000 degrees and teaching certificates had been earned by Western students in the 25 years since its origin. In 1929, the school proudly cited the 70 Western graduates serving as superintendents of schools and the 54 serving as high school principals.

The year 1929 became one of celebration for the Kalamazoo community. The city staged a mammoth festival in Bronson Park marking the centennial of its founding by Titus Bronson. It featured a historical pageant, a band concert, an "old timer's get-together" and a spectacular air circus at Lindbergh Field.

Western, too, held a gala celebration of its first 25 years. On June 14, the students of the pageantry class performed *Vision Unfolding*, a historical reenactment of the college's growth. The climax came as curtains parted to reveal a new painting of Waldo, followed by a choral interlude written by the dour, old Scottish chemistry professor William McCracken:

> *It stands upon a hill, four-square to all*
> *The winds that blow*
> *Behold in its splendor a sincere devotion*
> *To those ideals that attended its birth,*
> *Each column part of a vision unfolding,*
> *O Western, thou hast proved thy worth.*
>   *A monument in the hearts of the living,*
> *Its master architect, ye know,*
> *Behold on yon hilltop our loved alma mater,*
>   *Four-square to all the winds that blow,*
> *Four-square to all the winds that blow.*

Little did anyone know during that happy summer of celebration of the storm clouds gathering on the horizon and of the daunting challenges that would come. The October 23, 1929, issue of the *Herald* announced adoption of a hilarious new campus tradition. Henceforth, all freshmen would wear green beanies for the entire fall term. The following day's

In 1929, Western celebrated its 25th anniversary with a pageant *Vision Unfolding.*

Black Thursday ushered in a decade-long Great Depression, an economic catastrophe that would test Western to its limits.

Chapter 3

Depression & War, Challenges & Victory

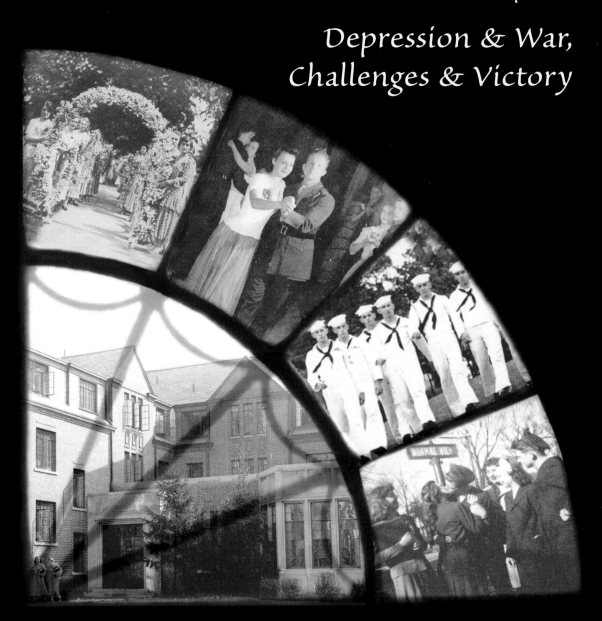

In 1930, the nation began its descent into what would become an entire decade of economic chaos. Yet, Western's fall enrollment actually rose more than seven percent over the previous year to 2,132 students. That student body was considerably less than diverse, however. Not more than half a dozen black faces peer from the pages of the 1930 *Brown and Gold* yearbook and that includes the two winners of the annual Women's League Masquerade Contest who appeared in blackface caricature as Aunt Jemima and Uncle Ben.

The varsity track team proved a notable exception with three African-American standouts. Dash man Edward Gaines and hurdler William Loving served as co-captains of the team. They, along with the six-foot-six-inch shotputter and discus thrower Henry Harper, consistently set new state records throughout the season. It was no accident that

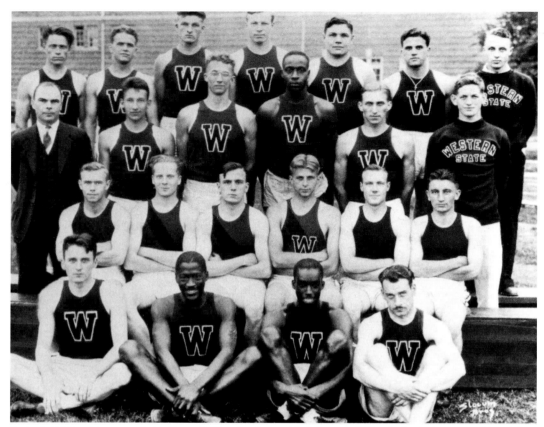

Western's 1930 track team, coached by Towner Smith, enjoyed an undefeated season. William Loving is shown second from left in the front row seated next to Edward Gaines. Henry Harper is standing.

these black athletes played for Western. Waldo had said more than once, "I may not be able to solve this racial thing, but I am going to have black players out there so people can see them." And he furthered that goal through recruitment.

Tom Briscoe, an outstanding black athlete of the early 1930s, recalled Waldo's techniques. When he read in the paper about the exploits of some black champion like Loving or Gaines from Gary, Indiana, he summoned Randall Fraser, a black Western graduate who had been able to secure no better a job than that of janitor in the school library, and said, "Go down there. I want that guy." Fraser would bring the athlete so Waldo could interview him and show him the campus. Waldo himself went to Indiana to recruit Loving and sat down to dinner with the family in the process, a rare social breakthrough in that era.

Sometimes, Waldo found himself competing for star athletes with other schools. Former

comptroller, Cornelius MacDonald, remembered how Harper, the big shot putter, had come to Western: "Fraser had talked to Harper at his home in Pontiac and he was coming to Western. All the arrangements had been made; he was accepted and he was coming. So Fraser went over to get him and found somebody from Ypsilanti had gone over and got him and took him over there. Fraser drove over to Ypsilanti and picked him up in a car and brought him over here. And he went here to school, and of course, Ypsilanti was mad." So mad, in fact, that Eastern Michigan College broke off athletic relations with Western.

Once in Kalamazoo, black athletes faced other challenges. No one would rent rooms to them because of their color. So Waldo, according to track coach Towner Smith, said to athletic director Judson Hyames, "You've got a couple of corner rooms down in the gym. Why don't you fix them up and let the colored boys live in there." One of those rooms was Waldo's

Towner Smith prepared to unleash his quarter-milers in 1934. Far left was John "Moon" Mullins next to Louis Mallard.

office in his beloved men's gym and his daughter, Dorothy, remembered his ransacking their home's attic to furnish the room.

Restaurants, too, remained segregated in Kalamazoo. Louis "Bo" Mallard, a superlative black football and track star who graduated in 1935, recalled: "We couldn't even eat downtown at the greasy spoon in the Coney Island Restaurant. They didn't even want to serve us and we had to eat at a pool room on Burdick Street, upstairs where guys used to hustle pool,

Henry Harper, in action in 1930, smashed the state record in the shot put.

called Jane's Place."

There were no cooking facilities in the gymnasium but as Mallard remembered: "Well, we got a hot plate and we weren't supposed to cook in there, they told us. So we used to cook eggs and stuff. You know in a place like that you smell it all over the place, all over heaven. So when they came in, we would cover it all up with a drop cloth. But they could smell the eggs and bacon sometimes and they said, 'You guys are cooking in here. 'Oh, no, we don't cook in here.' They said, 'The heck you don't, we smell that grease in here,' and so they made us stop. Eating was a problem back then."

Having to "shuffle like the devil to eat," Mallard found himself growing weak during track practice because he could not afford regular meals. The only form of scholarship an athlete received in the 1930s was payment of 25 cents an hour for working on campus. Coach Smith told Mallard to ask Waldo for

Edward Salter was a champion high jumper on the 1933-1935 track team.

the window and she couldn't see me. He was lying there asleep and so he looked up and saw me. He said, "Oh my God, what do you want now, Mallard?" I said, "Well, Mr. President, how are you feeling?" He said, "Never mind my health, how are you?" I said, "Well, I would like to have another little IOU, if you don't mind." So, he never refused me.

But when it came time for Mallard to graduate in 1935, he received a letter from Hoekje notifying him that he would not receive his diploma until he paid back the money he had borrowed. Fortunately, he succeeded in talking Hoekje into breaking the rules for once and letting him receive his diploma so that he could get a job and then repay the loans. Mallard went on to carve out a legendary career as a football, basketball and track coach at Roosevelt High School in Gary, Indiana.

Ordeals like Mallard's were not confined to black students. The bleak economic times brought hardship for nearly everyone. The depth of the Depression came in 1933. Industrial output had fallen by half since 1929 and construction by 70 percent. Thousands of farmers lost their land through mortgage foreclosures. One out of every four American breadwinners was unemployed and, by 1934, 25 percent of Americans received most of their subsistence from county, state and federal relief agencies. By 1932, suicide rates rose by nearly one-third.

In Kalamazoo, old established firms such as Henderson-Ames, a large fraternal uniform manufacturer, closed their doors forever. Yet, while the Depression tinged almost every aspect of the city's life, Kalamazoo did not suffer as severe effects as most of the nation, due largely to the diversified nature of its industry and the stability of the valley's many paper mills.

But for Michigan as a whole and, espe-

more working hours, and he did allot him an additional five hours. But that was still not enough to pay tuition and eat as well. So several times, he borrowed money directly from Waldo, signing an IOU. Waldo, in fact, got to know him pretty well, as a result.

One time, as Mallard recalled during a 1989 interview:

I went to go in and see the president and his secretary was sitting there at the desk, so I crawled under by

This 1930s view across brick-paved Oakland Drive with its trolley tracks still present includes the Electronics Building and the Science Building.

cially, Detroit's highly vulnerable automotive industry, the Depression proved overwhelming. Detroit's banking structure, in particular, teetered on the brink of collapse. With a rapidly spreading psychology of fear and consequent runs on Motor City banks, Michigan Governor William Comstock declared a "bank holiday" on February 14, 1933, and all the state's banks closed for eight days. Other states followed Michigan's lead, and two weeks later, incoming President Franklin D. Roosevelt extended the closings nationally. Unable to meet payroll obligations, Detroit, Grand Rapids, Kalamazoo and other cities issued script to employees. Fearing that his teachers might not be paid for months, Waldo sped to Lansing and brought back the school's payroll in cash by automobile.

Despite the rock bottom tuition rates during the Depression that had earned Western its reputation as "a poor man's college"—$12.50 a semester covered everything except room, board, and textbooks— many prospective students found it difficult to raise even that small amount. Zack York, who

grew up on an Ionia County farm, graduated from high school in 1930. He wanted to go to college, but "knew he couldn't. After all, we didn't have that kind of money." But when he won a $50 prize for selling subscriptions to the Lake Odessa newspaper, he borrowed another $150 from one of his high school teachers and with that $200 in hand, registered for Western in the fall of 1930. He secured lodging with a

Zack York taught a scene design class in 1957. Here he is readying the model for *Taming of the Shrew*.

A painting of the old Indian trail that once ran across campus was the frontispiece of the 1931 *Brown and Gold*.

Dutch family on Walwood Place. York and two other students lived in an unheated upstairs sleeping porch. They were allotted one bath per week and had to ask permission from their landlady who would then holler down the grate for one of her children to light the gas-fired hot water heater. York got a part-time job washing dishes at Bronson Hospital on John Street in exchange for meals, walking all the way downtown and back three times a day before, between and after classes. After three years, he was forced to leave Western to work full time, but he returned to graduate in 1937. Four years later, he began a distin-guished career in the speech department and later the theatre department, retiring as chairman in 1978.

Other students who attended Western during the Depression remembered the hard times with nostalgia. Nearly half a century later, Kenneth Beagle recalled his experiences living in Kalamazoo boarding houses:

> *The house mother was a widow. It was her house and she ran it accord-ingly, but she was a mother to us. And if anybody was there, she saw to it they had a little tender loving care. It was a good life. And it was economical, two dollars a week. And all the houses that I lived in, if you wanted to use them, there were light house-keeping privi-leges. In the basement, a kitchenette, you know, a sink and a stove, table and some chairs and generally four of us at least would form a little food co-op in the house. And four guys would get together and put a couple of dollars a week in the pot and buy the groceries you needed for a week. We flourished with that kind of an arrangement. And the good thing about it was, at Western, in those days, everyone else was in the same boat.*

Garrard Haworth recalled his experiences, typical of other Depression-era students. Following graduation from high school in 1930, he got a full-time job working at Peck's Drugstore in Benton Harbor for $3.75 a week. Three years later, he had saved up enough to pay tuition at Western. With three other students he rented a tiny third-floor apartment on Lovell Street. When the job he had been promised at Peck's Kalamazoo branch failed to materialize, he found himself hitchhiking home to Benton Harbor each Friday, working Friday night, Saturday and Sunday morning, and hitchhiking back to Kalamazoo for Monday morning classes. Eventually, he supplemented his income with additional part-time work on campus, parking cars under the direction of Hoekje. Haworth graduated from Western in four years, got a teaching job in Holland and eventually parlayed his wood-working hobby into a Fortune 500 Com-pany—Haworth, Inc., a leading manufacturer of office furnishings.

By the time Haworth started at Western, in the fall of 1933, student enrollment had shrunk from a high in 1927 of 2,316 to 1,388, a 40 percent decrease. At the same time, attendance at the campus Training School remained strong, despite the modest tuition charged. The sons and daughters of Western's faculty and staff, the offspring of some of Kalamazoo's prominent families and a leaven-ing of less-advantaged children continued to covet the superior grade school and high school education offered on the hill. The number of campus school graduates had risen throughout the 1920s from 32 in 1922 to 65 in 1929. By 1938, 78 State High graduates received their diplomas.

Declining enrollments and dwindling state revenues brought a precipitous slashing of the college's state appropriations by 59 percent in 1932, followed by another 31.5 percent in 1933. Western's budget stood at $503,874 that year, about half of its 1928 appropriation. Waldo and the other three teachers college

One of Western's stylish aerodynamic buses circa 1938

presidents had fought hard in Lansing to limit the 1933 cuts to 21 percent, but to no avail. Incensed at what he perceived as stubborn prejudice by many members of the state legislature, Waldo railed at the injustice of the teachers colleges receiving much greater reductions than the University of Michigan, Michigan State University and the Houghton College of Mines.

Powerless to prevent it, he watched as his own salary fell from $9,000 annually in 1931, to $4,000 two years later. During that same period, salaries of department heads fell by 40 percent to an average of $3,190 and middle range staff to an average of $2,400. Salaries of instructors with one to two years of experience dropped by 41 percent to $1,464 a year.

According to Waldo's youngest daughter, Dorothy Waldo Stapler, who was a student on campus at the time, the president called a faculty meeting and informed them that some would have to lose their jobs if they did not take pay cuts. They voted for the cuts. Actually, there was little the faculty could have done in protest anyway. As Leonard Kercher, who joined the Department of Sociology in 1928, noted:

The faculty had virtually no formal organization concerned with their interests and welfare. A Friendship Committee compassionately provided flowers on appropriate occasions. But beyond that, before and during the Depression years, there were no contracts, no tenure policy, no bargaining agents, no promotion policy, no grievance procedure, no appeal board, no academic rankings and no really effective faculty council. Each individual faculty member was dealt with personally as an individual by President Waldo and the concerned department head. Unless informed otherwise, one just assumed that he or she was reappointed each year. No one knew what his next year's salary would be until the first checks of the new college year appeared.

The cuts imposed by Waldo proved insufficient. He faced the agonizing decision of reducing the size of his beloved family of faculty. His top priority during the Depression became the preservation of as many faculty jobs as possible. He constantly juggled figures and positions to resolve the dilemma. Tech-

Coeds practiced in the pool in the basement below the East Hall gymnasium circa 1936.

niques included voluntary resignations, reduced teaching loads and pay, sabbatical leaves with or without half pay, leaves with small stipends and outright layoffs. Waldo gave Kercher, for example, a $600 stipend to work on his doctorate at the University of Michigan. A year later he was one of three the president hired back.

In 1930, ten instructors received sabbatical leaves with half pay and seven others took leaves with no pay. Although few, if any, faculty members were old enough to retire, 18 in the 1932-33 year made the difficult decision to resign voluntarily. If any funds remained at the end of the fiscal year, Waldo sent small checks to his most needy faculty. By 1933, the college faculty body had dropped from 141 to 113. Only 15 or so were permanently dismissed, and several of those had secured positions elsewhere through Waldo's assistance.

Even as Waldo battled to save as many of his faculty as possible, he found himself struggling to preserve his own job. During the state elections in the spring of 1933, Paul Voelker, president of Olivet College and Democratic candidate for state superintendent of public education, had openly declared that Waldo had refused to hire any Democrat on his faculty. Voelker won the election handily,

receiving a majority of votes except in rock-ribbed Republican southwest Michigan. He immediately launched a campaign to oust Waldo and replace him with Clayton Ettinger, a sociology professor whom Waldo had discharged the previous year for hobnobbing with local Democratic politicians. Voelker dispatched Edna Wilson from Saginaw, the other newly elected Democratic member of the State Board of Education, to investigate Waldo's fitness for retaining his position. At their initial meeting, according to Waldo, she requested his resignation because he had barred Democrats from the faculty, devoted too much time to lobbying in Lansing, was dictatorial and unfair to Catholics. Waldo produced an array of testimonials, letters of support and other documentary evidence that refuted her allegations. Then, as Waldo later told Ralph Ralston, a longtime supporter of Western from Kalamazoo:

> She came out and told me they wanted the position. I asked her what reason would I give for resigning. And she said to me, "Why, Mr. Waldo, you have had a little trouble recently. Say you're resigning for matters of health." She said, "You have had a little trouble

The demands of the Depression took their toll on the aging Waldo.

emptied state coffers, in his inaugural address to the state legislature on January 27, 1935, Governor Frank D. Fitzgerald announced that it was:

"an economic and educational fallacy to say that everyone should have a free college education ... There is little reason other than local pride for operating seven state colleges. Certainly it is illogical to have four teachers colleges turning out graduates at state expense for which our public school system has no crying need at this time. The closing of at least two state normals and the withdrawal of state aid to county normals is recommended in the interest of economics."

recently, haven't you, Mr. Waldo?" And I said, "Yes, I did have a little trouble, but that's entirely cleared up." She asked me, "Just what was your trouble, Mr. Waldo?" "Why, Mrs. Wilson, I had some trouble with my rectum." And, you know, I never heard another word about my health.

At a showdown meeting of the State Board of Education on July 31, 1933, the board members failed to unseat Waldo by a vote split along party lines.

Eighteen months later came the opening salvo of an even greater battle. Its outcome would determine the ultimate survival of Western. This time the threat came from Waldo's own Republican Party. As the effects of the Depression

Two weeks later, the *Detroit Free Press* announced that Voelker was backing Fitzgerald's plan and "as a start toward retrenchment, it has been proposed that Western State Teachers College in Kalamazoo be shut down." By then, Waldo had already begun marshalling his forces. Faculty members, alumni, business and civic leaders, state politicians and state and national educational leaders fired off volley after volley of letters, editorials, interviews, reports and speeches in favor of Western. Paul Sangren, who had been

An avid sportsman, Paul Sangren is seen here during a fishing adventure in Grand Traverse Bay.

In 1944, the huge boulder that Waldo had admired since he was a boy growing up near Plainwell was moved from north of Cooper to the site of the old Eames Mill through funds raised by Western's Men's Alumni Club. Here Carl Cooper, alumni secretary, is shown congratulating Hastings Truck Company personnel on their accomplishment.

a member of the Department of Education faculty since 1923 and had steadily risen up the ranks to become dean of administration, emerged as Waldo's stalwart during the campaign. When a senate committee visited Western in mid-January, Sangren delivered, according to a University of Chicago professor, "one of the ablest presentations he had ever heard."

The committee, headed by Senator Frank Mosier of Fennville, delivered its report to the Senate on January 30, citing, in part: "Western State Teachers College at Kalamazoo is considered one of the six leading teachers colleges in the United States... and that it is not feasible to consider the closing of Western or any of the other State Teachers Colleges." The resulting Senate vote handed Fitzgerald the first serious setback of his administration.

The Depression, the battles to save the jobs of his faculty, his own position and the

college itself took their toll on the 72-year-old warhorse. And there was truth to one of Edna Wilson's allegations—Waldo's health was slipping. He suffered from the effects of Parkinson's disease, and his walking and other movements grew stiffer and stiffer. Furthermore, he seemed to be getting more eccentric as the 1930s wore on. Rural education director Robinson recalled that by the Depression, Waldo's traditional open-door policy for faculty and students did not always mean he would pay attention to the conversation if he were preoccupied. Track coach Smith remembered that when one of his athletes was having trouble passing a course, Waldo called in the professor and asked him, "Why can't you teach him good enough for him to get a decent grade so that he can be eligible?"

And then there was the famous Ike Miller story cited by half a dozen contemporaries. Distinguished English professor William

Waldo with his parrot, Jimmy Boy, who sometimes rode on his shoulder as he walked around town

Waldo conducted the program. As he announced each name, a senior stood up and received recognition for this kind of honor and another senior stood up and received recognition for that kind of honor. About half way through, Mr. Waldo looked over his glasses at the seniors in front of him, and said "Is Ike Miller here?" Ike Miller was an athlete from Indiana, and Mr. Waldo had heard that Ike had won a contest in a county fair the previous fall. Ike stood up and Mr. Waldo said, "Ike, I understand that you won a hog calling contest last fall; is that right?" Ike admitted that it was. Mr. Waldo pointed his finger at him and said, "Ike, will you come up on the platform?" And Ike came up on the platform, stood in front of Dr. Brown and Lavina Spindler and the other dignitaries and Mr. Waldo said, "Ike, I want you to show these people how you won that hog calling contest." And, I think, much to Ike's embarrassment and certainly to Dr. Brown's and Miss Spindler's, Ike gave the champion hog call on the Senior Honors Day program.

Brown and Lavina Spindler, head of the Department of Counseling, had planned a Senior Honors Day assembly to be held one Tuesday morning in the women's gymnasium. They had told Waldo that it should be a very dignified and proper occasion to impress on the student body the significance of their achievements. History professor Charles Starring, who was there, recalled what happened:

> *They had the senior class sitting down toward the front in their caps and gowns with some of the senior dignitaries on the platform, as were Dr. Brown, Miss Spindler and Mr. Waldo. Mr.*

Lavina Spindler was the dean of women in 1917.

Western's administrative offices in East Hall looked like this in the late 1930s.

Waldo's daughter Dorothy recalled that during the Depression her father sought relaxation by reading pulp fiction, mysteries and Westerns, in particular. He increasingly attended downtown movie houses, preferring low-cost, high-action Westerns, and he always sat on the left side of the theatre. After a hard day on campus, Waldo invariably walked to his home at 151 Thompson Street. Part way there,

After his retirement in 1936, Waldo enjoyed traveling to historic sites. A lifelong and ardent Republican, here he stands at the site of the Lincoln-Douglas debates.

Dorothy remembered, would be waiting his parrot, Jimmy Boy, who called Waldo "Dad." The sight of a distinguished college president walking around town and talking to a parrot on his shoulder must have seemed more than a little odd.

The truth of the matter is that Waldo knew full well he was failing. He had been ready to retire since 1934, but he would not relinquish the reins until he knew for sure that the college he had built from the ground up would be in good hands. Those hands, Waldo had become convinced, belonged to Paul Sangren, the man he had been grooming for the job for several years and whose valiant defense of the school during the closing crisis had clinched his succession.

Born in the Muskegon County village of Ravenna in 1898, Sangren attended Ferris Institute and Indiana University before serving six months in the army during World War I. Following his discharge, he earned a bachelor's degree from Eastern Michigan Normal College at Ypsilanti in 1920 and a master's degree from the University of Michigan two years later. He was serving as superintendent of Zeeland schools in 1923 when Waldo hired him as an education

Waldo Stadium is shown under construction in the late 1930s.

instructor. He soon distinguished himself through his scholarly articles. Following a leave of absence during which he completed his doctorate at the University of Michigan, Waldo named him director of the Bureau of Education Research in 1926, and a year later elevated him to chairman of the Department of Education. In 1934, he filled the newly created position, dean of administration.

Waldo breathed a great sigh of relief in 1936. He wrote his education instructor Roxanna Steele on August 5: "A week ago yesterday, the State Board of Education reached the heights of statesmanship at Marquette when they elected Dr. Sangren president and am I glad? It was the most statesmanlike thing the State Board of Education has done for 37 years."

Waldo retired as president emeritus, and the state legislature voted him a pension of $3,000 a year. As his disease worsened, he walked more rigidly, unable to move his head

to the right or the left. Still, as long as his strength permitted, he reported daily to the little "cubbyhole" of an office Sangren allotted him. Sadly, they became estranged, as Waldo grew disillusioned over the changes in administrative policy Sangren made, especially as Western began its metamorphic rise from a single-purpose teachers college to a multifunctional institution.

By 1938, Waldo spent more and more of his time traveling and collecting Native American artifacts, geological specimens, shells, rare books and documents he envisioned would form a Western Michigan College museum. In October 1939, he fell and broke his hip and on October 29, he died of pneumonia in Bronson Hospital. He was cremated and his ashes placed within a cornerstone of East Hall, beneath the office that had been the nerve center of Western for so many years.

Just prior to his death, Waldo had

The Woman's League room on the main floor of Walwood Union was fitted with fine furnishings and decorations.

consented to the naming of a new football stadium in his honor. The Depression had brought a halt to any new construction on campus, but in December 1936, the State Board of Education approved the development of a stadium and football field. The stadium project marked the beginning of a planned building program as well as a progressive means of financing through self-liquidating bonds. The initial modest project called for Western to raise $33,000 "through contributions from alumni and friends of the institution, and fees from students," to be matched by a $16,200 Works Project Administration (WPA) grant for labor and supervision. But over the succeeding three years, the project ballooned into an expenditure of over $270,000, with $200,000 from the federal government via a WPA grant. The State Highway Department paid $32,000 for the long-desired acquisition of a right of way for the rerouting of crooked U.S. 12 (now

Stadium Drive), the Upjohn Civic Trust gave $3,000, and the Kalamazoo Chamber of Commerce raised $25,000 with a campaign subscribed to by local citizens. That left $10,000 in alumni contributions to make it "a debt-free stadium at the time of dedication." Western's alumni clubs campaigned hard. They minted souvenir coins with Waldo's image and the phrase, "It's the extra drive that wins," and they mailed 2,000 little wooden barrels to alumni so they could drop a couple of coins in daily and return the filled bank. Despite their efforts, by the time of the dedication on November 4, 1939, they remained $4,000 short of their goal.

The completed athletic complex was touted as "one of the finest at any teachers college in the country." The original gridiron and 440-yard cinder track were moved to the southwest because of the rerouted highway. Concrete stands on each side accommodated 15,000 spectators, including 52 eight-person

Vandercook Hall is shown here in 1939.

boxes, as well as concession stands, locker rooms, coaches' and officials' rooms, toilets and a press box. Extensive excavation of the hillside to the west allowed erection of a 2,500-seat, covered, concrete grandstand and the realigned baseball diamond.

Prior to the dedication of the athletic complex, other similarly funded structures had risen on the hilltop. The first to be completed, in September 1938, stood at the intersection of Oakland Drive and Austin Street, the former site of the Fletcher Sanitarium, which had burned in 1914. Named Walwood Hall, an amalgam of Waldo and Leslie Wood, the U-shaped structure housed the campus' first dormitory, accommodating 115 women in one wing and the union building in the other. The main floor of the union wing contained the general lounge, the Women's League room, a powder room, coat-check room, soda fountain, cafeteria, faculty dining area and kitchen. On the second floor lay a 100-foot-by-50-foot ballroom with raised stage, two Men's Union

rooms, and a Student Council room. Rare vases, hanging artwork and furniture accented the Philippine mahogany woodwork. A Pewabic tile fireplace highlighted the commons room. Lydia Seidschlag, head of the art department, and her staff decorated Walwood's interior.

Ironically, Waldo's old nemesis, Edna Wilson, spoke on "beauty" at the October 8, 1938, dedication. Four years later, art instructor Kathyrn Keillor painted a mural depicting the

Fine arts instructor Lydia Seidschlag in 1926

evolution of the college on the northwest wall of the union building. During the first year of its operation, the cafeteria served nearly

The camera captured a view of Western's classic quadrangle about 1940.

85,000 meals, and the popular soda bar catered to more than 141,000 patrons. An attraction that lured students as well as local citizens to the soda fountain was, as 1930s student Kenneth Beagle remembered, "the best piece of pie with a quarter of a pound of ice cream on top of it for 15 cents!" Sixty-five students worked an average of 16 hours per week in the union building to earn 30 cents an hour. When it opened, room and board in Walwood Hall cost $7.50 per week.

On October 13, 1939, Western's first male dormitory, originally called simply the Hall for Men and the following year renamed Vandercook Hall after the former legislator considered Western's father, was dedicated. Located on the west side of Oakland Drive, the Tudor-style brick structure cost $285,000 and accommodated 215 students. It included communal kitchenettes and bathrooms on each dormitory floor, a barbershop and a small auditorium that originally housed displays of Native American artifacts that Waldo had collected.

Another structure finished in the fall of 1939, the Health and Personnel Building (now the Charles Van Riper Speech and Hearing Clinic), would complete the classic quadrangle atop Prospect Hill.

Students pose before the entrance to Spindler Hall shortly after it opened in 1940.

This aerial view captures the appearance of the hilltop campus prior to the building spree of the late 1930s.

The daisy chain was for many years the highlight of the campus social calendar. Here is pictured the daisy chain of 1945.

With the opening of the structure, a 17-bed infirmary and a nursing staff of five under Dr. Wallace Borgman replaced the one bed and two cots "in a dark corner of a dark room" in the basement of the Science Building that had previously sufficed for the college's health services. Soon, additional physicians held dental, skin and orthopedic clinics.

The ground floor of the building contained classrooms and offices, primarily for student advisory activities. Health services occupied the first floor, and the second floor accommodated special testing and educational efforts such as the Psycho-Educational Clinic, speech correction laboratories, classrooms and psychological offices.

Before the year that witnessed the dedication of these four new complexes had ended, the State Board of Education approved construction of yet another structure, an additional women's dormitory. Completed in late 1940, the three-story building with a capacity for almost 200 residents was named Spindler Hall in honor of the longtime education instructor and first dean of women hired by Waldo in 1906.

With the completion of that spate of buildings during the last of the Depression years, Western's hilltop setting achieved the golden era of its beauty. The campus that Will

Rogers reputedly dubbed "the Acropolis of Kalamazoo" looked out over the city's vistas, and Kalamazooans gazed back with pride at their college. Betty Virgo, who had been born in Kalamazoo in 1923 and attended the Training School from kindergarten through high school before earning a degree from Western, recalled the appearance of the campus in the 1930s during an interview nearly 60 years later:

> *The whole Davis Street campus was very well landscaped; it was beautiful. The configuration of the hill was different than it is now; it was*

more terraced. There was a very deep terrace at the top. At the bottom of that terrace was what looked like a path. No one ever walked around it; I suppose it was for mowing purpose. Then after one more terrace, the hill gradually went down. There were huge beautiful trees and very nice thick bushes there at the top that screened the bottom of the buildings when you looked up the hill. Everyone in the city used that hill in the winter for sliding. The adults skied there. They would go down from that steep terrace at a diagonal; it was quite a good shot, about two-and-a-half

By the mid 1930s, the members of the Women's Glee Club had overwhelmingly adopted bobbed hair.

blocks long. The trolley was on that campus, which made it interesting looking. There was also what was called the horseshoe; one set of steps that came down that very steep terrace at the top and separated into a horseshoe on each side. It came down from the Administration Building and had all kinds of trees and bushes. There were very thick lilacs on campus. There was a little half street, bordering Davis Street, that went up toward the trolley. The lilacs were right in front of that. In the middle of those thick lilacs was a huge green maintenance box where they kept mowers and equipment and all the tennis court supplies. There were four clay courts on campus. The lilacs were so gorgeous.

Another form of campus pulchritude remembered by Virgo and numerous others was the annual daisy chain. The grand finale in the Women's League social calendar for each year, the daisy chain formed a prelude to the Women's June Breakfast. Freshmen women honor students and members of the Women's

League, clad in diaphanous gowns, escorted faculty, guests and upperclass women in a procession extending from the winding wishbone-shaped walk on Davis Street to the women's gymnasium where the festivities were held. Hazel Cleveland Saye, a 1932 graduate of Western, never forgot her participation in the daisy chain:

It was an honor but, part of it was we had to get up early in the morning and go out and pick the daisies and make the chain, which was a long rope that we tied daisies to—half-a-mile! The daisy chain formed at the foot of Western's hill at Davis Street. There was an arch that everybody was to walk through when we got to the top. We formed a chain, walked up the hill, dressed in formals, hats and gloves. The breakfast was held about 10:00 or 10:30.

With the opening of Walwood Hall, the Women's League moved the program there. The daisy chain began at the flag quadrangle behind East Hall and proceeded to Walwood. Another feature of the June Breakfast begun in

1941 was the Arista tapping. Organized to highlight outstanding junior women who had achieved excellence in scholarship, leadership and character, Arista, Greek for "the best," membership became a highly coveted honor. At the breakfast, alumni members in caps and gowns marched around the tables to suddenly tap on the shoulders, amid shrieks of surprise and pleasure, those selected to be inducted into the organization. Currently, this tradition continues with the Mortar Board organization.

Some other Western organizations offered considerably more ribald inductions. By the late 1930s, three fraternities had been allowed to exist at Western. Kenneth Beagle remembered the hazing to which his fraternity brothers subjected new pledges. They took the unlucky captives out in the country five miles or more and unloaded them without a stitch of clothing, expecting them to get back to the fraternity house on their own. Despite that run in the raw, fraternity life in the 1930s was pretty tame. Beagle remembered his Phi Sigma Rho fraternity house, located at 516 South Westnedge Avenue, as a big three-story structure where the members paid $2 a week for a room. "We had a good house mother," he recalled, "she was very active and very able to look after 25 or 30 guys in terms of any medical care we needed. She saw to it that we kept our faces clean and that we kept our rooms cleaned up. The rules, of course, were obvious. No girls in that fraternity house, ever!"

In addition to those initial fraternities and sororities, Western's campus of the 1930s offered a rich variety of organizations. There was the Women's League and after 1936, its male counterpart, the Men's Union. Classmates could serve on the Student Council, help compile the *Brown and Gold* yearbook and the *Herald,* join the Men's or Women's Debate Squads or participate in interpretive reading contests. Thespians had the Players and the musically inclined the Men's Glee Club, the Women's Glee Club, the Teachers College Choir, the College Symphony Orchestra and the College Band. Varsity-letter winners belonged to the "W" Club and while archery was not an official college sport, its advocates formed the Western Merrie Bowmen. The oldest organization on campus, the Country Life Club, dated from 1904. Other clubs catered to diverse interests such as commerce, early elementary teaching, industrial arts, home economics, international relations, science, arts and crafts and agriculture. The Inglis Club was for secondary education students. Future physicians joined the Circulus Premedicus. Foreign language boosters could chose from Le Cercle Francais, Der Deutsche Verein, El Círculo Español or the Classical Club for Latin admirers. There was a Dance Club, the Square and Compass Club for Free Masons and its female counterpart the Eastern Star Club, an Eldorado Club for writers and last but not least, the Oteyojwa Club, Algonquin for "gathering of friends in a strange land," devised by homesick "Yoopers" (from the Upper Peninsula) attending Western.

Among those from the Upper Peninsula in the late 1930s was an amazingly powerful athlete named Ray Bray, who was born in Caspian and later moved to Vulcan, both in the Upper Peninsula's rugged iron country. The 220-pound Bray started on both the offensive and defensive football teams as guard from 1936 to 1938. Known to his teammates as "Muscles," Bray single-handedly held up the college pickup truck as a tire was changed. He was one of the toughest linemen in Western's history. In 1939, the Chicago Bears drafted Bray and, with the exception of three years of military service during World War II, "the strong man of football" played on professional teams into the middle 1950s.

Despite Bray's outstanding efforts, some of the late 1930s teams failed to compile winning seasons. At one of the annual football banquets, Sangren announced that, in spite of the mediocre season, he was satisfied because the team had given its best. He added that,

Herbert W. "Buck" Read, Western's famous basketball coach, is shown here explaining the moves of a set play to his team, circa 1933.

"Western did not believe in imitating other institutions who dropped their coaches after several unsuccessful seasons." When the following year's team suffered an even poorer season, Sangren reminded the attendees at the football banquet of his previous statement. Then turning to head coach Mike Gary, he said, "That statement should not be taken too literally."

Western added golf to football, basketball, baseball, track and tennis as varsity sports in 1936. "Buck" Read served as golf coach the first year and was succeeded by Fred Huff in 1937. Gary resigned as head football coach in 1942 to enlist in the Navy's physical fitness program. John Gill, who had been his assistant, replaced him. Three years before, Gill had won the contest to replace Western's traditional nicknames, "Hillsmen" or "Hilltoppers," because they were being confused with similar names used by other colleges. Gill came up with Broncos, "as distinctive, descriptive and apropos of the purpose and spirit of athletes on Western's campus."

That new name symbolized changes in other aspects of Western's development. In

Mitchell "Mike" Gary served as head football coach from 1929-1942. In 1949, Sangren named him director of athletics and physical education.

The 1939 golf team, coached by Fred Huff, won 10 matches, lost three, tied one.

Beginning in 1935, students seeking admittance to the Occupational Therapy School, begun by Marion Spear at the Kalamazoo State Hospital in 1922, were required to complete two years of courses on Western's campus. Continued rapport between Spear's school and Western would result in its transfer to Western in 1944, with Spear and her assistant, Jane Thomas, joining the college staff with faculty status. That fall, 20

1934, the first students who did not intend to become teachers were admitted, and each year thereafter saw an increase in that category. By 1936, Western offered a non-specific "general degree" and pre-professional courses in medicine, dentistry, business administration, engineering, forestry, journalism, law and pharmacy.

Backfield coach John Gill succeeded Mike Gary as head coach in 1942. Three years before, he had suggested "Broncos" as Western's new nickname.

students enrolled in Western's new Department of Occupational Therapy, then housed in the rickety old World War I barracks called the "Temporary Building."

Another new endeavor that would ultimately bring Western international laurels began in 1936, when

Marion Spear in 1956

Sangren hired Dr. Charles Van Riper to launch a speech pathology program. Born in 1905 in the Upper Peninsula village of Champion, Van Riper had experienced a miserable childhood because of a severe stuttering affliction. The primitive cures inflicted on him did more harm than good. Eventually, after attending Northern Michigan Teachers College and the University of Michigan, where he earned a master's degree in 1930, Van Riper developed his own techniques to turn his disability into an asset that would revolutionize the discipline of speech pathology.

Van Riper had just finished his doctorate in psychology at the University of Iowa in 1936, when he learned of an opening at

In 1947, Dr. Charles Van Riper's speech therapy students enjoyed a guest lecture. Van Riper used the child's speech development as an object lesson.

Western. "Sangren," Van Riper recalled in 1990, "had a nephew who stuttered badly. His nephew had been put through the same crud that I had been as a youngster. I was sent to some quack institutions, just as he had been—fraudulent ones. Sangren knew about the quack institutions and understood the devastation that stuttering can do to a person. He wanted to establish a reputable, scientifically-based speech clinic, which was relatively unheard of in those days."

Sangren interviewed Van Riper on May 7, 1938, and the following day offered him a position with the simple instructions, "build a clinic and a profession." Van Riper installed his clinic in a shed "with broken windows and rats" attached to the old Eames Mill at the foot of Oakland Drive. He devoted his initial years to recruiting students, designing courses and acquainting the public with the services offered. Van Riper also began operating a mobile speech clinic which traveled throughout the Lower Peninsula diagnosing children's

speech disorders and assisting teachers, principals and parents in understanding the problems faced by those who could not speak or hear normally. In 1939, Van Riper relocated his speech clinic to the third floor of

Dr. Charles Van Riper in 1943

the newly erected health services building. Over the following four decades, prior to his retirement in 1976, Van Riper more than accomplished Sangren's charge through his teaching, the many textbooks he wrote and his travels around the globe promoting his profession. In 1965, he headed up the new Department of Speech Pathology and Audiology established by the Board of Trustees. In May 1983, the trustees voted to rename the health and services building the Van Riper

Speech and Hearing Clinic.

The year that Van Riper first moved his clinic into that building, 1939, proved another landmark for Western's evolution when the college offered its first graduate courses. Originally, the graduate division was under the guidance of the University of Michigan, which approved courses, instructors and student credentials. A number of University of Michigan personnel harbored doubts about Western's qualifications for teaching graduate courses and their elitist attitude resulted in a degree of friction over the succeeding decade. Elmer H. Wilds was appointed the first director of the graduate division. One hundred and eleven students enrolled in the initial four graduate courses during the winter semester of 1939. Two of those first courses were in education, one in European history and another in "The Modern Novel." Tuition for a full load of graduate studies cost $55 a semester. The curriculum had expanded to eleven courses with an enrollment of 154 by the summer session of 1939.

By 1939, the country had shaken off the worst effects of the Depression thanks largely to the increased industrial production spurred by federal government and Allied spending for war material. Employment reached heights unattained since the bright days of the 1920s. In 1940 and 1941, the nation as a whole enjoyed boom years. Russell Seibert, who had been hired to teach history by Sangren in 1936 for what Seibert thought was a magnificent salary of $2,400 a year, remembered about 1939: "I suddenly thought to myself, these students look well fed, and I became aware of the fact that all of the students I had been teaching looked underfed prior to that. Now that is what the Depression had done."

But as the Depression ended and the unsolved problems inherited from the previous generation's world war avalanched into another global conflict, fear of war replaced economic uncertainty. Although, initially, the American mood overwhelmingly reflected neutrality,

Elmer Weaver developed Western's initial programs in aviation in 1940.

when world events reverberated with the thud of goose steps and the Banzai battle cry, echoes of preparedness mingled with the hum of industrial machinery.

Some on campus clearly saw the writing on the wall. Early in 1939, mechanical trades instructor Elmer Weaver launched a program to train aviation mechanics. Because flying was of special interest to him, he also began training pilots at about that same time. In

Dr. Elmer Wilds, shown here at his desk in 1948, was Western's first director of the Graduate Division.

As depicted in the *Brown and Gold* for 1944, 1,230 Western men and women were in uniform by that year and 37 had paid the supreme price.

doing when they first heard the awful news. Dorothy Osborn, the wife of chemistry professor Gerald Osborn (later dean of the College of Arts and Sciences and acting president of the University in 1960), remembered she was one of the thousand-voice choir being led in practice by Harper Maybee in the men's gymnasium. She finished the rehearsal for the Christmas program just as Hoekje announced that Pearl Harbor had been bombed. Someone, she recalled, asked, "Where is Pearl Harbor?"

1942, trustees of the W.E. Upjohn Foundation gave Western $60,000 to develop an aviation center at the Kalamazoo Municipal Airport. By the fall of 1942, approximately 200 Western-trained pilots were flying for the U.S. Army, Navy and Marines. Also in 1940, Weaver began training skilled mechanics, inspectors and foremen to work in vital war production industries. In 1941, Weaver moved his programs into the newly constructed Mechanical Trades Building on Stadium Drive, northeast of Waldo Stadium. Some 3,000 men had been prepared for factory war work by the fall of 1942, and the program was in the process of expanding to include the training of "Rosie the Riveters."

On December 7, 1941, Japan's attack on Pearl Harbor ended the nation's uncertainty, and the United States faced its greatest challenge since the days of the Revolution. Few forgot where they were or what they were

Few Americans would ask that question again as "Remember Pearl Harbor" became the rallying cry. Kalamazoo County answered President Franklin Roosevelt's call to arms with overwhelming enthusiasm. More than 12,000 men and women from the county served in the armed forces during the long 44 months of America's involvement in the war. Western's campus echoed that patriotic fervor. Fifty-four of the approximately 1,200 male students on campus quit school within the first month to join the service. On January 1, 1942, Western suffered its first casualty of the war when Lt. Charles Van Eeuwen dove his plane into a sand pit near Mitchell Field, New York, to avoid crashing into a heavily populated residential area. He was awarded the Distinguished Flying Cross, and, in 1945, Western's first veteran's club was named in his honor.

Soon after "the day that will live in

Left to right, Thelma Bacon, Shirley Mowder and Arnold Brown helped conduct a benefit ball to assist the homefront war effort in 1942.

the initial decisions of the council was to accelerate the training of students so that a greater number of men might finish their degrees before entering the military. The plan allowed students to complete their bachelor's degree in three years. The entire physical education program was also revamped to include types of training which would better prepare the male students for the demands of military service as well as a special "hardening program" of daily exercises. Leaves of absence for faculty members were immediately discontinued except for those who left for the service or vital government war research. By the fall of 1942, 15 faculty members had joined the military and many more would follow.

The home front received more emphasis than it had in any previous war. Families of faculty and students alike proudly displayed

infamy," Sangren called a meeting of the faculty to determine the role the college would play during the war. He appointed faculty members to a Committee on Defense, which was soon renamed the War Council. One of

Western's Bond Queen contestants posed in 1945.

The school bore the name, Western State Teachers College, from 1927 to 1941. This decal was discovered in a 1938 *Brown and Gold*.

service flags in their home windows with a star for every member in the service. As price controls and rationing of food, tires and gasoline became a way of life, men patched up their old cars, women their nylons, and victory gardens grew on vacant lots. The college elected "Campus Bond Queens" and conducted drives that sold enormous quantities of bonds and war stamps. Students and faculty collected books to be sent to prisoners of war. As Civil War cannons and antique pewter fell victim to scrap drives, in the fall of 1942, the men of Vandercook Hall piled on to a scrap heap the ancient 150-pound Victory Bell that had tolled the glad tidings of Bronco athletic successes. The students announced they "would rather hear it ringing against the side of a Jap bomber than pealing forth triumph of even the most coveted athletic victory." The State High students contributed as well, rolling bandages, conducting defense stamp drives and collecting magazines for wounded soldiers at Percy Jones Army Hospital in Battle Creek.

The homecoming parade that fall featured floats carrying the message, "We Build For Defense." Defense stamp corsages became the rage at student parties such as the annual "Mistletoe Hop" and "Sadie Hawkins Day." In April 1943, the Players presented a musical production titled *This is the Campus*, featuring such numbers as Irving Berlin's *Oh, How I Hate to Get Up in the Morning* and *This Is the Army*. Staged in the newly constructed, 350-seat theatre, (later called The Little Theatre and briefly Oakland Recital Hall) and written by theatre instructor Wallace Garneau, it parodied life on a wartime campus. Rehearsal for the production began with both men and women in the cast. By the time of its presentation, the male members of the Players had been inducted in the service and it became an all-female revue. The show included the song *Western Keeps Marching Along*. One stanza sung to the tune of *Off We Go, Into the Wild Blue Yonder* captured Western's home-front mood:

> *Here are we—left on the hill that's Western,*
> *Chins up high—sturdy and strong.*
> *Finding work—we who are left at Western,*
> *Finding work—and singing a song.*
> *When you're back—back on the hill that's Western,*
> *After taking care of our foes,*
> *We'll still march on, as we did before.*
> *Shout! Nothing'll stop the Western Broncos!'*

During the war years, clothing styles changed abruptly. Robert Burgoyne, a student at Western in the early 1940s, remembered the sartorial trends resulting partly from wartime rationing and the need for women to shoulder more of the traditional male responsibilities and partly because of a simple change in fashion:

Commander John T. Tuthill conducted a regimental review of Western's V-5 and V-12 enrollees in May, 1944.

Cuffless trousers, no pleats or belted backs, narrower lapels and tighter fits were adopted by the men. Feminine apparel changed also. Silk hose began to be a real luxury and the "jeans and plaid shirt" era was ushered in. Bare legs and leg make-up became common custom; full skirts were out as were wide sleeves, flared collars, extra accessories and long jackets. Our coeds took on a more casual, trimmer appearance. Sophistication was more a matter of tailoring than of adornment.

But some campus customs resisted change. In 1942, Dean of Women Bertha Davis still held conferences with all freshman female students, counseling them on proper etiquette in representing Western's dignity on and off campus, including the mandatory wearing of hats and gloves downtown. Women in pants, even stylish slacks, remained taboo and jeans were not even a speck on the horizon of acceptable fashion. It took Mother Nature to bend Davis' dictates. The winter of 1943, a particularly brutal one, did the trick. As Betty Jane Virgo recalled: "We'd have to go down all those steps, across Oakland Drive, either to the Men's Gym or the old barracks, and we'd just freeze to death with the wind and snow whipping around. Finally Mrs. Davis said yes,

we could wear slacks until that cold snap was over. But that broke the ice because from then on people wore slacks when they wanted to."

Slacks or not, by 1943 Western's campus had taken on a decidedly feminine look as more and more male students and faculty left for the war. Those left behind busied themselves with war work. They made cookies for the USO, sewed and knitted for the Red Cross, provided volunteer assistance to the local rationing board, folded bandages, contributed nickels and dimes so penniless servicemen could call home, made speeches to sell war bonds, enrolled in air raid warden courses and then spent untold hours scanning the skies for enemy bombers. Two Western women helped relieve the manpower shortage for campus maintenance by volunteering to repaint college scoreboards and signs. Some women grumbled when asked to turn over their ration books for dormitory kitchens, but most complied.

The male shortage changed abruptly on July 1, 1943, with the arrival of approximately

Bertha Davis in 1917

Western's V-12 marines are shown here buying war bonds.

900 members of the U.S. Navy's V-5 and V-12 programs. About 150 of those men had enrolled in the naval program known as V-5 and would spend three months on campus receiving ground and flight instruction in order to become Navy flight officers. The V-12 unit, comprising the remainder of the military personnel assigned to Western, would spend from one to four semesters on campus (depending on their prior college credits), while taking general college courses leading to a degree. They then became Marine officers or Navy deck officers.

Because the V-12 organization required year-round operation, the college shifted to three, 16-week semesters and a shorter summer term. The regular students were routed out of Walwood, Spindler and Vandercook dormitories to provide housing for the military. Some of the displaced coeds found cramped lodging in the five residences on Walwood Place acquired by the college. On campus, the trainees endured musters, watches, reviews,

inspections and demerit cards. One too many demerits for "fouling up" resulted in loss of weekend liberty off campus. The V-12 Marines resided in Spindler Hall. Being Marines, they required a particularly difficult obstacle course constructed on the northwest side of the railroad tracks along Stadium Drive. During physical education classes in Oakland Gym, contingents of Marines raced down the hill, darted over the highway by the tracks, splashed across Arcadia Creek, grunted through the course twice and ran back up the hill.

Beyond military protocol and specific Navy courses taught by Navy and Marine personnel, Western's faculty taught all other courses. The V-12 students participated in college athletics, worked on the *Herald,* acted in school plays, sang in the choir and played in the orchestra.

The V-12s ate meals in the Walwood Union and always marched there in double columns from their respective dormitories. Ben Wheatley, a former V-12 trainee, remembered:

Western's campus sported a decided military appearance after July 1, 1943.

This illustration from the 1944 *Brown and Gold* showed that military life on campus had its compensations.

In the winter, with their dark blue uniforms, they gave the appearance of trains arriving at the big city terminal from points on the map. In the springtime, when weather required that gray raincoats be worn, the columns looked like regimented, white-tufted ducks waddling up Oakland Drive. Their steps were more cautious when the weather was bad, for every step that splashed meant white uniforms had to be laundered.

Long queues of men in uniform waiting to eat at Walwood became a common sight during the war. They ate in the main cafeteria with the tables rearranged in long lines like a typical mess hall. Toward the end of the war, more freedom was allowed and the tables returned to their normal placement. The academic regulations also grew more liberal, and some V-12 students were allowed to substitute courses more in line with their post-war interests. More classes became a mixture of civilians, Navy personnel and veterans.

The V-12 unit was disbanded on November 1, 1945. Many of those in V-12 during the war returned to Western to finish their degrees after discharge. William Kowalski spent three semesters in the V-12 program at Western in 1943 and 1944, before serving on active duty in the Pacific as a Marine officer. He returned to campus in the fall of 1947, earned his bachelor's degree a year later and his master's in 1952. After decades of service to the college, he retired in 1986 as director of campus planning.

Chapter 4

Sangren's Folly

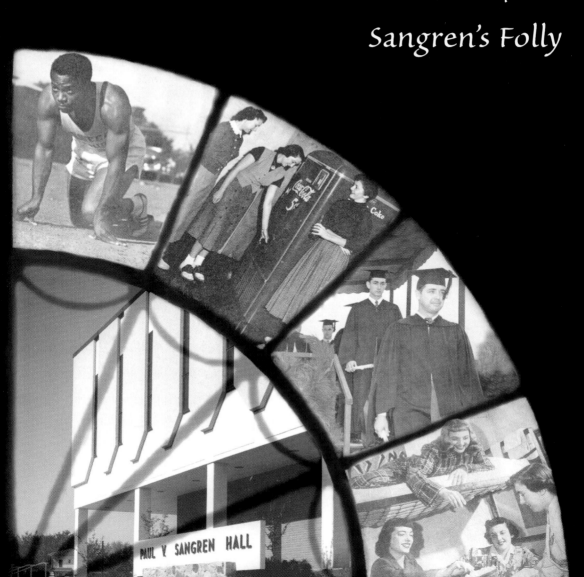

PAUL V SANGREN HALL

F ranklin D. Roosevelt had guided the nation through the Great Depression and the most terrible war in history. Before he could finish that last task came the stunning news on April 12, 1945—the president was dead! Shocked and grieving students crowded the women's gymnasium to capacity the following day for the memorial service in his honor. Of all the remarkable accomplishments of Roosevelt's unparalleled three full terms served in office, his calm reasoning, the "alphabet programs" that got the country through the Depression, social security, his leadership in prosecuting a two-ocean war, none would be more important than the document he signed on June 22, 1944,—the Serviceman's Readjustment Act of 1944, soon dubbed the "GI Bill of Rights."

Western's graduating class of 1945 entered a changed world.

Following World War I, four million returning soldiers had been dumped penniless on street corners by their government. Roosevelt and liberal members of Congress intended that American servicemen and service women's sacrifices would not be similarly forgotten. The original GI Bill contained six titles providing, among other measures, government-backed mortgages for buying homes, businesses and farms; a year of unemployment benefits at $20 per week; and most significantly, monetary assistance for training and education of all types. The bill offered payment of tuition, fees and textbooks up to $500 a year and a monthly subsistence check of $50, or $65 if the veteran was married. In 1947, those amounts were raised to $75 and $105, respectively.

The GI Bill revolutionized higher education in America. For the first time, it enabled millions of working-class citizens to consider acquiring a college education as a realistic expectation rather than an impossible dream. It became "the great American mobility machine," democratizing access to the ivy-covered walls. It became the "most admired and least criticized federal program of the twentieth century," while accomplishing changes in society comparable to the Industrial Revolution. Nearly eight million World War II veterans took advantage of the GI Bill to enhance their education or job training. In the late 1930s, approximately 160,000 Americans graduated from college annually. By 1950, nearly half a million did so. On the 50th anniversary of its signing, President Bill Clinton credited the GI Bill with creating "the world's largest middle class, the world's strongest economy."

Well before the war ended, Western's administrators had begun planning for the anticipated influx of veterans. In 1944, history

Anna Kanley presents Sangren with her check for $50,000 in 1944, a gift that helped make possible the development of the west campus.

Sangren had the foresight to realize that the campus would need to expand dramatically. But it was hemmed in on the hill through the difficulty of access and the prohibitive cost of acquisition of the surrounding residential neighborhoods. The best available land lay westward, a mile distant and across Stadium Drive and the railroad. In 1944, Sangren secured a $75,000 appropriation for the acquisition of property. Shortly thereafter, Anna Kanley, whose son William had played football for Western in 1911, presented Sangren with a $50,000 check to establish a park in memory of her husband Fred.

In 1944, with that combined funding, Sangren purchased a 70-acre tract comprising nine holes of the old Arcadia Brook Golf Course. Kanley Park, at the triangle formed by Michigan Avenue and Stadium Drive, was laid

professor Charles Starring announced in an article in Western's *News Magazine* that the "college considers it a privilege as well as a duty to participate to the limits of its ability in this program of service to veterans."

At an unveiling in 1946, officers of the class of 1942 presented Sangren with the flag pole dedicated to "all men of Western in the Armed Services" during WW II.

The old Arcadia Brook Golf Course Clubhouse later became the headquarters for Western's Safety and Security Department.

out that year. Along with the golf course purchase came the 1869 Italianate residence known as the Oaklands, which would become Sangren's and wife Flossie's home. The following year, Sangren used a $10,000 grant from the Upjohn Foundation, in part, to purchase an additional 40 acres, the rolling Gateway Golf Course or "Goat Hill," as it was known.

Few faculty members saw the wisdom of those land acquisitions. "Sangren's Folly" they termed the tract. Nevertheless, Sangren proceeded to lease a quantity of small house trailers and place them on the new property for married student housing. The following year saw construction of one-story houses for married veterans. Sangren also established a veteran's counseling and guidance center in the fall of 1945, just in time for the rush to begin.

Robert Burgoyne, a Western student at the time, later described the hectic years right after the war:

I think in some instances that the campus underwent a more rapid and drastic change after the war during

Kanley Park and Western's "proposed new campus" looked like this in 1947. Note the trailer village that provided housing for married students.

1946 and 1947 than it did following the outbreak of the war. It seemed like the returning servicemen literally swarmed back on campus in endless waves. They filled the rooming houses, the dorms, the trailer camp and every available housing unit until I'm sure that Dean Pellet and Miss Margaret Feather were on the verge of nervous breakdowns. The return of the men to campus brought with it numerous new attitudes that flared and died quickly. Combinations of uniforms, shirts, officer's pinks, GI shoes, battle jackets and coats served as the only available clothing due to shortages. The girls were agog with the sudden abundance of male escorts. The campus was again filled with strolling couples, classes more balanced and Vandercook was once again filled with masculine voices and the smell of shaving soap; and the switchboard was carrying out more calls than were being sent in.

The tradition of "no smoking" on campus fell by the wayside with the return of war weary GIs and the Campus Book Store was forced to undertake the Veterans' Administration procedure for selling books and materials to veterans under the GI Bill. The GIs, for the most part, brought into the classroom a new seriousness, a determination to get their education and get on with the life that had been so suddenly snatched away from them two, three or four years before. The fellows were older, some in years, some in experience and some in both. These were men with a new purpose, men with families, wives, with a definite goal in mind: to get on with the business of living and learning. Western "grew up" over night."

Married student life was not without its distractions, as this student daddy is about to discover.

The post-war period brought a growing international student enrollment. More than a dozen nations were represented in this 1949 student grouping.

The trailers where married students resided after the war offered private but "snug" accommodations, as this 1946 photograph testifies.

As Western's enrollment boomed during the post-war years, the Little Theatre on Oakland Drive doubled as a classroom.

Grew up it did. From 1946 through 1950, Western's annual enrollment topped 4,000, more than double the attendance in 1945. With a similar avalanche of veteran students at colleges and universities nationwide, faculty positions became increasingly difficult to fill. Desperate department heads pressed faculty wives into teaching courses for which they were sometimes little prepared. Textbooks, too, continued in great demand. Dorothy Osborn, who taught freshman English courses on an emergency basis, remembered textbooks ordered but not arriving until the course was more than half over. And by 1946, parking on campus had become a huge problem that resulted in the advent of the first numbered windshield stickers.

Despite the difficulty in finding instructors, Western continued to broaden its curriculum and class offerings during the post-war years. In 1945, for example, the Department of History and Social Studies burgeoned into four distinct departments—history, economics, sociology and political science. In

1946, Sangren outlined the growth in curricula over the first ten years of his presidency. From nine non-teaching curricula in 1936, the college now offered at least 35. He itemized some deserving special mentions:

> The Music Department has three curricula leading to a general degree. Four-year curricula are offered in occupational therapy, in business administration and in secretarial science. A five-year curriculum in

Students crowded the snack bar at Walwood Union in 1947.

nursing is offered in collaboration with Bronson Hospital. Among the new shorter curricula, not leading to a degree, the ones in trade and industrial education are especially noteworthy. Here the school offers training in aircraft mechanics, air conditioning and refrigeration, radio mechanics, pattern making, cabinet making, two-year courses in homemaking, and half a dozen other allied fields. Retailing and secretarial training should also be mentioned.

The opening of the fall semester of 1945 brought the establishment of the Department of Library Education. Financed with the assistance of the W.K. Kellogg Foundation, the program sought to "properly prepare teacher librarians for public service and to stimulate the development of school and community libraries and library services." Alice Louise LeFevre, a Wellesley College graduate, arrived from Brooklyn, New York, to head the department. Hundreds of Western-trained personnel ultimately staffed community and school libraries across the state. In 1953, the first graduate courses in librarianship were offered, and two years later, the graduate program became the main component of the department.

Sponsored and partially funded by the huge papermaking industry of the Kalamazoo River Valley, the initial course in pulp and paper technology appeared in 1948. Six years later, the Paper Technology Department became a separate entity. Western's pioneering efforts in paper technology would also prove important in establishing ongoing rapport with influential members of the Kalamazoo business community. Dwight Stocker, president of the Kalamazoo Vegetable Parchment Company, for example, assisted the college in numerous ways. Private money would continue to further develop Western's papermaking program and an auxiliary program in

Western's aircraft mechanics program expanded after the war.

Alfred Nadelman, head of the Paper Technology Program, demonstrated the use of a hydrapulper in this 1953 photograph.

printing technology.

Western's aviation program continued to develop after the war. In 1947 came the formation of the Sky Broncos, a club formed to promote flying and to help interested students acquire a commercial license. In 1951, the college branched into a related field

Eddie Powless posed by the short street connecting Stadium Drive and Oakland Drive that was named in his honor in 1956. Powless began driving bus for the college in 1942 and became a beloved personality, shuttling students between campuses until his retirement in 1975.

when it began offering a four-year curriculum geared to training airline stewardesses. In an era when sexism that would be intolerable today was the norm, the "airline hostess" curriculum specified special entrance requirements: "Height: five-feet minimum, five-feet, six-inches maximum; weight: proportionate to height, 100 to 125 pounds; eyesight: not requiring glasses; appearance: well proportioned, good carriage, neat and attractive; voice: well modulated, pleasing tone; marital status: single, never married."

Another vital link with the Kalamazoo area business community came with the expansion of Western's courses in business. In 1947, a business professor teaching at the University of Minnesota named Arnold Schneider arrived on campus for a job interview with Sangren. Sangren liked his style and offered him a position at $4,700 a year. Even though the University of Minnesota

was willing to meet that offer to retain him, Schneider opted for Western because, as he recalled in a 1990 interview, "Something told me that this is the place of the future." Schneider took charge of a program with four instructors and a little over 300 students. Classes met in the basement of the library and in the Walwood Union. Soon, classes were moved to a series of old army barracks the college acquired and set up above Waldo Stadium. Richard Chormann, a business student about that time, remembered those barracks as "just white sheds, uncomfortably hot in the fall, spring and summer and unbearably cold or overheated in the winter."

Schneider had a vision for the development of Western's business program, and in 1948, without authorization, he changed its name in the catalog from business education to business studies. Summoned to explain his actions by Western's first vice president, Dr.

Wynand Wichers, Schneider admitted making the change unilaterally, but that it had been Wichers's office that sent the catalog to the printer. That ended the reprimand. Schneider credits that name change as "the first major step in moving toward a College of Business."

Part of Schneider's success in developing the department came through his ability to stand up to conservative administrators defending the *status quo*. Schneider never forgot his initial encounter with crusty old John Hoekje:

Dean John Hoekje flipped a coin to decide the winner of the Men's Union leadership, as shown in this 1945 photograph.

> *In the course of my first year I was making a lot of decisions ad hoc because I had to. I was here maybe three or four months, and Hoekje was going to put me in my proper place in relationship to his authority. He called up on the phone and he said, "This is Dean Hoekje."*

And I said, "Yes, sir." And he said to me, "You know, you made three mistakes," and enumerated them. And I said, "Yes, sir." I said, "Dean Hoekje, you know they tell me that you are a great sports enthusiast." And he said, "Yes." And I said, "Well, you didn't ask me how many things I did, how many times I went to the plate." And he said, "What's that got to do with it?" And I

Business students developed their adding machine skills in this classroom in an old army barracks, circa 1946.

Campus School students enjoyed learning about rabbits while under the watchful eyes of practice teachers in this 1946 photograph.

business administration degrees, the first former normal in Michigan and one of the first in the nation to do so. It was about that time, to the disbelief of fellow faculty members, that Schneider began predicting that Western would soon become a university.

Western pioneered in another discipline in 1958, with the establishment of the nation's first Department of Religion and Philosophy in a state-owned college, with Dr. Cornelius Lowe as its head. Actively promoted by the dean of the College of Arts and Sciences, Gerald Osborn, the movement took root in 1951 with the construction on the West Campus of Kanley Chapel, then one of only two such religious buildings owned and operated by tax-supported institutions of higher learning in Michigan. In 1944, several donors had contributed toward a chapel with gifts of war bonds in memory of relatives killed in the service. Five years later, the estate of William Kanley, an alumnus of Western's first decade, presented the college with a $200,000 bequest to build

said, "Dean Hoekje, I stepped up to the plate 10 times, and I swung out on three, according to you, and hit safely on seven and I am batting 700 percent. What do you think of that figure?" He never called me again for the rest of my career.

In 1950, Schneider wrote Sangren a letter telling him, "We have a lot of veterans and these veterans are not going to be teachers and in the best interest of these students we have an obligation to give them a degree in business." Based on that letter and further communications, Sangren pursued the matter with the State Board of Education, and in 1952, Western began granting its first bachelor of

Students played golf on Western's "Goat Hill" course in 1957. Kanley Chapel is visible in the background.

Western's 1953 Homecoming featured a parade that commemorated the college's 50th birthday.

the structure. Patterned after the ancient basilica type architecture, the building contained an upper chapel seating 300, a lower chapel seating 80 and a social room accommodating 100 people. From its square clock tower, electronic Westminster chimes hourly pealed across the West Campus.

In 1954, as part of a Danforth Foundation grant, Western became one of 15 pilot centers to explore the integration of religion with teacher education. Sangren appointed a committee to guide the project, and among its recommendations was the eventual establishment of a Department of Religion and Philosophy. In the interim, two initial religion courses were approved in 1954.

Prior to that, Western had held an "Exploration of Faith Week" on campus each March with numerous religious speakers from various denominations. By 1961, the event had become the "Religious Emphasis Week."

Religion in the 1950s was definitely emphasized on Western's campus, sometimes too much so. Claude Phillips, for many years a distinguished political science professor at Western, never forgot the day in 1957 when he was waiting to be interviewed for a position outside Dean Osborn's office, and he heard Osborn's voice boom out in argument, "He wants a promotion and he doesn't even go to

Dr. James O. Knauss, who joined Western history faculty in 1926, wrote the first two histories of the college.

Hugh H. Anderson received the college's first master's degree diploma from Sangren in 1953.

oriented course as part of the required general education of students. Phillips became director of the Institute of Regional Studies to campaign for that course, and finally, in 1964, Western's curriculum required one non-western course for graduation. The University had become the first major institution of higher learning in America to make that requirement.

By the winter semester of 1952, Western's graduate-level courses had grown to 28 offerings. The following fall, the University of Michigan relinquished control of Western's graduate programs and the college was authorized to grant its own graduate degrees. Dr. George Mallinson, who had been named head of graduate advisors in 1952, succeeded Elmer Wilds as director of the graduate division in 1955. Over the succeeding 27 years, Mallinson ran what evolved into the Graduate College as a "tight ship." His toughness in demanding absolute standards in theses and dissertations (he thoroughly read every one himself) and his abrasive encounters with those on and off campus who failed to appreciate his unrelenting zeal were proverbial. Among the many accomplishments of his tenure were the securing of much-needed funding via grants and the acquisition of sophisticated equipment such as the eight-million-volt Van de Graaf accelerator.

Meanwhile, Western students were busy creating extracurricular traditions. Back in the fall of 1945, four students had conceived the idea of producing a variety show made up of Western talent. They approached the Student Council and secured its approval. The call for talent met an overwhelming response. The show, named the *Brown and Gold Fantasies*, was advertised as a three-act musical to be performed in the Kalamazoo Central High School Auditorium on April 30, 1946. One of

church!" Despite misgivings, Phillips accepted the position, and the following year he helped establish a less parochial emphasis in the curriculum. As he recalled in a 1990 interview:

> In May of 1958, I walked into Russell Seibert's (vice president for academic affairs) office and I said, "I have been here a year and I want to tell you what I think of this place," I said, "There is tremendous potential … but it is just amazing that you can educate 7,000 people each year and there is not a course in the catalog that will get them out of western civilization."

Seibert, too, had been concerned with the lack of courses about the non-western world, and that fall, he appointed Phillips to chair a committee to look into the problem. The committee recommended the creation and implementation of at least one non-western

The wearing of freshman beanies to foster school spirit first became a campus tradition in 1929. Dropped during WW II, the custom was reintroduced in 1949.

the performers and a Western graduate of 1948, Dick Kishpaugh, recalled the problems that developed:

> *Somehow, in the confusion of putting the show together, the task of assembling a third act was overlooked. Since the show had been billed as a three-act musical, the directors decided (one day before the opening) that they had better add a third act. The union soda bar was quickly named as the scene. The show went on as scheduled for its one-night stand. Admission was free, and a near-capacity crowd of students and townspeople filled the auditorium. While the audience laughed its way through the first two*

Western's famous trolley was still running strong in this circa 1946 snapshot.

Deep Are the Roots, performed by Western's Players in 1947, was the first non-professional production of this play by a racially mixed cast in the United States.

acts, it was unaware of the frantic work going on backstage—the now-famous third act wasn't ready yet!

Time would not wait for the performers, so the third-act curtain rose on a strictly impromptu presentation. To delay the curtain, we pulled the old gag of asking one row of the audience to move, leading them out of the auditorium, down another aisle, and right back to the same seats. Despite the fact that no one knew from one minute to the next what was going to take place on the stage, the audience enjoyed the proceedings, judging from the applause. To close the show, another old stage joke was employed. Stagehands took down the scenery without closing the curtain, and the audience stayed in the belief that it was a part of the third act.

Thus launched, the *Brown and Gold Fantasies* became a highlight of the college

year. The 1947 presentation featured as a finale a popular song written by Jim Barber and Tom Fulton of Kalamazoo, *The Girl from the College on the Hill*.

Western's speech department made history in 1947 when the Players presented as their midwinter play *Deep Are the Roots* by Arnaud d'Usseau and James Gow. That year's *Brown and Gold* noted that "the play's message concerning the seemingly ever-existent problem of racial prejudice was strong and impressive." Western's performance of the play about a returning black veteran's encounter with racial intolerance in the South became the first non-professional production of this play with a racially mixed cast in the United States. Six years later, James Earl Jones starred in a University of Michigan production of that same play.

Integration became a major issue in the post-war period. In 1947, Jackie Robinson broke the color barrier in professional baseball, and the following year, President Harry Truman issued his executive order that prohibited segregation in the military. Black athletes had long starred on Western's football and track teams but, with the exception of the baseball prowess of Sam Dunlap in the early 1920s and Ed Salter in the middle 1930s, the other varsity sports remained white bastions until 1947, when Charles Bassett Brown became the Bronco's first black basketball player. He scored 15 points against Central Michigan College in his first game.

Born and raised in Benton Harbor, Brown returned to his hometown following his graduation from Western and the completion of his medical studies to begin a long and successful career as an oral surgeon. In 1989, he recorded his experiences while at Western:

The Delta Chi Christmas Ball of 1959 featured trumpet playing by the immortal Louis Armstrong.

> I remember Western as a big family of about 2,000 students, and racism was not prevalent as far as the student body was concerned. We were not included in the fraternities, but we didn't miss it. We also were not allowed to live in the dorms, but many of us could not have afforded to live there anyway. Psychologically it was no impediment to us because we always had our friends, and we were there to get an education. Our social consciousness was great, but that was not our main objective for being in school.
>
> Western was a beautiful experience for me, and being on the basketball team was great because everybody likes a winner, and we were winners. I had no trouble with the guys on the team, and I want to stress that's how it was with the students. Everybody knew everybody and everybody spoke to one another. I had had the same experience in high school. I was not programmed to fail. People treated me as their equal in high school, and the same thing happened to me at Western. It's just that institutions often lag behind people.

Even institutions guided by progressive leaders sometimes fall behind because of a reluctance to change with changing times. In his determination to build Western's future outward from the hill, Sangren faced a good deal of opposition. With the exception of the adaptive reuse of some residences and temporary buildings, the first real construction west of Stadium Drive took place in 1948. Two brick apartment buildings, known as Hillside Apartments, opened in June of that year to provide living quarters for 32 faculty members. A Greek Revival-style brick clubhouse for the golf course was converted into a cafeteria and faculty clubroom.

WESTERN MICHIGAN COLLEGE

EDUCATION BLDG.
HEALTH SERVICE BLDG.
HIGH and ELEMENTARY SCHOOL
LIBRARY
MAINTENANCE BLDG.
MEN'S GYMNASIUM
NATURAL SCIENCE BLDG.
SPINDLER HALL
THE THEATRE
UNION BLDG.
VANDERCOOK HALL
WALWOOD HALL

ADMINISTRATION BLDG.
ARCADIA CAFETERIA
BURNHAM HALLS
DRAPER : SIEDSCHLAG HALLS
HILLSIDE APARTMENTS
INDUSTRIAL ARTS BLDG.
KANLEY CHAPEL
McCRACKEN HALL
MAYBEE HALL
MECHANICAL TRADES BLDG.
R.O.T.C. BLDGS.
TEMP. HOUSING VILLAGE

Erected in 1952 at the intersection of Oakland and Stadium drives, this huge sign demonstrated the confusing nature of the split campus.

In 1949, twin dormitories opened on West Campus to provide housing for 500 students. They were named in honor of brothers, Ernest and Smith Burnham. The latter had served as a member of the history department for 20 years, beginning in 1919. Because the pent-up demand by consumers for furniture during the post-war years made it nearly impossible to furnish the dormitories, the college solved the problem by securing furniture manufactured by inmates in Jackson State Prison.

Living quarters away from the hilltop campus were one matter, but when Sangren revealed plans to construct a much-needed classroom, Western's first "Million Dollar Building," on the West Campus, that was something else. Cornelius MacDonald, college comptroller under Sangren, recalled in 1963: "When Doc Sangren first said that he was going to put a new arts and science building way over there, the opposition from faculty and everybody—not everybody, but a large number—was tremendous. And it shows his wisdom and his strong Swedish jaw that said, 'We're going to move over there. We're going to need the room.' And he was very wise." Completed in 1949 and named McCracken Hall in honor of William McCracken, head of the chemistry department from 1907 to 1939, the four-story structure initially housed the departments of chemistry, physics, art, home economics, occupational therapy and paper technology.

The second classroom structure to open in 1949, the Harper Maybee Music Hall, commemorated the 32 years of service (beginning in 1913) of the near-legendary head of the music department. Costing more than $500,000 and built with state-of-the-art acoustics, the Maybee Music Hall contained 35 practice cubicles, eight ensemble rehearsal rooms, a music library, offices, classrooms and studios.

The fall of 1949 witnessed the dedication of another pair of connected dormitories for women. Named in honor of Lydia Siedschlag, longtime art professor, and Blanche Draper, who had performed publicity work for the college for 32 years, the dormitories provided housing for more than 500 women at a construction cost of $2 million.

Life in Western's dormitories of the 1950s was a far cry from that of today. Housemothers ran a tight ship with plenty of "do nots." The Associated Women Students published a little handbook in the 1950s that defined some of the expected behavior:

The Hillside Apartments, now demolished, were built in 1948 for faculty housing.

Harper Maybee Music Hall, constructed in 1949, was demolished to make room for the new University Computer Center.

This photograph offers a peek into a "four-girl study suite" in Siedschlag Hall in 1950.

The Walwood Union cafeteria was a bustling place in the 1950s.

Yelling in the halls and out of windows suggests a lack of femininity and is considered poor taste.

For our evening meal, we remain standing until all the girls at our table are ready to be seated. In consideration of others, we do not eat our dessert until the rest of the girls are ready to begin. After we have completed our meal, we leave the table in a group.

It is thoughtful to greet professors first when you see them outside of class, for it is sometimes difficult for them to remember all of your names.

Students entering their rooming places, whether residence halls or private houses, under the influence of liquor, and students who introduce liquor or liquor bottles into any rooming place or college building will be subject to dismissal from college.

Western likes young love, but "huggin and kissin" on the campus, up-

town or in residence halls tends to cheapen your affection and be embarrassing to the onlookers. One of our favorite slogans to remember is...

Kissing in the lobby
Is not a good hobby

Bermudas, shorts or slacks are never worn in classes, administration buildings or in the lobbies of our dormitories. They can be worn for studying in the library, however, as long as good taste is used. These types of apparel, when worn too tight, always prove embarrassing to yourself and to the onlooker.

Western rules demand dressing for dinner on Sunday, and you will find that the extra time spent that this takes will apply good dividends in mental uplift and relaxation. Simple dresses, suits, or skirts with your best blouses or dressy sweaters wear well at dinner. And unless you want to take the chance of missing your meal entirely, never try to sneak in with anklets.

So much for the rules, but what was campus life really like in the early to middle 1950s? Carol Waszkiewicz, who entered Western as a freshman in 1955 and who in the 1980s would serve as chairperson of the University's Board of Trustees, remembered:

> *We had the hitching line from the west to the east campus and you would see people standing there hitching rides to the other side of campus in slacks... everyone had slacks on. Another thing that I well remember is that you had been initiated one way or another as a college student if you had been to the boondocks. Wherever that was... they were out west of town. There was very little development west of town, so west of campus out in some field people went there and had beer parties.*

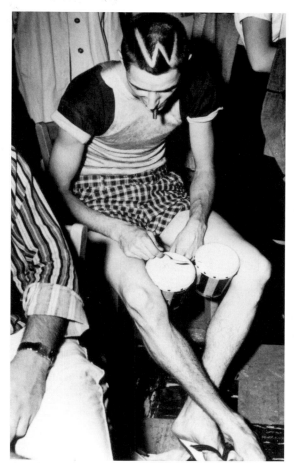

During Western's 1959 Homecoming, Hoedown Day provided students the opportunity to portray themselves as "beatniks."

Tom Coyne, who graduated from Western in 1955 and who would retire as vice president for student services in 1990, recalled that the spring of 1952 "brought the first panty raids to Western Michigan as the boys from the Burnhams decided to check out the upper floors of Draper and Siedschlag. They simply didn't want to be behind the times in comparison to other colleges." By that era, another campus tradition had emerged—a female student was not an official coed until she had been kissed while under the cupola of the old administration building (East Hall).

Coyne, who met his steady girl friend Monique Jako at Western and married her following their graduation in 1955, recalled taking her to football and basketball games and "sock-hops" in Walwood Union. He remembered some humorous aspects of the dating scene during a 1993 interview:

Joy Harrison celebrates Hoedown Day at Western's 1959 Homecoming.

After the sock-hop came the problem of reclaiming the right footgear, as this 1953 photograph demonstrates.

Dating in the fifties was quite different. If you dated a girl on campus, she had hours. The guys didn't. It was a double standard. The women had to be in by 10:30 p.m. during the week. The time was different on the weekends. I believe that the time was 12:00 or 12:30 a.m.

Every night around 10:15 p.m. the dorms looked like a scene out of a World War II movie. The troops were at the train station kissing their sweethearts good-bye, because they were, perhaps, never going to see them again. It was like something out of a B movie.

What happened, of course, would be that at 10:30 all of the women would go inside, and the guys would make a beeline for the halls. We had only one phone per floor. The next thing you know there would be some guy on the phone to the gal that he had just been passionately kissing good-bye five minutes before. In retrospect, it was quite funny.

In 1952, the college dedicated its new $1.2 million administration building (later named in honor of Russell Seibert). The lowest floor of the modernistic structure housed the campus bookstore and the post office for all faculty. The remaining three floors provided much-needed administrative offices and classes for social sciences and languages and literature. The Division of Adult Education and Extension occupied the penthouse.

Davis Hall, named for Bertha Davis, music professor and longtime dean of women, opened as a residence hall for women in 1954. The following year Zimmerman Hall, honoring Elizabeth Zimmerman, who taught German on campus for more than 40 years beginning in 1905, added an additional five stories of dormitories for 300 women.

The camera captured this happy moment during the 1948 Senior Cabaret Dance.

These fashionably dressed students attended a 1950 Western football game. Note the freshman beanie.

In 1953, the college acquired another 42-acre site surrounding a majestic century-old Italianate structure, formerly a private mental sanatorium known as the Wilbur Home. In June 1955, wreckers battered down the grand old building, and the following month Sangren announced an $8 million building program for the site. That summer, giant earth-moving machines created lung-choking clouds of dust as they leveled 30-foot-high hills and filled in valleys. By the following year, the first of the structures to cover the site, Ellsworth Hall, a 440-bed men's dormitory, stood completed. The year 1957 witnessed the dedication of the centerpiece of the development, the student center (later named for President John T. Bernhard), complete with cafeteria, bookstore, snack bar, bowling alleys, pool hall, lounges and meeting rooms. Henry Hall flanked the student center on the left in 1957, and by 1961, Hoekje Hall and Bigelow Hall (named for longtime economics professor Howard Bigelow) had completed the semi-

The Seibert Administration Building was nearing completion in this 1952 photograph.

This 1956 aerial view shows the Bernhard Student Union and adjacent buildings under construction.

Newly constructed Hoekje Hall was the subject of this 1959 photo.

circle of dormitories around to the student union.

In 1954, Kalamazoo City Manager Clarence Elliott presented head librarian Katherine Stokes with Western's 100,000th book. Appropriate to the Cold War era, *Tomorrow* by Philip Wylie was written to "awaken in Americans a real sense of the probabilities of atomic warfare." Four years later, Western's library held 125,000 volumes housed in an avant-garde new structure on the West Campus named in honor of Dwight B. Waldo. The three-story structure, with a capacity for 225,000 volumes, featured open stacks, a welcome relief from the page-retrieval system of the old East Campus library.

The Cold War escalated in 1950 when the Korean War broke out. That year the campus became the scene, for the third time, of the thud of marching feet and the harsh commands of drill sergeants, as Western's first ROTC program was organized. Initially, its ROTC units specialized in quartermaster training. Western experienced some loss of enroll-ment due to veteran students reentering the armed forces and the psychological effects of the draft on college-age men. The fall enrollment of 1951 dropped to 3,702, but the following year, it rebounded to 4,145 and would continue to increase throughout the decade to 8,000.

The year 1950 brought another challenge for Western in the form of a "financial crisis." Promised salary increases for the college's 377 employees vanished when the legislature cut Western's budget. Willis Dunbar, program director of the Fetzer Broadcasting Company and later head of Western's Department of History, delivered a personal radio appeal about the situation in November 1950. He noted that Western's employees had been getting "a raw deal" since the early Depression-era cuts. Subsequent to that, their wages had

Dr. William Brown, English Department head, lectured on Shakespeare in a class on the third floor of the Administration Building, about 1955.

Vice President Wynand Wichers posed beside the war memorial constructed near Kanley Chapel in 1954.

not kept up with the cost-of-living increases. In 1950, Western's instructors averaged $3,237 a year, assistant professors $3,824 and full professors $4,968. Salaries would gradually creep upward during the 1950s, but this would not be the last financial crisis faced by Western.

Throughout the decade, Western also went through an intensive reorganization to keep up with the burgeoning student enrollment. In 1951, for example, when Dr. George Kohrman arrived on campus to become director of the Division of Practical Arts and Vocational Education, he had under his jurisdiction a diverse jumble of disciplines, including agriculture, home economics, occupational therapy, distributive education, all business courses and the ROTC. He even had responsibility for the Pine Lake Technical School, then operated by Western for the rehabilitation of veterans. To revamp the traditional unwieldy college administration, which was essentially a one-man rule, a major reorganization occurred on July 1, 1956, with the creation of the offices of vice president for

Waldo Library in 1961

The interior of Waldo Library looked like this when it first opened in 1958.

Western's library, then located on the East Campus, acquired its pioneer microfilm reader in 1952.

academic affairs and vice president for student services and public relations. Deans were appointed to head five new academic schools: applied arts and sciences, business, education, liberal arts and sciences, and graduate studies.

Also in 1956, Dr. Robert Limpus was appointed director of the Basic Studies Program. Amid a near-constant barrage of student resentment over having to pay for and take courses that were not directed at their specific educational goals, Limpus campaigned long and hard to insure that Western graduates had attained a university degree that provided "the knowledge, the techniques and the desire to live a reflective and discriminating life." Nine years later, the Board of Trustees approved the establishment of a School of General Studies with Limpus as its dean. Unfortunately, competition from other schools and departments protecting what they perceived as their turf and fragmentation of general studies requirements between what was offered by the School of General Studies and the various departments continued. It and the other five university schools then in existence became colleges in 1970. Two years later, Dr. Norman Greenberg succeeded Limpus. In 1989, Provost and Vice President for Academic Affairs George M.

Read Fieldhouse was nearing completion in 1957.

Dennison announced the dissolution of the College of General Studies and the establishment of the Department of General Studies in the College of Arts and Sciences. Affected faculty were given the opportunity to stay with the new department or transfer to other departments within the University.

Returning to the events of 1956, in October, at the dedication of the $1.5 million Gary Center, a men's physical education facility named in honor of athletic director Mitchell "Mike" Gary, Senator Carlton H. Morris casually inserted into his speech an off-hand remark that set off a rapid chain reaction.

Morris said that he would be happy to enact a bill to rename Western a university at any time desired by the college. Sangren acted quickly to make the dream a reality. Presidents of the state's three other universities, at Ann Arbor, East Lansing and Detroit, sent letters of support, a brief pamphlet presenting Western's case was produced and circulated and the State Board of Education recommended the action. So little opposition emerged that Sangren expressed concern that he knew not where to "point the gun." The Michigan Senate passed the bill 28 to 0, and two weeks later, the House did likewise. On February 26, 1957, Governor G. Mennen Williams signed the bill designating Western Michigan University. Art professor John G. Kemper hastily scrawled on the back of a faculty I.D. card the design for a new seal to replace the Western Michigan College seal adopted in 1955, and ten days later the new emblem was unveiled. The seal featured a tree with its roots firmly planted in the year 1903 surmounted by five stars signifying the five

In 1957, the opening tip off of the first game played in the new Read Fieldhouse pitted Western against Northwestern.

The Morris Dancers, comprised of campus women, danced around a Maypole in this photograph taken about 1946.

As Sangren looked on, Michigan Governor G. Mennen "Soapy" Williams signed the 1957 bill creating Western Michigan University.

particularly as a demonstration of how it could be used to enhance education. In 1950, workmen hoisted a 72-foot tower atop Maybee Hall, and testing started. Regular broadcasting of the 400-watt station, at 91.1 FM, began in January 1951. Listeners within 25 miles of campus could tune into a two-hour morning broadcast of taped classroom lectures by professors, talks by assembly speakers and student recitals. A grant from the W.K. Kellogg Foundation allowed the station to increase its power to 36,000 watts and move up the broadcast band to 102.1 FM. Garrard D. Macleod, who joined the staff as the first full-time announcer in 1959, recalled the primitive nature of the arrangement:

> *The fans used for circulation of air within the building made so much noise that whenever I wanted to make a recording, it was necessary to turn the fans off. Meanwhile everyone in the building suffered during warm weather.*

Another problem was funding for repairs of the antiquated equipment. Macleod remembered calling around the country to other stations trying to locate replacement parts for obsolete transmitters. As the 1950s wore on, WMCR's broadcast schedule expanded to include coverage of Western's many athletic events.

While the 1950s often proved disappointing to fans of Western's football and basketball teams, in other sports they proved remarkable years. Western had joined the Mid-American Conference in 1948 (from 1927 to 1931 it belonged to the Michigan Collegiate Conference before it was disbanded), and coach Hap Sorensen's tennis players took eight MAC first places in the 1950s. Coach Charles Maher's baseball team won many a game, thanks to the likes of All-American outfielder Bill Lajoie and pitcher Jack Rumohr. Swimming became a major intercollegiate sport at Western,

academic colleges created the year before.

When the college became a university, WMCR (Western Michigan College Radio) station manager Wallace Garneau realized those call letters were no longer appropriate. In 1961, when the opportunity emerged, Western's radio station became WMUK-FM. Since the early 1930s, the campus had been involved in radio broadcasts. From a private studio located on the west side of the gallery of the women's gymnasium, students and faculty broadcast college news and talks about specialized topics of public interest via local airwave pioneer John Fetzer's WKZO radio. Garneau, a member of the Speech Department, began teaching a course called "Introduction to Radio Speaking" in 1941, and other radio-related activities followed.

Sangren liked the idea of Western's involvement in the new concept of FM radio,

This 1950s era Western radio production included plenty of sound effects.

beginning in 1957. Five-foot-four-inch Ira Murchison, the "Tiny Terror," joined the ranks of a long tradition of great black Western track stars. Prior to getting drafted into the army during his sophomore year at Western, he broke all existing sprint records. While racing in Berlin in 1956, he ran the 100-meter dash in 10.1 seconds to break Jesse Owens' record set there 20 years before. At the Melbourne, Australia, Olympics that year, he won a gold medal as a member of the world-record-setting, 400-meter relay team. In a 1986 interview, Murchison credited much of his success to Western track coach George Dales:

> *He was a beautiful coach and like a father to us. He taught us what we had to do to be successful not only on the track but also later in life. He urged us to put everything into our training so we would get the most out of it. He always said, "If you don't put something into the bank, you can't get anything out of it." I've never forgotten that and many are the times I've said the same thing to the kids I've coached over the years.*

In the fall of 1959, the University held a contest to adopt a new fight song and alma mater. A jury composed of faculty and

WMCR Station Manager Wallace Garneau discussed tube replacements with Chief Engineer Glen Bishop in 1955.

Western's 1951 MAC championship baseball team posed with Coach Charles Maher.

students selected as the fight song the words and music submitted by senior Walt Gilbert:

Fight on, fight on for Western Michigan,
Take the ball, make a score, win the game.
Onward for the Brown and Gold,
Push'em back, push'em back, bring us fame.
Fight on, fight on and we will conquer them
Over one, over all we will reign.
Fight, Broncos, fight,
show them all your might,
Western, win this game.

Coached by Hap Sorensen, Western's 1952 tennis team took the MAC crown.

James Bull, a 1957 graduate, wrote the new alma mater:

Western, we sing to you,
Brown and Gold;
Western, we bring to you,
Faith untold:
You challenge and inspire;
Your hope is our desire;
We sing to you, our Alma Mater,
Brown and Gold.

A few months later, on December 13, 1959, WMCR broadcast the breaking news that Sangren had announced his retirement, effective June 30, 1960. For years he had been suffering from the same debilitating illness that had taken his predecessor, Parkinson's disease.

As his condition grew worse, in May 1959, he underwent corrective surgery in Grand Rapids, but to little avail. When he stepped down in 1960, Sangren outlined the many accomplishments of his 25-year tenure. The college had shifted from the heights of Prospect Hill to sprawl across the former golf courses, as dozens of modern new buildings took shape. The student body rose some 570 percent from 1,454 to 8,303. The faculty grew correspondingly from 188 to 468. Five academic schools offered hundreds of new courses in disciplines unheard of a quarter century before. Seven hundred graduate students pursued master's degrees in education, biology, chemistry, economics, English, history, librarianship, political science, psychology, sociology and business administration.

Sangren crowned Homecoming Queen Myra Brieve in 1953.

Ira Murchinson, Western's "Tiny Terror," ran the 100-yard dash in 9.8 seconds when this photograph was snapped on May 18, 1957.

In 1964, at the dedication of the sprawling new classroom structure named Sangren Hall, Russell Seibert, vice president for academic affairs under Sangren, summed up the quality of his leadership:

> There are numerous factors that help to account for the highly successful administration of President Sangren. I sometimes said with a high degree of truth, that he "made haste slowly." He was a man of patience who knew how to move forward steadily but with persistence. He had a clear vision of where he was going and with administrative wisdom and tact carried his faculty with him. He might at times delay a difficult decision for weeks or months, but then having once made up

his mind acted with unusual vigor and straightforwardness. The changes that took place at Western were evolutionary in character rather than revolutionary, but change was constant and in keeping with the times.

President Emeritus Paul Sangren died in 1967. Sangren's retirement seven years before marked a milestone in the University's development in more than one way. As the institution continued to evolve from a college with its primary goal to educate teachers into a major university with myriad and complex specialties, as it grew physically and in enrollment and as it endured increased budgetary and administrative concerns, it, by necessity, changed. With growth also came loss. Dr. Philip Denenfeld, who arrived on

Western's august History Department posed in 1957. (Left to right) front row are: Cornelius Lowe, Margaret MacMillan, Alan Brown, Howard Mowen, Robert Friedmann and Edyth Mange, back row: Sherwood Cordier, Nicholas Hamner, Edward Elsasser, Charles Starring, Gilbert Morrell and Willis Dunbar

Sangren and wife, Flossie, sat with their dogs on the steps of the Oaklands in 1957.

These Vandercook Hall residents gladly bade the college farewell as they left for the summer of 1953.

campus as a English instructor in 1956 and rose through the administrative hierarchy to become vice president for academic affairs in the 1980s, looked back at the sea change that had occurred during a speech at a 1986 Academic Convocation. He lamented the lost sense of community, and the disappearance of the big-family atmosphere in which everyone knew almost everyone else on campus. He saw it as an inevitable loss, but one that "changed the nature of campus relationships and thereby the nature of the institution." By necessity, though regretfully, this story of Western will reflect those changes by detailing less social history in order to encompass the rapidly expanding nature of the institution during the final third of the 20th century.

Chapter 5

The Sixties Sizzle and the Seventies Fizzle

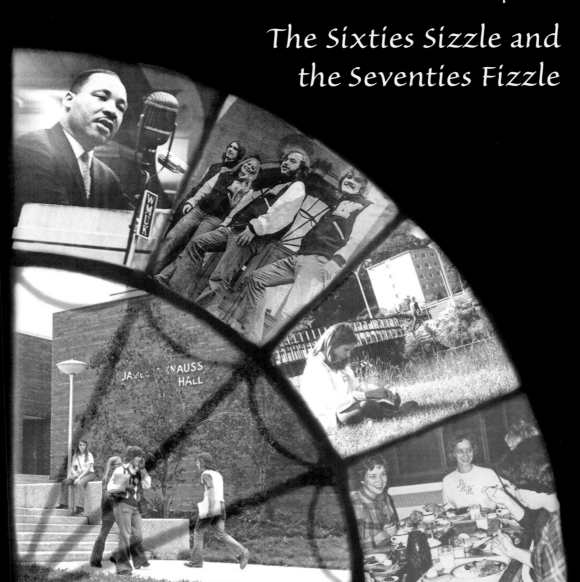

The decade of the 1960s dawned with the bright promise of the John F. Kennedy administration, then darkened into one of the most turbulent periods in American history. Headlines screamed of assassinations, protest demonstrations, flag burnings, race riots and the Vietnam War. Americans learned new geography: The Bay of Pigs and Da Nang, Woodstock and Kent State. They drove Mustang convertibles and Volkswagon vans, donned Beatle boots and miniskirts, listened to Bob Dylan, Motown, the Mamas and the Papas, and the Beach Boys. LBJ and Tricky Dick, flower power and long hair, school desegregation and draft dodging disrupted and divided American society. In 1963, Martin Luther King, Jr. told Kalamazooans that "Americans must live as brothers or perish as fools." Five years

Dr. Willis Dunbar of the History Department presided at the campus convocation to honor President John F. Kennedy following his assassination in 1963.

later, the Detroit Tigers clinched the World Series and helped heal hometown scarred by the race riots of the summer before. The decade also saw America rise above the difficulties of life on earth to begin the conquest of outer space.

During that tumultuous era, the University would need a fair, even-handed, yet firm hand at the helm. It would need a statesman with an inquiring mind, a willingness to listen and a refusal to sidestep issues. Western found those qualities and more in its third president, Dr. James W. Miller.

Born April 7, 1913, in Brockton, Massachusetts, Miller grew up in the same community that spawned Rocky Marciano, the only undefeated heavyweight-boxing champion in history. Miller liked to joke about his connection with Marciano:

"I pushed him all over the park one day. He really wasn't so tough." Then he would deliver the punch line:

"Of course, I was a 15-year-old ballplayer

and Rocky was only four years old. Even then, it was a split decision."

Miller graduated, cum laude, with a bachelor of arts degree from nearby Amherst College in 1935. After studying in Germany and England for two years, he earned his master of arts degree from the University of Minnesota in 1938 and ten years later, his Ph.D. In the meantime he found employment as a teaching assistant at Minnesota before joining the political science faculty at Michigan State University in 1940. Two years later, he enlisted in the U.S. Coast Guard and emerged from the service as an officer in 1946. He returned to MSU, becoming a full professor of political science in 1953. The following year, he was named to the post of director of teacher education.

Governor G. Mennen Williams appointed Miller state controller in 1955. His responsibilities included preparing the entire state budget as well as directing state purchasing, properties, buildings and office services.

The Rev. Martin Luther King spoke on campus December 18, 1963.

During the nearly six years he spent in Lansing, Miller learned a good deal about practical politics. One of his favorite tactics was to say, "Look, I'm not a politician and I'm not running for office. This is what state agencies say they need and I think they need the money for these reasons ... " Miller soon earned a reputation as a sincere and honest state employee with good judgment and ideas. In June 1960, he left state government to become secretary to the MSU board of trustees.

That was precisely the time when Sangren's retirement took effect. Dr. Gerald Osborn, dean of the School of Liberal Arts and Sciences, took over the reins as acting president. Meanwhile, the State Board of Education's search for a new president floundered amid political consider-ations. The four-

As state controller, Dr. James W. Miller briefed a group about budgetary concerns in 1956.

The Oaklands looked like this about the time President Miller and his family moved there in 1961.

space in Ellsworth Hall for the displaced faculty, and soon expert restorers began work on the majestic structure. When the Miller family moved in, the Oaklands emerged as the historic jewel of the West Campus.

Miller wasted little time in confronting what he perceived as the major problems of the ensuing decade. With campus enrollment burgeoning by 10 to 15 percent each year, Miller announced, "The basic challenge is two-fold in nature: namely, how to accommodate the increasingly larger number of students seeking training at our institution, and at the same time to sustain, and in some areas, improve the quality of our education ... In addition to our concern about a level of operation which will assure sound programs of teaching, research and extension, we are also vitally concerned about our building program from which we must obtain additional space for classroom teaching, laboratory

member board, three Democrats and one Republican, simply could not agree on a unanimous choice. Besides Miller, Vice President for Academic Affairs Russell Seibert and State Superintendent of Public Instruction Lynn M. Bartlett were contenders. Bartlett was the leading candidate until he withdrew from consideration in August. On September 29, 1960, the board announced Miller its choice "by unanimous action." He would assume the $25,000 a year post on January 1, 1961.

One of Miller's first endeavors was to secure housing for himself, wife Jane and their three children. He decided to reclaim the Oaklands, which, following Sangren's retirement, had been assigned to 16 faculty members for offices. He found

The Miller family was pictured at home in the Oaklands in 1953. Left to right are Jane, David, Mary Beth, John and President Miller.

Bigelow Hall was completed in 1961.

use, research and desperately needed office space."

The succeeding 13 years of Miller's presidency would see a frenzied building boom that studded the campus with scores of architecturally significant structures. The campus, too, would grow from 387 acres to 513 acres, with another outlying 322 acres. First came Bigelow Hall in 1961. Each of the next four years brought the dedication of a new residence hall. In 1962, Moore Hall, a women's dormitory, opened. It was named jointly for sisters Grace and Mary Moore, in recognition of their many years in the home

economics department and the campus cafeteria.

Goldsworth Valley, named for former physical plant director John Goldsworth, emerged as a celebrated campus beauty spot in the 1960s. The initial construction had been a series of married student housing apartments built in 1959. Four years later, the first residence hall complex was dedicated. Its four component halls, Hadley, Shilling, Britton and Ackley, honor the many years of service of biology professor Theodosia Hadley, political science professor David C. Shilling, Leoti C. Britton of the music department and mathematics professor Hugh Ackley. Goldsworth Valley II opened in 1964, followed by Goldsworth Valley III the next year. That made a total of $13.7 million spent on construction of the Valley dormitories, exclusive of expenditures for landscaping, roadways, development of the pond, tennis courts and an eye-catching pavilion presented by the University Alumni Association.

Harvey Hall, part of the Goldsworth II complex, was pictured here the year following its construction in 1964.

Before the advent of advance registration, students endured the travails of long lines in Read Fieldhouse during registration days.

Even that hectic pace of construction was not enough to accommodate the onslaught of baby-boomers. In 1967 alone, enrollment jumped by 2,000 to 18,447 students. Russell Gabier, who served as assistant director of admissions in the 1960s, remembered:

> At times we would be receiving 100 applications a day and we had a small staff; in fact, the first summer that I arrived they had applications downstairs at the Administration Building sitting around on window sills, just all over the place. Clayton Maus [the registrar] and Dr. Keith Smith were the only two people working on it, and they just could not deal with it, could not handle it. We would get calls from parents and they would say, "Well, my son or daughter submitted an application back in April and we still have not heard from Western." The girls in the office would start tearing around and trying to locate the application because, you know, sometimes we could not get them into the file cabinets they were coming so fast."

The registrar was not the only one receiving phone calls from irate parents. The president's phone rang constantly with calls inquiring where sons and daughters would be living on campus. Thomas Carr, longtime director of housing, never forgot the day in 1967 when he and Maus were summoned to Miller's office:

> He [Miller] walked through the door, walked over, sat down at the table and he hit that table like this, which I'd witnessed him do a couple of other times when he was in a little bit of a rage, and he said, "I want to know what in the hell is going on here!" And

The Bronco cheerleading squad practiced in Goldsworth Valley, circa 1966.

A familiar campus sight, the hitching line, was the subject of this September 1965 photo.

here I was, and there Clayton was, and thank God he turned to Clayton Maus first. And for the next, I don't know how long, 30 minutes maybe, he just tore Clayton Maus up and down. "How could you ever let these students in this University? What am I supposed to do as president?"

After he got done with that, fortunately he had ground down a little bit, he turned to me and he said, "Tom, how are we ever going to take care of all this?" He knew our maximum was 7,000. Here we had 8,500 kids we had to house. And I said, "Well, here's what I've done so far. I've put up every bed we could find in recreation rooms in residence halls, 50 of them in this common room." The kids had to live in there, upper and lower bunks, bags under their bunks next to them, no

protection for anything. "And I called Michigan State yesterday to my counterpart and I said, 'We've really got a problem. We've got 8,500 kids and we've run out of beds. Do you have 500 beds by any chance?' State was the biggest system in the country. If anybody had them, it would be State. And they were also very generous and good people, the State people. And they immediately said, "Tom, don't worry about it. We'll have 500 beds delivered to your campus by no later than tomorrow. Don't even bother to send your own trucks, you have enough problems. We can take care of our kids; we're going to help you take care of yours." And they did. Next day, man! In came 500 beds. Which we immediately put up in the residence halls in the Valley. There was no damn way you could put an additional bed in

The University Student Center, now the Bernhard Center, was doubled in size and revamped in 1964.

the room, but we did it because we had to find a place for these kids. And we ended up housing more than 8,500 kids that fall, which was a monumental thing. Just almost broke this University's back.

With the exception of the Stadium Drive Apartments for married housing completed in 1969, the opening of Goldsworth Valley III brought to a close Western's dormitory building spree. A drop in enrollment in the early 1970s and the decision by the Board of Trustees to permit students to live off campus decreased the demand. Additional dormitories had been projected west of the Valley, but the University dropped the project when it lost a lawsuit over the land on which they were to be erected. That proved fortunate because, as it developed, they would have been superfluous.

In 1962, Wood Hall, the first instructional building of the 1960s decade, opened. Two years later, the newly opened Sangren Hall provided space for the College of Education, the art, history, sociology, political science and economics departments and for

the award-winning Educational Resources Center.

In 1964, also, the redesigned student center opened, having been doubled in size, air-conditioned and its front facade totally altered. A nearly $2 million enlargement of Read Fieldhouse increased seating capacity from 4,500 to 10,000. An adjacent intramural building included basketball and handball courts as well as a dirt floor area (later paved) for indoor practice.

To better utilize its existing structures and other resources, in 1965, Western adopted a calendar consisting of 15-week fall and winter semesters and spring and summer sessions of seven-and-one-half-weeks each. Public schools were requesting more of Western's student teachers, thereby offering sufficient opportunities for directed teaching in the classroom. The administration made the difficult decision to close the University High School in 1966, bringing to an end a vibrant educational opportunity that had produced many of the community's and college's leaders. Three years later, the University's elementary school also closed.

election of Dr. Milton Greenberg by his colleagues as chairman of the Department of Political Science. Previously, department heads (the traditional title) had been appointed by the president or one of the deans to serve at their will. Department heads acted as supervisors and managed departments as they saw fit with little, if any, input from faculty underlings. In 2002, Greenberg assessed the significance of his election as chairman for a term of four years:

> *The [Western] faculty came out of the World War II generation, products of prestigious graduate schools, scholars of varied and specialized disciplines and more geared to their standing as professionals and as members of elite academic disciplines in arts and sciences, business, applied arts as well as teacher education. They began to demand what they observed and experienced at major universities where faculty control of their departments and destiny was commonplace. They were dissatisfied with the professional (not personal) quality of many of the department heads who had emerged from a different time and place.*
>
> *The Department of Political Science led the way to the change of the*

Some residents proudly posed before Draper Hall in 1966. The fallout shelter logo in the background was a sign of the times during the Cold War era.

But even as the 1960s witnessed the demise of some cherished Western traditions, such as the campus school system, different ones arose. The beginnings of a quiet revolution in departmental administration, for example, came in March 1965, with the

Sangren Hall neared completion in the spring of 1964.

Homecoming Queen Cindy DeMarest of Coldwater posed with her court in 1968.

As President Miller and the Board of Trustees looked on, Trustee Alfred Connable threw the ceremonial shovelful during the groundbreaking for the Industrial and Engineering Technology Building in January 1965.

*form of departmental leadership.
Success was not sudden nor without
anxiety. It involved a challenge to the
head who had hired us and a challenge,
in effect, to every other department
head in the University. The central
administration was uncomfortable and
quietly resistant.*

*Change began within the depart-
ment itself as faculty called for more
departmental meetings, more participation in hiring and curriculum and
eventually for a change in chair
selection through election for a limited
term. Self-governance was to be
encouraged by the establishment of an
executive committee elected from among
the departmental faculty to advise the
chairman.*

*Tensions ran high from time to
time but eventually the resignation of
the head led to agreement by the
administration. Subsequently, as each
head left office, chairs were elected in
many departments by the late 1960s*

*and by the remainder in the early
1970s.*

*Though seemingly innocuous, this
democratic change was a significant
feature of University growth, clearly
supported by the faculty and symbolic of
a mature university.*

The year following Greenberg's election as chairman, the academic area of the campus ranged even further west with completion of the industrial and engineering technology building (named in honor of longtime dean, George Kohrman, in 1980) and the distributive education building (later named for Adrian Trimpe, chairman of the Department of Distributive Education from 1957 to 1975). Those buildings allowed migration of several departments of the College of Applied Sciences to the West Campus as well as the removal of distributive education from the ramshackle "temporary building." The year 1966 also witnessed completion of the first Waldo Library expansion with its modernistic all-glass facade and attractive landscaping.

The Liberal Arts Complex as it looked in March 1969

The following year, William R. Brown Hall, containing classrooms, language laboratories and studios, opened. It was connected to the 10-story faculty office building named for longtime English professor George Sprau. Also in 1967, came the unveiling of a fully equipped 600-seat theatre for student productions named for legendary speech professor Laura V. Shaw.

But the major development of what would be the nucleus of the liberal arts complex came with completion, in 1967, of the University Auditorium (renamed James W. Miller Auditorium in 1971). Considered one of the "finest facilities of its kind in the nation," it included 3,550 seats in continental style, a large stage and state-of-the-art lighting and

sound systems. The availability of Miller Auditorium almost immediately put Kalamazoo on the map as a venue for some of the world's finest artists and performers. In January 1968, a gala, two-week-long inaugural "grand opening festival" demonstrated the structure's diverse capacities. In 1969, the auditorium became the home of a gigantic, portable pipe organ, costing $65,000 and containing 44 ranks and 2,363 pipes. A year later, the Talbert and Leota Abrams Foundation of Lansing donated a huge automated globe for the auditorium lobby.

A new health center completed in 1969 would later be named for donors Gordon and Elizabeth Sindecuse. The year 1970 brought construction of the first 600-vehicle parking

In 1972, some students admired the huge globe that had been installed in Miller Auditorium two years before.

structure as part of a campus development plan that would ultimately result in the closing of West Michigan Avenue to through traffic and the rerouting of Howard Street to achieve a pedestrian campus.

The accomplishments resulted in 1970 being heralded as "the most significant year in the University's history, from a standpoint of construction completion." The remodeling and expansion of McCracken Hall was finished, which doubled its size for the needs of the burgeoning chemistry and paper technology departments. The physics, mathematics and physical sciences departments moved into shining new quarters in Paul Rood Hall. Its companion structure, John P. Everett Tower, housed faculty offices. The new student services building, later named for Vice President for Student Services L. Dale Faunce, also opened its doors that year.

The year 1972 brought dedication of three more instructional buildings. Clustered about an amphitheater court to form a pleasant academic complex, both architecturally attractive and functionally efficient, Willis F. Dunbar Hall, Robert Friedmann Hall, and James O. Knauss Hall, named for three distinguished historians, provided additional

The remodeled and expanded McCracken Hall is shown in this 1970 photograph.

Dr. Alan Brown, Western's first archivist and a beloved member of the History Department, examined a volume of 19th-century Michigan newspapers with head librarian Katherine Stokes in 1963.

impressed with the quality of the faculty and student achievements in the years that I've been here, than I am with the brick and mortar."

An event that had allowed Miller to guide Western in a manner more suitable to its perceived role came in 1963, when Michigan adopted a new state constitution replacing the 1908 version. Under the 1963 Constitution, Western received its own governing body, removing it from direct supervision of the State Board of Education. On February 7, 1964, Governor George W. Romney appointed the original eight members of Western's new governing board: Alfred B. Connable, vice chairman, Fred W. Adams, Dorothy Upjohn Dalton, John Dykema, Dr. Julius Franks, Mildred Swanson Johnson, Dwight L. Stocker and Philip N. Watterson. To his credit, Romney selected a particularly outstanding board, ably representing education, business, industry, the arts and the professions. Adopting the title, the Western Michigan University Board of Trustees, it held its first meeting on March 20, 1964. Miller, who served ex-offico as chairman of the board, noted in his 1970 *Portrait of a*

classroom for nearly 3,000 students and offices for 160 faculty members.

As proud as Miller was of the massive building program he oversaw, the enhanced architectural signature and pleasant landscaping, other accomplishments took precedence. During a 1974 interview he said: "I'm far more

Western's original Board of Trustees posed with university administrators in 1964.

A fashionably mini-skirted student strolled by the newly dedicated Dunbar Hall in 1973.

Decade: "With the appointment of the governing board Western took on a new personality. Its policies were being established by trustees whose sole allegiance was to Western Michigan University."

With its new freedom of self-determination, Western might well have retreated toward more parochialism, but instead it continued to look outward, to expand further into the international arena. There had been a few notable foreign study opportunities, such as an Oxford Seminar in Great Britain during the 1950s, but the 1960s would see a dramatic expansion of student and faculty overseas programs. In 1960, The Institute of Regional Studies' Director Claude Phillips, secured a $144,000 grant from the Carnegie Foundation that provided opportunities for numerous faculty members to study in Africa, Asia, Latin America and other parts of the non-Western world little understood by Americans. They would then develop campus courses to disseminate their new knowledge. The renamed Institute of International and Area Studies also brought foreign scholars to the campus for lectures and seminars. Similarly, in 1962, the International Teacher Development Program began bringing 28 educators from around the world for a three-month residence in Kalamazoo to foster a better understanding of American life. At the same time, exchange programs were developed to provide opportunities for Western students to study in Berlin, Belgrade, Japan, India and East Africa. Groups of students studied geography and social studies in Central America, theatre in England and classical cultures in the Mediterranean. The Varsity Vagabonds and other Western musical groups participated in USO-sponsored tours to Europe, Asia, Iceland and the Caribbean. The development of new interdisciplinary undergraduate programs in African, Asian, Latin American and Slavic studies came as a direct result of Western's faculty and students broadening their international horizons.

Another facet of Western's world outreach began in 1960, with a phone call to the dean of the College of Applied Sciences, George Kohrman, from a representative of the Federal

Dean of the College of Applied Sciences Dr. George Kohrman, in white, is posed with some Western ROTC students in 1962.

Agency for International Development. Thus began Western's grand adventure in Nigeria, an eight-year program to develop from the ground up a technical college in Ibadan. There, teams of advisors from Western helped establish programs in electrical, civil and mechanical technology, business studies and city planning. When Western completed its work in 1968, it left a fully functioning technical college staffed by indigenous instructors and attended by more than 500 Nigerian students. During the ceremonies marking the end of Western's involvement, the Nigerian authorities named the street in front of the college Kalamazoo Way, in recognition of the Western faculty who had shown "the way" to educate their country's badly needed technicians.

By 1965, more than 40 Western alumni had joined the Peace Corps, serving in Africa and Asia as teachers, community developers and medics. That year, U.S. Congressman Paul Todd, Jr. from Kalamazoo announced that the University had been selected as a training site for Peace Corps volunteers. Under the direction of Dr. Claude S. Phillips, nearly 150 volunteers studied the principal languages of Nigeria during a 12-week summer course in preparation

A Western instructor explained mechanical principles to a group of students in Ibadan, Nigeria, in 1966.

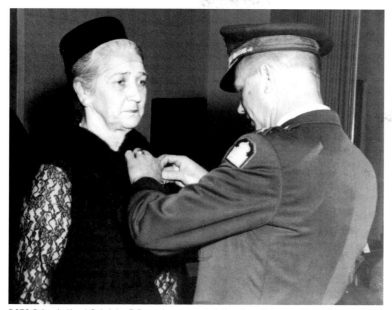

ROTC Brigade Head Col. John F. Brownlow presented Mrs. Erna Lubavs with the bronze star posthumously awarded her son Lt. Konstantins A. Lubavs in 1966. He was the first Western alumnus to die in Vietnam.

of International Education—Reader's Digest Foundation University Award in 1966.

Even as Western's faculty and students grew in their understanding of the international arena and its problems, hundreds of thousands of other college-age Americans underwent tours to a part of the world most would rather not have known—the jungles of Vietnam. In February 1966, Lt. Konstantins A. Lubavs became the first Western alumnus to give his life for his country in Vietnam. The Latvian immigrant was posthumously awarded the bronze star. As the war intensified, colleges across the nation became epicenters of protest with demonstrations, sit-ins, love-ins, teach-ins, flag-burnings, vituperation and violence. Miller noted in his 1970 report on the previous decade's events:

for teaching assignments in schools there. In June 1965, the Peace Corps and Western announced a cooperative program enabling students to continue to earn academic credits while serving overseas. That endeavor failed to live up to expectations. Nevertheless, by 1970 more than 145 Western alumni and students had served in the Peace Corps.

In recognition of the breadth and excellence of its diverse international efforts, Western was awarded the prestigious Institute

> *Western felt the spin-off from the centers of excitement, but here the destructiveness, divisiveness and polarization were minimal. The occasions that did arise here during the last 10 years were of short duration and far from severe. For this situation, I credit our faculty and students, the overwhelming majority of whom showed calm consideration and judicious temperaments that*

Peace Corps Director R. Sargent Shriver visited campus in 1965.

In 1970, the two fingered peace sign was a familiar sight on campus.

allayed situations that easily could have become extremely serious.

One of the reasons why Western remained largely aloof from the more violent Vietnam War protests was that its student body, by and large, understood how fortunate it was to be in college rather than the battlefield. In 1974, a year after he had retired as vice president for academic affairs, Russell Seibert recalled: "Everyone knew, and I was very much aware of it, the president was very much aware of it, the kids that had enough money to go to college didn't go to Vietnam, and the students were pretty much aware of that. I think some of them probably had a guilty conscience."

The student activism that did materialize on Western's campus in the 1960s developed into a dichotomy between antiwar protesters and the black power movement. Those separate movements shared little contact between each other because they differed in their basic goals. Thomas Coyne, who served as Miller's assistant in the late 1960s, succinctly

summed up the situation during a 1989 interview:

The reason was that the black students were not fooled. They recognized that the Vietnam War movement had a large portion in it comprised of white students who feared that if they did not stop the war, they would wind up in Vietnam. They could protest all

Western's Safety and Security officers made sure this 1970s demonstration remained peaceful. Note, they carried no guns then.

Students gathered for folk songs and anti-war protests in front of the Student Union, circa 1969.

they wanted and they could wear the old dungarees and the old clothes, unshaven and the long hair, but the minute they needed a job all they needed to do was shave and get a haircut and put on a white shirt and tie. But the black students were going to remain black. Black students had an agenda and knew what they wanted. White students, by and large, protested for protest's sake. They enjoyed the excitement of the protest. Black students wanted a piece of the pie and the white students wanted to get rid of the pie. Black students were becoming aware of the need to organize and make America aware of their needs and concerns. White students were saying stop the war because I don't want to go. This was a laudable concern, but I don't think many of them were aware that this was an evil war.

Michael Phelan, a student radical on campus during the late 1960s and early 1970s, recalled the Vietnam protesters' rationale and techniques:

We had a sense of powerlessness, a sense of helplessness that events were rushing headlong; we were being tossed into this with no feedback, no attempt at dialogue, and no chance. There were constant demonstrations. "Teach-in" was a big term. What that meant was someone would get up and start speaking, without a microphone or anything, and just start haranguing the crowd, and people would stop and listen, or pass on. We would do this wherever: in the union, out in front of the union, in the grass on the hill. One was in front of the flagpole at the administration building. We also disrupted classes. It didn't matter which

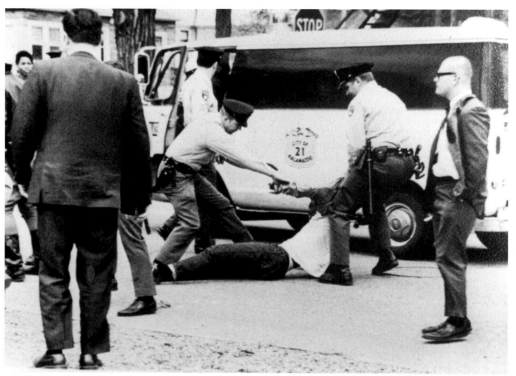

In 1970, an anti-war protest became violent.

class it was. It would be simply a math class, or whatever. Disrupting business classes was the best because we hated the business field. We'd go in and we would say, "We are not going to talk about this; this is irrelevant. People are dying in Southeast Asia. This does not have any bearing on our lives. For the next twenty minutes we are going to talk about Southeast Asia whether you want to or not." In general, the students were more antagonistic than the faculty members; the faculty would usually stand aside. The students, some of them were very antagonistic, some to the point of physical violence. Some of the people would say, "I paid for this class and you are not going to disrupt it." No administrator ever stopped us. President Miller was truly an intellectual, and even if he didn't agree with you, you could see a gleam in his eye that at least his students were right up there with everybody else. So no one was ever stopped.

But the situation did nearly get out of hand several times, thanks largely to visiting agitators from more militant campuses. One night, someone threw a Molotov cocktail into the ROTC building. Fortunately, it failed to ignite. Bomb threats initially disrupted classes and events, but when the administration decided not to evacuate buildings when a bomb threat was called in, that tactic was effectively defused. Local police quickly quelled student protests in the streets of Kalamazoo after the 1970 Kent State killings by the Ohio National Guard. Probably the most violent situation came in 1970, when unarmed antiwar protesters took over the student union. The Kalamazoo and state police formed a line from the Oaklands to the student union and began a sweep. They fired tear gas, and the students evacuated with little damage to the union except for petty pilfering of food.

The war protesters were emulating a tactic first used by black students on campus after the assassination of Dr. Martin Luther King, Jr. on April 4, 1968. The following morning, a number of grief-stricken students entered the student union and chained the door closed. Miller showed courage and diplomacy in personally entering the union to calm the situation and this remains one of the hallmarks of his presidency. Miller, in 1974, remembered the troubling events that followed:

The war was not the only item being protested in 1970.

A lot of people said that was a terrible day. I thought it was a remarkable day. It was a day in which the trauma of the assassination of Martin Luther King reached whites as well as blacks. The young blacks started going in there about 6:30 a.m. I saw them right at the beginning because I had my dogs out at that time, a couple of little Scotties. And they weren't in the mood to talk to anybody, they were just upset, they had to do something dramatic, and they were doing it. They went in and barricaded themselves in the building. I was in touch with them throughout the day, and I went in the building and people said it was difficult and I said, "Gee, there was only one thing difficult about it and that was all these whites who were leering and peering in at the blacks." And had those whites not been contained by Milt Greenberg (chairman of the Department of Political Science) and some other leaders in the

Some Western students took an active role in the 1970 campaign to place a mandatory deposit on cans and bottles.

faculty, we might have had a real confrontation, a very unfortunate one. We had white kids out there that were pointing fingers at the blacks inside. They made their trauma, just aggravated it something terrible, had dogs out there barking, urging them to bark at the black students. And if I'd had any doubts about there being strong racist elements within our society, they were all wiped out in that short period of time. But what the people inside had in mind didn't seem unreasonable to me at all. One of the things they wanted

These happy students were about to receive their diplomas during the August 1967 commencement.

was to have the University send three or four of them to the funeral. And I remember saying at the time that there was no way I could get University funds for that purpose, but I have every reason to believe that I could get private funds and I had the private funds within ten minutes.

Miller secured those private funds via a quick call to his friend Dan Ryan, editor of the *Kalamazoo Gazette.* The protesters left the union at 2:00 p.m., having cleaned it spotless and paid for the candy they consumed.

Prior to the protest, Western had been involved in a number of programs to assist the "educationally disadvantaged," including the federally funded Upward Bound program and a basic skills educational program at the Fort Custer Job Corps Center. King's death and the reaction to it spurred Miller to implement a program that would "encourage black students who have the desire, the curiosity and ability for college work, but with no hope of continuing beyond high school, to enter Western." He contacted several local benefactors and within

days of the assassination, the Martin Luther King Fund had been established. The fund grew and money from other sources was also utilized to create "financial packages." Recruiters visited high schools in southwestern Michigan and in the Detroit area, seeking eligible applicants. In the fall semester of 1968, 76 students entered Western under the Martin Luther King Fund project. In addition to financial assistance, they utilized a special study center, tutors and counselors to achieve a remarkable record. Of the 76 students, 74 earned an academic grade point average of 2.0 or better.

The Black Americana Studies Program also emerged as a result of an awareness of the need to increase students' understanding of the contributions by blacks to American life and culture. Begun in 1970 under the direction of Dr. Carleton Lee, the interdisciplinary program offered a minor somewhat like the African Studies Program previously developed by the Institute of International and Area Studies. In 1973, Dr. LeRoi Ray came to Western to take charge of the Black Americana

These students were intent on the lecture during a Black Americana Studies class in 1969.

Studies Program. His hard work and dedication soon invigorated it. When he discovered but few science majors among the more than 1,000 black students on campus, he started a hands-on science program. Next he implemented a similar program to assist black students in the College of Arts and Sciences, which later became a University-wide endeavor. He also inaugurated an annual Minority Leadership Conference. In 1995, Ray proudly recalled some of the other accomplishments:

We put on an annual rodeo that has been very successful. We collected a lot on the history of blacks in southwest Michigan. We started a black community theatre, which has been a very successful main stage production. We started the Martin Luther King creative projects contest where students do a paper and get a scholarship. We also started the W. Peter Boyd Black Contribution to Western Luncheon.

Before Ray's arrival, a controversy had flared up in the fall of 1971. The University had decided to coordinate the Martin Luther King Program, minority student services, Project '73 and Upward Bound under the direction of a new assistant to the vice president for academic affairs. The position was offered to Troy Allen, but when he refused it because

Erlinda Rolls, shown here installing a display in Waldo Library in 1969, was the University's first black librarian.

Blind Rehabilitation Teacher Program instructor, Stanley Suterko, guided a student across Kalamazoo's Michigan Avenue in 1961.

of some unacceptable terms, Chauncey Brinn from the Office of Student Financial Aid was selected. Two weeks later, Allen decided he wanted the position, and the Black Action Movement and more than 500 black students supported him. The situation grew tense with demonstrations and a sit-in in Miller's office. Ultimately, the storm blew over. Brinn would continue to excel in his administrative capacity, earning promotion to secretary to the Board of Trustees in 1981 and vice president for university relations in 1984.

Among other innovations that marked the decade of the 1960s, the formation of the honors college has proved a continuing success. Created in 1962 as the honors school because, as its first director, Dr. Sam Clark, remembered, "We needed a way to compete with other institutions for some of the really bright kids," the program initially included

active recruitment of honors students, financial support and academic counseling for them. Then came the development of general education honors curricula and seminars and enhancement of the visibility of the college through special events. With limited funding, under Clark's leadership, the college began offering academic seminars, special athletic and recreational opportunities and educational trips within the United States and abroad.

Dr. Sam Clark, founder of the honors college, conferred with this student in 1969.

Membership in the honors college grew from 176 in 1964 to 608 ten years later. By 1972, more than 160 freshmen enrolled in the honors college each fall.

Another program to emerge in the early 1960s, and one that would earn Western international acclaim, originated when a coterie of professors in various departments realized they shared a common interest in the Middle Ages. Spearheaded by history professor John Sommerfeldt, the colleagues submitted a proposal for an interdisciplinary program, including an undergraduate major and minor, that would lead to a master's degree in the study of the medieval period. The administration liked the idea, and by the fall of 1961, Sommerfeldt directed the prototype of the Medieval Institute, which offered the nation's first interdisciplinary master's degree in medieval studies.

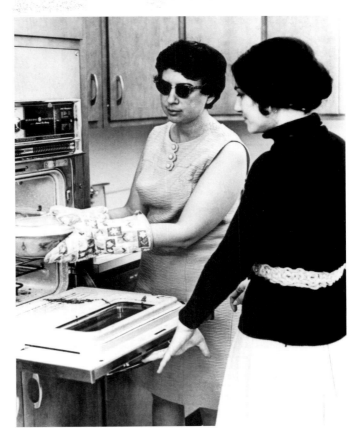

A Western Institute of Blind Rehabilitation student learned to master domestic science techniques in 1973.

In 1962, the institute sponsored its first International Congress on Medieval Studies. That small regional gathering in the student union, originally held every other year, burgeoned over the decades to become, by 1998, a three-and-one-half-day mega-conference, the largest of its kind in the world, drawing over 3,000 international scholars who presented 1,600 papers on their specialties. Otto Grundler, who succeeded Sommerfeldt as director of the institute in 1975, also established a premiere press at Western called Medieval Institute Publications, which further broadened Western's reputation as the world's center for medieval studies.

Another of Western's unique programs began in 1960, when the Office of Vocational Rehabilitation and the VA Hospital in Hines, Illinois, collaborated with the University to create a curriculum for the training of orienta- tion and mobility specialists for the blind. In July 1961, Donald Blasch arrived to direct Western's newly established Center of Orientation and Mobility. Two years later, with the addition of a rehabilitation teacher program, the name of the center became Programs for Blind Rehabilitation. To understand the problems of those without sight, students must experience the life of the blind. Soon, blindfolded students tapping white canes along the campus sidewalks and crossing busy downtown intersections became a familiar sight. Also in 1963, Western launched a master's program for the training of home teachers for the adult blind. Two years later, six Western graduates received the first master's degrees in home teaching of the adult blind ever awarded by any university or college. In 1967, the Programs for Blind Rehabilitation became the Institute of Blind Rehabilitation. Five years later, it joined the newly established College of Health and Human Services under Dean

A Bronco cheerleader led fans in a cheer for the Bronco football team during its 1966 championship season.

William Burian.

Western's programs for the training of teachers of the blind were among 41 different degree programs offered at the master's or specialist level in 1964. The following year, the State Board of Education approved the establishment of doctoral programs in educational leadership, science education and special education. Within two years, the University offered doctorates in four programs. In 1966, the total University enrollment stood at 16,470, and for the first time, graduate students exceeded 2,000. In 1968, the University launched its fifth doctoral program (in mathematics) and offered 56 master's and 13 specialist degree programs.

In 1970, the School of Graduate Studies became the Graduate College under the direction of Dean George Mallinson. Graduate enrollment topped 3,000 in 1971. New doctoral programs in psychology and environ-

mental science were added the following year. In 1974, Western's total enrollment had decreased by about 700 students (from a high of 21,846 three years before), but graduate student enrollment had risen by an astonishing 35 percent over the same period to stand at 4,139. That year, 450 graduate students received nearly $900,000 in financial assistance through fellowships, assistantships and grants.

By that time, many additional athletes were receiving scholarships as well. When Bill Doolittle came to Western as head football coach in 1964, only 15 members of Western's team received scholarships. He soon talked athletic director Mike Gary into doubling that number, and throughout the 1960s and 1970s, more athletic scholarships for football and other sports were added. Under Doolittle's coaching, Western's team, sparked by defensive tackle Bob Rowe, won the co-championship of the Mid-American Conference in 1966. Rowe

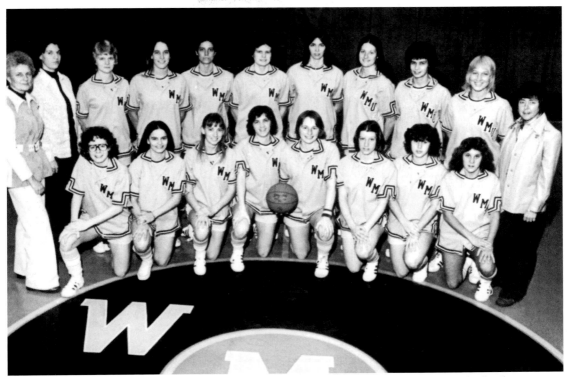

Western's women athletes took the Michigan Collegiate Basketball Championship in 1976, with Coach Fran Ebert leading them.

went on to play 10 years with the St. Louis Cardinals. Doolittle left coaching in 1974 to become more involved with fund raising, and in 1975 he became director of the Mike Gary Fund. His initial fund drive netted $25,000. When he stepped down as its director 15 years later, he was bringing in $500,000 annually.

During the 1960s and 1970s, Western's baseball, track, tennis, cross country and swim teams compiled enviable records. Western's cross country runners won NCAA team championships in 1964 and 1965. Coach Eldon Miller's basketball players won the MAC championship in 1976. Ranked tenth nationally, they became the first Bronco team to play in the NCAA Basketball Tournament that year. Other Bronco teams began competing in the intercollegiate

Guard Pattie Rendine drove in for the score during a 1980 game.

Gold Pride was the homecoming theme in 1976.

In 1978, when this photograph of the Bronco women's volleyball team was taken, Western's female athletes competed in 10 intercollegiate sports.

arena as well. Gymnastics came in 1967, soccer four years later, and in 1973, Western's hockey fans first cheered their intercollegiate home skaters.

In 1971, Western fielded women's intercollegiate teams in basketball, golf, volleyball, and field hockey. Thanks largely to the passage of the Education Act of 1972, known as Title IX (a federal law that requires equal opportunities for all persons in educational experiences), women's sports began to receive more emphasis. By 1975, women's swimming, gymnastics, bowling and indoor track and field had been added. That year, the men's and women's physical education departments merged and the athletics program was separated from the physical education department. In the fall of 1977, Western awarded its initial 31 tuition scholarships to women athletes. By 1978, Bronco women

competed in 10 intercollegiate sports, including cross country, softball and synchronized swimming. That year, equipment, uniforms and travel, once available only to men's teams, became an integral part of the women's programs. Playing schedules were enlarged to allow longer trips to meet higher-quality women opponents. Support services, such as athletic training programs, were further expanded to better serve female athletes. Two new women's locker rooms opened in the Gary Center, and schedules were developed that allowed for the sharing of existing facilities by men's and women's teams.

Even as Western's men and women athletes won laurels in increasingly diverse sports, Western pioneered in another arena popular with spectators—the creation of the state's first College of Fine Arts. The University had progressed far beyond its original role of providing fine arts as simply a background for teachers. The time had come to give students more exciting and relevant instruction so that they had the option of pursuing professional careers in various artistic endeavors.

In 1972, Robert Holmes was appointed dean of the newly created College of Fine Arts. Dance was transferred from the College of Education, and art and music from the College of Arts and Sciences. In 1976, theatre left the Department of Communication to join the College of Fine Arts. Over the succeeding decades, the college expanded its offerings, attracted more students, graduated world-class practitioners of the arts and produced as many as 1,200 exhibitions, performances and events to combined audiences of more than 400,000 annually.

By 1973, Miller had overseen the growth of the campus to encompass more than $100 million worth of new buildings. Enrollment had grown from 9,327 in 1960 to nearly 22,000 in 1971. That included the first few students from Malaysia to enroll at Western. Outreach efforts there and in Guam and the People's Republic of China, in particular, as well as a growing number of students from oil-rich Middle Eastern nations, would swell international student enrollment to more than

1,000 a decade later. The academic hub of the University, Waldo Library, had been expanded and its holdings increased from 145,000 volumes in 1960 to approximately 800,000 in 1973, including nationally significant special collections in regional history, ecology, the history and culture of Africa and black America, and maps. Rood Hall housed a twelve-million-volt electron linear accelerator and a massive state-of-the-art PDP-10 computer. The auditorium named in Miller's honor was the envy of all other Michigan institutions of higher learning. Important new University positions had been created, such as the appointment in 1970 of Milton Brawer as the first ombudsman. Miller turned 60 in April. Having skillfully guided the University through the turbulent 1960s and early 1970s, it was time to step down and enjoy life in Kalamazoo and his beloved cabin in Minnesota. He announced his retirement, effective December 31, 1973. Miller would enjoy 20 more years of active retirement before his death at the age of 80.

In one of his last communications to the University at large, Miller stated: "The tasks ahead for Western will be different from those in its immediate past. The period of great growth in enrollment and the dramatic expansion of physical facilities is over." As farsighted as that prognostication was— based on the obvious decrease in baby boomers enrolling in college and the impact of greater numbers of students attending junior colleges—Miller could not have foreseen the severity of the economic climate of the middle to late 1970s, as the nation and Michigan, in

The university's first ombudsman, Dr. Milton Brawer, notified a student that his problem was resolved in this 1971 meeting.

Frisbees and fun in the sun were the focus of this summer day in the mid-70s.

Myron L. Coulter (center) served as interim president between the tenures of President James Miller (right) and President John Bernhard.

particular, faced the worst recession since the Depression.

The Michigan economy had long been overly dependent on the automobile industry. In the early 1970s, that industry enjoyed boom times when federal economic policies substantially increased the price of competing foreign imports. Then, in the middle 1970s, came the Arab oil embargo, a severe gasoline shortage and sudden dramatic increases of prices at the pump. For many consumers, the additional cost of operating an automobile made buying a new car unfeasible. And those who could, turned to purchasing the less expensive, more fuel-efficient compact cars, which brought less profit to the manufacturers. Rapid declines in traditional car sales led to massive layoffs in the auto plants and component factories. Michigan's budget ran red, and state support to its universities plummeted. For much of his tenure, Miller's successor would face as his biggest challenge trying to make the most out of shrinking dollars.

Vice President for Institutional Services Myron L. Coulter replaced Miller on a temporary basis when the latter left the

campus at the end of 1973. In the meantime, the Board of Trustees had appointed a committee composed of three of its members, alumni, faculty, students and administrators to launch a nationwide search for the new president. During the selection process, the committee emphasized the role of the future president in fund raising, especially from private sources. Some 70 educators from across the nation applied for the job. The committee narrowed that number to five, who were brought to campus for interviews. After nearly a year of intensive effort, the search committee announced its choice. Effective September 1, 1974, Dr. John T. Bernhard would become Western's fourth president in its 70-year history.

Bernhard came to the job with a wide range of experience and training. The son of Danish immigrants, he was born in New York City in 1920. He grew up in the concrete jungle, but through involvement in the Boy Scouts, he developed a love of the outdoors. Following graduation from an all-male high school in the city, he enrolled at Utah State University to study forestry. There, he met his

President John Bernhard at his desk, circa 1974

future wife, Ramona. Prior to graduating, he worked as a lumberjack in northern Idaho, and after earning his degree in forestry, he labored as a lead miner in Utah and as a forester for the U.S. Indian Service, surveying timber on the huge reservations that sprawled across Arizona and New Mexico. During World War II, Bernhard joined the U.S. Coast Guard and saw duty in the North Atlantic.

Following the war, he utilized the GI Bill to pursue graduate studies, ultimately earning a master's and doctorate in political science from UCLA. An acquaintance with a fellow graduate student helped secure him a job as a political and public relations assistant to Howard Hughes, the wealthy aircraft pioneer who, by then, had become a mysterious recluse. Bernhard worked for Hughes from

1951 to 1954 and again from 1957 to 1959, but during that period he saw him only three times. It was a well-paying, but dead-end job. In 1960, he returned to campus life, serving successively as chairman of the political science department at Brigham Young University, dean of its College of Humanities and dean of the College of Social Sciences. Appointed to fill an unexpired term in the Utah State Senate in 1962, Bernhard won election as a Republican for a four-year term in his own right. In 1968, he was selected to serve as president of Western Illinois University, a position he held until coming to Kalamazoo.

The year Bernhard arrived on campus, *Barron's Educational Series* published an in-depth profile of Western. It offered a snapshot in time of the University. An undergraduate

Students enjoyed beer and pizza at a hot spot near campus, circa 1972. From 1972 to 1978, the Michigan drinking age was lowered to 18.

student body comprising 7,717 men and 6,506 women utilized the 600-acre campus with its 80 structures. Ninety-two percent of the students hailed from Michigan and 7 percent were from minority groups. Six hundred and fifty students from 60 foreign countries attended Western. More than two out of three students lived off campus. The remainder occupied 20 dormitories, each with 250 to 500 occupants. They comprised three types: single-sex, coed by alternate floors and coed by alternate suites. Each residence hall determined its own rules. Most allowed 24-hour visitation, and alcohol was permitted on a regular basis (Michigan lowered the legal drinking age to 18 from 1972 to 1978). Yearly tuition and fees for in-state students averaged $600. Room and board in the dormitories cost $1,280. The total yearly expense for attending Western, including books, supplies, travel and so on, was estimated at $2,500. Nearly one-half of all students received financial aid, and

freshmen averaged $1,110 in financial assistance.

Fifty-five percent of the 1,105 faculty members held doctorates. The overall faculty-student ratio stood at 17-to-1. Five libraries on campus contained 1,180,903 volumes. Students belonged to some 180 special interest clubs and organizations. The Broncos fielded 12 varsity athletic teams. Numerous intramural events were also available. Athletic facilities included the newly opened Lawson Ice Arena and Gabel Natatorium, five intramural fields, handball courts, 20 asphalt tennis courts and several gymnasiums, including the Oakland Gymnasium for women's athletics.

The students were mostly from middle-class families and, according to one administrator, seemed less idealistic than students in the 1960s. They appeared more goal-oriented and tended to choose Western because of its specialized programs that would put them on a career track. Other factors included the relative

Evenings like the one in the preceding picture, often led to mornings like the one shown above.

Lawson Ice Arena and Gabel Natatorium opened in 1974.

inexpensiveness of attending Western, compared to many other colleges; its location, halfway between the urban centers of Detroit and Chicago; and the Kalamazoo community itself, which offered part-time job opportunities and cultural and entertainment facilities. So compelling was the allure of what had become known as the "Mall City," that many students expressed a desire to remain in Kalamazoo after graduation.

If the University community benefited from the numerous attractions of Kalamazoo,

then a city of 85,555, it was a symbiotic relationship. A study conducted by Western's College of Business in 1977 found that the University had a nearly $80 million impact on the economy of Kalamazoo County. Western's more than 21,000 students and 2,500 employees spent the equivalent of 10 percent of the county's estimated retail sales of $756.3 million in 1976, which translated into the creation of 1,173 jobs in the surrounding community.

Increasingly, an appreciative community

In the late 1960s, a mural painted by Jack Ramsey Bennett decorated the Student Union Snack Bar.

was returning some of those proceeds to Western as well. Bernhard announced that 1974 had been a banner year for fund raising, with alumni and local friends of the University contributing nearly $950,000 plus more than $1 million in deferred gifts. He increased the Annual Fund goal to $1 million for 1975. While previous presidents had dabbled in fund raising, it would become an increasingly important element of Bernhard's duties.

In 1975, Bernhard assigned two part-time assistants to Secretary to the Board of Trustees Robert Hannah, in order to enhance his lobbying efforts in Lansing. That year also saw the launching of the President's Club. At a gala in the Oaklands and student center in May, Bernhard honored 61 charter members of the new club. Membership in the prestigious organization was by invitation only, based on a minimum cash contribution of $15,000 or a deferred gift of $25,000. Dr. Russell Seibert, retired vice president for academic affairs, headed up a campaign to identify prospective members of the President's Club.

Increased emphasis on private funding became a necessity as the hot summer of 1975 wore on. When Michigan's economic plight worsened, Governor William G. Milliken began slashing the state budget. Western was granted a token 1.8 percent increase in state appropriations over the previous year. That amounted to an additional $588,000 in a year when the estimated increase in campus utility bills, alone, stood at $574,000. That left a mere $14,000 in new money available for salaries of faculty and staff, increased cost of supplies, new programs, equipment and other necessary operating costs.

Bernhard protested against the injustice of Western's appropriation, citing the fact that, while the University was the fourth largest in the state, it ranked 14th in appropriated dollars per fiscal-year-equated student. He traveled to Lansing to meet with the state budget director who seemed sympathetic, but indicated his hands were tied because of the state's fiscal plight.

On September 26, Western's Board of Trustees approved a balanced general fund budget based on the 1.8 percent increase with an additional $1.50 in tuition per credit hour. Charles H. Ludlow, chairman of the board's budget and finance committee, noted, "the final balancing factor was an across-the-board cut to all departments. Every part of the University has been affected; the departments in being required to operate in an inflationary period with less funds; the staff in receiving salary adjustments at rates less than we had hoped could be made; and the students through an increase in their tuition."

The ink was hardly dry on that bare bones budget when Milliken announced another $10 million cut for institutions of higher earning. Western's share would be a decrease of $750,000. Forty-five full-time, non-faculty positions had already been stripped from the budget by not filling vacancies. Ultimately, there seemed no recourse but to lay off faculty. Vice President for Academic Affairs Stephen R. Mitchell, who had replaced Seibert when the latter retired in 1973, announced that the University intended to "pink slip" between 150 and 175 faculty members, effective the end of April 1976.

The timing for that announcement could hardly have been worse. Shortly after taking his position, Mitchell had begun a campaign to realign the number of faculty and financial support of some programs in favor of more popular ones. The adversely affected faculty naturally fought those efforts. Mitchell's personality posed another problem; he was often less than diplomatic in his pronounce-ments. As a result, an adversarial relationship soon developed between him and many faculty members.

If the 1960s were a period of student revolt, the 1970s proved a decade of faculty unrest. In February 1975, the faculty voted to accept the American Association of University Professors (AAUP) as its bargaining agent.

Fifteen years later, political science professor Claude Phillips recalled some of the problems with that election: "I was convinced that the union was formed for the wrong reason. I understand why it was formed; it was mainly aimed at Steve Mitchell, but it was formed without a majority of the faculty approving it. You see, it won by 44 percent of the faculty vote. Unfortunately, that was 51 percent of those who bothered to vote. So it never had the mandate of the majority of the faculty."

The union produced a schism among Western's faculty. Pro-union advocates cited its need to give them clout in bargaining for salary increases and job security. Opponents basically felt that a college professor was not an appropriate profession to belong to a labor union. History professor Lewis Carlson remembered some of the consequences of the dissension: "There were tremendous tensions within departments. I was in two departments at that time, history and then, of course, because of being laid off by Mitchell, I was moved over to general studies, and I saw a

Dr. Russell Seibert, vice president emeritus for academic affairs, circa 1975

Students stuffed themselves during the 1971 Homecoming Fritter Fest.

faculty split. It was sort of like the Vietnam War. It was hard to be neutral ... One of the negative factors in the fallout was that we split faculty. There was resentment on both sides."

The first collective bargaining negotiations between the AAUP and the administration began in May 1975. Things did not go smoothly. In February 1976, the AAUP filed unfair labor practice charges against the administration with the Michigan Employment Relations Commission. That muddied the controversy until the following October when both sides resolved those charges. In the meantime, the Board of Trustees and the union signed a one-year contract on September 20 that had been negotiated that summer.

In the spring of 1977, the editor of the *Western News* noted that the negotiations for that first contract had been "marked by tension and some turmoil on campus. That was partially because bargaining creates an adversarial relationship between employee and

employer, partially because of angry words and accusations, and partially because of the uncertainty about the ramifications of decisions made upon the future."

The situation worsened in August 1977, when the contract came up for renewal. Negotiations broke off and the union membership narrowly passed a strike vote. On the first day of classes, about 225 of Western's 850 faculty members walked off their jobs and onto the picket line. Some students joined the picketers, milling around the entrance to classrooms, and nearly 400 students and faculty members rallied in front of the administration building. English professor William Combs remembered some of the strikers: "There were people like Jean Malmstrom, one of the distinguished members of the English department, crippled because of hip problems. There she was with her cane walking around Sprau Tower and Brown Hall with a picket sign with her courtly husband,

Vince Malmstrom who didn't approve of the faculty union. But she did, and there she was, a crippled woman."

The strike ended early the next morning as a result of a 16-hour marathon bargaining session that produced a tentative one-year agreement. Many of the participants of that first strike viewed it as "a kind of holiday." But in 1984, negotiations again took an ugly turn and a real strike ensued. Approximately half of the faculty on campus walked the picket line or simply failed to show up for class. The University remained open for the duration of the four-day strike by implementing a contingency plan. Strikers returned to their teaching posts following this Bernhard announcement: "Persons who strike will not be paid if they do not meet their normal responsibilities to the University."

In the meantime, economic problems continued to plague Bernhard's tenure. In 1976, he wrote: "Our budgetary crunch remains severe, not terminal. I am convinced that we will see a distinct improvement in state funding by 1977. However, the interim period will be extremely difficult to live through—especially in view of growing needs and inflation pressures." Tuition rates rose $3 per credit hour and room-and-board rates by $30 per semester in the fall of 1976. Galloping increases in tuition and dormitory rates, to keep pace with the inflationary spiral and lack of increased state support, became familiar but unpleasant news to students and parents almost yearly. The financial troubles abated somewhat in the late 1970s, but returned with a vengeance in the early 1980s.

The popular Gold Rush clowns of the 1981 Homecoming celebration are pictured here.

The 1960s and 1970s witnessed campus appearances by some of the nation's most prominent politicians, including Hubert Humphrey in 1964(above) and Richard Nixon in 1966 (below).

In his September 11, 1980, "State of the University" address, Bernhard warned that Western faced a "financial crisis [that] is both imminent and indefinite in duration ... By all indications, the next few years—at least—will be unlike any period that any of us have faced at Western in the demands that will be imposed upon us." By April 1981, the situation had, in his words, become a "financial siege." Milliken had recommended a nine percent budget increase for Western for the 1980-81 fiscal year, but by the time the axe had fallen, the University sustained an actual reduction of six percent—the first time it had received less funding than the previous year since the Great Depression. In 1982, came news that newly elected Governor James Blanchard was deferring payment of an entire three months' state appropriations checks, amounting to a $12.3 million blow to

Western. By 1983, Michigan had fallen to a rank of 39th among the states in per-capita state appropriations for higher learning, and yearly tuition increases had brought the cost of attending its public colleges and universities to a level more than 50 percent higher than the average of other states.

Western fought to decrease its expenditures in as many ways possible, reducing funding for services and service personnel, supplies, maintenance and non-academic units. A University Energy Management Program saved more than $1 million in energy costs in 1980 alone. Some of the slack, especially in the realm of construction of new facilities, was taken up by the University's first major capital campaign, "Partners in Progress." By 1982, the campaign had raised more than $8 million from faculty, staff, emeriti and friends and through matching gifts from corporations.

All those efforts proved insufficient. Bernhard's thinly veiled intimation in 1980 that "in academic areas we have nibbled at the edges, rather than the heart, of faculty positions" (which made up the bulk of the academic base budget), would become

Entertainers Martha Reeves and the Vandellas performed at a 1966 Homecoming concert.

transparent that year with the hiring of Dr. Elwood Ehrle to replace Cornelius Lowe as vice president for academic affairs. The first to hold that position, Russell Seibert, had been greatly valued and respected by the faculty; but many loathed his successor, Stephen Mitchell. Cornelius Lowe, who was ill for much of his tenure, had been tolerated. Ehrle, whose role was soon perceived to be that of "hatchet man," would find little affection or support.

Ehrle began by implementing the University Priorities Project, which included a massive encyclopedia of every position on campus with a detailed job description, as well as a rationale for all programs and activities. The compilation of that report proved to be a challenging activity, consuming much time

and energy. Many thought it irritating "busy work" and, unfortunately, many participants such as Claude Phillips came to believe: "It didn't do one bit of good as near as I can tell—the years we spent creating that monstrous thing. As far as I can see, not one ounce of good came out of it; not one decision was made that depended upon all that effort that we put into it."

The actual impact of the University Priorities Project on the forthcoming retrenchment efforts remains debatable, but one thing is certain—hard decisions were made. In 1982, came the euphemistic announcement, "seventy-eight activities may be modified." Of the 1,600 "activities" identified in the priorities project, those to be cut included two non-

Bill Cosby performed at Miller Auditorium in 1969.

revenue sports, the student center barber shop, late-night urgent care service at the health center, two doctoral programs, seven specialist degree programs, 17 master's degree programs and 13 undergraduate programs. Ehrle estimated savings of between $500,000 and $1 million in eliminating those 39 academic programs. The next devastating news came when Bernhard reported to the Board of Trustees that 172 positions, including 100 academic, would be dropped from the 1983-84 budget. "The most wrenching feature of our current down-sizing mode," he told the trustees, "of course, is the human factor. The very process of retrenchment unfortunately brings with it heightened anxiety, painful insecurity, loss of income and disruption of career plans." Over the period from 1979 to 1983, Western made over $10 million in base-budget reductions and an additional $5.6 million in one-time cuts.

An especially mourned casualty of the retrenchment came in 1983 with announcement of the closing of Western's School of Librarianship. That left, to the discouragement of many prospective librarians, only two institutions—both on the eastern side of the state—where a librarianship degree could be earned in the state of Michigan. To the present day, this decision continues to haunt the University.

In 1996, Ehrle recalled his feelings about the demanding role he had been assigned: "Faculty positions at WMU were reduced, and I was in charge of executing a plan that would make these reductions even steeper. It was awful. And I tired quickly of the whole administrative business." Ehrle resigned in 1983 and returned to the classroom as a valued member of Western's Department of Biology. His successor, Dr. Philip S. Denenfeld, had joined Western as an English professor in 1956 and worked his way up the ranks to become assistant to Seibert in 1972. He had been patiently waiting in the wings as assistant to the three succeeding vice presidents for academic affairs, and he brought to the position fairness, intelligence and a gentlemanly style deeply appreciated by the faculty.

The dark economic clouds suddenly parted in 1983, and the sun burst forth with Governor Blanchard's recommendation of a 7.5 percent budget increase for Western for the forthcoming fiscal year. As the state's economy further improved, Lansing continued to loosen its purse strings. In 1985, came legislative approval for $27.1 million in campus improvements, including a $15 million renovation and expansion of Waldo Library, a $12.1 million building on West Campus to house the College of Business, construction of the Robert A. Welborn Printing Management and Research Center at $2.8 million and a $1.2 million addition to McCracken Hall. Blanchard warned Western, however, that there would be no additional funds for overruns.

Presidential candidate George McGovern spoke on campus in 1972.

Then-Vice President Gerald Ford visited WMU in 1973.

Those projects brought an end to the drought in state money for new construction on campus that had shriveled budgets for more than a decade. The last structure to go up on campus solely from state money had been the Lawson Ice Arena and Gabel Natatorium in 1974. Ground breaking for the fine arts center in 1980 became a reality only because of $1 million in seed money from an anonymous donor. The $16.2 million structure, which completed the projected arts plaza, was named in honor of charter trustee and longtime patron of the arts, Dorothy Upjohn Dalton, following her death in 1981. The Dalton Center, "widely regarded as one of the finest instructional facilities for the arts in the nation," was dedicated in October 1982. The three-story structure housed a mammoth multimedia room with an 80-foot diameter performance space, 112 practice rooms and teaching studios, a 500-seat recital hall, lecture

Jesse Jackson was on campus and was interviewed by WMUK News Director Tony Griffin in 1974.

halls, band and chorus rehearsal rooms, and the music and dance library. The Dalton Center emerged as a major focus for the performing arts and music in southwest Michigan.

Another magnificent structure, dedicated the following year, owed its existence to financial support from alumni, businesses and foundations contributed through the highly successful "Partners in Progress" campaign. In 1981, local broadcast pioneer and Detroit Tigers owner John T. Fetzer gave $1 million to the project. The $4.2 million Fetzer Center honors his achievements and generosity. The structure included a specially designed auditorium with executive-style seating and a unique enclosed exhibit area in the lobby documenting through text, photographs and artifacts Fetzer's diverse career in radio, television and sports. The Fetzer Center auditorium was named in memory of C.W. Kirsh, founder of the Sturgis-based Kirsh Company, then the world's largest manufac-

turer of drapery hardware.

Bernhard's drive to secure greater funding from private sources reaped benefits in other ways as well. In 1983, the University announced the establishment of the Medallion Scholarships. The most prestigious scholarship awarded to first-year students, each carried a stipend of $5,000 annually for four years. Created by private donations through the WMU Foundation, the Medallion Scholarships demonstrated "Western's commitment to encourage and recognize superior intellectual achievement." The first two scholarships, to be awarded by a committee appointed by Bernhard, were funded through donations from Guido Binda, a noted Battle Creek architect and his wife Elizabeth, a well-known civic leader, and Merze Tate, a 1927 graduate of Western and a retired faculty member of Howard University.

The campaign to secure funding for the Fetzer Center and its utilization by area industry leaders brought the University closer to the Kalamazoo business community, furthering a mutually advantageous relationship. Richard Chormann, CEO of Kalamazoo's First of America Bank Corporation, recalled how the situation had changed after he returned to Kalamazoo in 1984, following a four-year absence: "I observed a significant change in the involvement of people at Western in things like the Percolator Club, the Chamber of Commerce and so forth. There was involvement prior to that, but as Western changed its focus and as the business school grew in prominence, it created more of a natural tie to the business community in Kalamazoo."

In 1984, Bernhard paused to reflect on his achievements during a decade of leadership. He considered his role in development, a euphemism for fund raising, critically important because:

We'll never be able to count on the public funds we once enjoyed. As a consequence, private fund raising provides that margin of excellence needed to sustain quality. For example, I think that if we didn't have the Fetzer Center, and the other aspects of the recent "Partners in Progress" capital campaign, we really would be slipping backwards. But as a result of that successful campaign, I honestly feel we've been able to ward off any backsliding. We've had a tough time consolidating and retrenching, but overall, as I see the institution, I don't believe we have suffered irreparably. In some important ways, we've gained strength. I also think that the College of Business has been greatly enriched by the Fetzer Center, which I consider the keystone of our development program, and we're just beginning to see what that center is going to mean to Western and the community.

Another program dear to Bernhard's heart was affirmative action. Within months after he took office, the University approved a plan to improve the number and status of women and minority group employees. The affirmative action plan set goals for hiring and promoting and implemented procedures for filing complaints based on discrimination because of race, sex, age, creed, religion or national origin. The "action-oriented" plan also promoted in-service skills training programs to enable employees to move into higher positions, as well as training programs for supervisors about affirmative action goals and techniques.

As the women's movement gained strength nationally, stressing equality for women, as early as 1972 the Commission on the Status of Women at Western began to publicize the special needs of women students, faculty and staff. Two years later, the Susan B. Anthony Center offered programs and counseling to students. It merged with a Continuing Education for Women program in 1976 to create the Center for Women's Services to serve both campus and community.

The University developed additional programs in the 1980s to promote the advancement of women. The first of the annual Women Researchers Conferences began in 1980. Two years later, came an annual Career Opportunities for Women at Western conference. Also in 1982, Bernhard commissioned an Affirmative Action Advisory Committee that cooperated closely with women's groups and championed equality issues.

In 1983, the Hispanic Student Organization on campus grew out of the Chicano Student Movement founded in 1971. This marked recognition of the growing number of students from Spanish-speaking backgrounds attending Western. The first known Hispanic student, Rosa E. Noble, graduated with an education degree in 1936. Following World War II, a number of students from Puerto Rico earned degrees in occupational therapy. The 1960s and 1970s witnessed a surge of American-born Latino students as well as greater

In 1947, these Western students hailed from Costa Rica, Puerto Rico, Guatemala and Bolivia.

enrollments from Honduras, Guatemala, El Salvador, Chile, Peru, Panama, Venezuela, Spain and the Caribbean Islands. In the 1980s and 1990s, increasing numbers of Latinos would earn doctoral degrees from Western.

In 1985, Bernhard appointed Allene Dietrich, director of the Center for Women's Services, to head a committee to develop an affirmative operating plan to enhance the status of Latinos, blacks, women and non-traditional students. Throughout the 1980s and 1990s, the University continued to make rapid strides toward implementing its affirma-tive-action goals.

In 1986, the College of Health and Human Services celebrated its first decade of existence. Western had been the first U.S. school to formally combine the curricula of health and human services. Under Dean William A. Burian, the college melded the

School of Social Work, the departments of Occupational Therapy, Speech Pathology and Audiology, Blind Rehabilitation and Mobility, and programs for physician assistants, alcohol and drug abuse, multi-clinic, medical technol-ogy and gerontology. Two years later, the college founded the Community Information System for Human Services, a database and source for technical assistance data collecting that became a nationally recognized model project. In 1985, the prestigious Robert Wood Johnson Foundation awarded the college's Department of Speech Pathology and Audiol-ogy the largest grant it had ever given Western. By 1986, the internationally acclaimed college had added special programs in holistic health care administration.

For many on campus during the year the College of Health and Human Services was created, the most memorable events related to the American bicentennial celebration. In 1976, the nation, Michigan and Western shrugged aside the recession to stage an incomparable tribute to America's first 200 years. Western's participation was "unrivaled on any campus in the state." In the planning stage for three years, the celebration featured 38 projects involving students, faculty and staff, including a traveling vaudeville show wagon, a series of radio shows about Michigan history and a multimedia work, "Proud Music of the Storm," which incorporated a 62-piece orchestra, a mixed chorus of 60, a brass band, a woodwind band, 12 dancers, electronic sounds, films and slides.

Assistant Dean of Fine Arts Robert Luscombe, who chaired the University's Bicentennial Committee, did such a good job that Bernhard appointed him to head the Diamond Jubilee Committee in charge of Western's 75-year birthday celebration in

Robert Luscombe (left) headed Western's Diamond Jubilee Committee in 1978.

1978. The kickoff event was the Broadway play, *The Ponder Heart,* held in Shaw Theatre for a week in May. It featured Western Theatre Department alumni who had won fame in movies, television and Broadway. Among the celebrity performers were David Wayne, Mary Jackson, John Zaremba, Alfred Hinckley, Sherman Lloyd and Barbara Marineau.

This student prepared for class atop the university's U.S. Bicentennial Time Capsule.

Barbara Marineau, who parlayed her WMU theatre training into a successful Broadway career, starred in the 1970 production of *Ten Nights in a Barroom*.

Anyone on campus the January before remembers well another occasion when classes were canceled—the Great Blizzard of '78. Students rose the morning of January 26 to find the campus, as well as much of lower Michigan, smothered under 25 inches of dense, wind-blown snow. Huge drifts crippled the campus and a state of emergency declared by area authorities prohibited non-emergency automobile travel for three days. Few off-campus personnel could have reported for work, even had they wanted to, during the first few days. On January 26, only six of 140 dormitory food service workers struggled through the drifts. The campus remained closed for five days.

Another dose of Mother Nature at her worst struck on the afternoon of May 13, 1980, when a killer tornado roared from the west toward Kalamazoo. The whirlwind struck the center of the city, splintering 150-year-old trees in Bronson Park and devastating scores of structures. It left five people dead, hundreds homeless and $50 million in property destruction. Miraculously, the campus escaped serious damage. The University offered storm victims temporary housing in dormitories, where an additional 350 state police and 75 power company linemen stayed while they labored to restore order.

Proceeds from the performances went to the David Wayne Scholarship and toward creating a new scholarship for drama students honoring Laura Shaw, the nonagenarian director emeritus of Western's theatrical activities. In September, the celebration continued with a Chautauqua recreation; art fair; street dance; jazz, folk and rock concerts; and art exhibits. Students, in particular, enjoyed the gala because classes were canceled for the day.

Assistance in time of disaster was a natural response, but it was also an example of the many ways Western increasingly performed public service activities in the 1980s. A water-

The Great Blizzard of January 1978 closed the campus for five days.

quality project, for example, jointly administered by the departments of Geology, Geography and Chemistry, rendered Western the leading water-research facility in the state, especially in the study and protection of groundwater. As the program developed via grant support during the 1980s, it offered the public sector answers to questions ranging from where to build a factory that would not pollute the water supply, to how large an area around a well field needed to be protected.

To coordinate and facilitate the University's diverse expertise on subjects of concern to the public, in 1981 Western established WESTOPS, the WMU Office of Public Service. Created to assist the University in its goal of "becoming more important to more people," the office soon found itself fielding calls and diverting them to the proper source for help in identifying fossils, determining the difference between the sex of amphibians, exploring the possibility of setting up a specialized training program in a local industry and advising consumers on what kind of personal computer to purchase.

The University itself jumped with both feet into the beckoning world of the computer revolution in 1982 with the start-up of Project EXCITE (Expanding with Computers and Information Technology). A campuswide

Students trudged through a snow-clogged parking lot in a scene typical of January 1967.

emphasis on the computer, the project required all students to learn basic computer literacy prior to graduation. Western became the first U.S. public university to adopt that requirement. Computer literacy classes for faculty and staff were also implemented, as was a communications network that linked all computers on campus. The program, which put Western in the forefront of public institutions emphasizing the computer, brought John G. Kemeny, co-inventor of the BASIC computer language and a leading architect of the computer age, to campus in February 1983, to receive an honorary degree as a WMU Foundation Fellow. In his convocation address, Kemeny made some prophetic statements: "Within 20 years, persons without computer literacy will not be employable ... In the next 20 years people will have the same access to national databases as they do to their local libraries ... the way we live our lives will be drastically changed ... computers will allow people to work outside of centralized offices, even at home."

As computers became an integral part of Western's operations, they offered the opportunity to do a better job at various tasks. In 1982, for example, Bernhard asked Dean of the College of Continuing Education Richard Burke to take on an additional role as the University's coordinator of student recruitment in an attempt to stem the steady decline in enrollment. Burke discovered that, in addition to a dropping enrollment, Western was also losing its market share of potential students to other Michigan universities. He quickly introduced a new state-of-the-art computerized system, which allowed his office to better identify students who had been recruited and then, through additional communication, "clinch the deal" to get them to commit to Western. Burke's use of the computer and other techniques helped reverse the trend. In 1985, enrollment grew for the first time since 1980 and the state increased Western's appropriation by 12.4 percent.

By that year, it had become obvious that Western had weathered the storm and could look forward to another period of growth and development. Bernhard had guided the University through one of its most adverse decades, one of plummeting enrollments, economic uncertainty and faculty discord. He would turn 65 in 1985. He announced his retirement, effective June 30, telling the Board of Trustees, "I have given the presidency my very best, but today it's time to turn the page." The Bernhards remained in the community they had come to love, and he returned to the classroom as a tenured professor of political science.

Jack Meagher (middle), shown here with the primitive, by modern standards, University computer in 1965, was an early champion of the computer revolution.

President John Bernhard retired in 1985, after guiding the University through one of its worst economic crises.

Chapter 6

Into the Millennium and Beyond

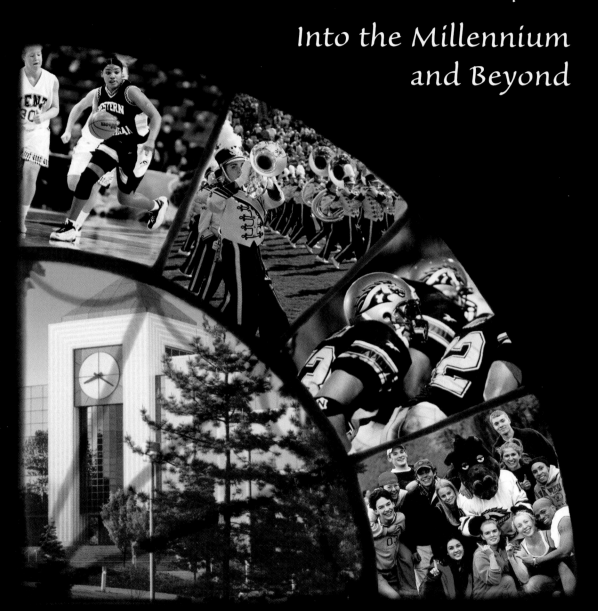

The 1980s brought to maturity a more complacent generation, seemingly lacking the protesting zeal that had characterized the previous two decades. Mountain bikes and bungee jumping, Cabbage Patch dolls and Teenage Mutant Ninja Turtles, Madonna, Bruce Springsteen and rap music enlivened popular culture. Increasingly, health conscious Americans ate less red meat, kicked the smoking habit and drank lite beer. They began to focus on the world's deteriorating environment, depletion of the ozone layer, global warming and the rape of the rain forests, Ronald Reagan won an overwhelming reelection in 1984, despite runaway military spending, yawning budget deficits, a huge foreign trade gap and extensive cuts in social programs. His second term would be plagued by revelation of the Iran-Contra debacle and other embarrassing scandals, while the effects of Reaganomics would continue to foster sky-high federal deficits.

The 1980s and 1990s witnessed a computer revolution on campus.

By the November 1984 presidential election that pitted Reagan and George Bush against Walter Mondale and Geraldine Ferraro, more than 100 candidates had applied for the new presidency of Western. The university hired the international consulting firm Korn/Ferry to help its screening committee winnow down that number. By spring, 1985, three finalists remained in the running. On May 17, 1985, the Board of Trustees voted unanimously to appoint Dr. Diether H. Haenicke the university's fifth president at a salary of $95,000, as well as the traditional use of a home and automobile.

Born in central Germany in 1935, Haenicke moved to the northern German town of Witzenhausen when Hitler inflamed Europe in war four years later. Ironically, in view of the fact that he would come to Kalamazoo (once the world's leading paper maker), that German city's major industry was a paper mill owned by the family of Haenicke's mother. He grew up in a wealthy environment, and thanks to his mother's social clout, he was frequently excused from attending the mandatory Hitler Youth Corps rallies. During a 1985

interview, Haenicke vividly remembered: "When I was commuting to school by train, we were frequently machine gunned by incoming aircraft. The pilots in those planes didn't know there were kids on board. They were looking for targets and it could have been a troop train. Passengers were killed all the time. I was never hit. It was war. When people shoot at each other, people get killed."

The citizens of Witzenhausen spent the final nine months of the war in constant fear of an invasion, which did not materialize. Following the war, Haenicke and an entire generation of German youth endured the trauma of coming to grips with the incomparable evil their elders had unleashed on the world. In his quest for understanding, he turned to the study of history and of other cultures and came to realize that America's "was the ideal form of government."

Haenicke completed the German high school equivalent, "gymnasium," in 1955 and enrolled in the University of Gottingen. Seven years later, he completed his doctorate at the University of Munich. In the meantime, he had met the daughter of a Wayne State

University professor working in Germany. In 1962, he married Carol Colditz and the following year arrived at Wayne State as a Fulbright lecturer. He liked the Detroit campus so well that he stayed for the succeeding 15 years, working his way up the hierarchy to become vice president and provost. In 1978, Haenicke accepted the position of dean of the College of Humanities at Ohio State University, and five years later, he became vice president for academic affairs and provost. Haenicke left that 60,000 student campus for Western, in part, because he wanted to preside over a school of a size "he could

By the 1990s, the Student Union snack bar had been completely revamped.

A Western tradition that students have always wanted do without

embrace." Then, too, he, Carol and their two teenaged children also missed Michigan's many splendors.

Haenicke "put his arms around Western," and he put his feet to use, as well. During an August 12, 1985, news interview, he described his management style as MBWA—management by walking around. He would pop up, unannounced, seemingly anywhere on campus. He took a self-guided tour of Waldo Library one day and ambled through the recesses of the Bernhard Center on another. He arrived unheralded to sit in on a doctoral oral examination and left remarking, "Impressed."

Within the first year Haenicke could say, "There isn't a department or a building or a site on the University that I haven't seen. I have attended classes, examinations, parties. I have been eating in student dormitories."

A few shocks awaited him on his inspections, such as the dilapidated conditions, with plaster falling from the ceiling and walls, of some of Western's original historic structures on the hill. He would later use the dismal condition of East Hall to his advantage. William Parfet, a local business leader who had headed the University's highly successful Campaign for Excellence fund drive, remembered the day Haenicke had led a group of area business moguls through the crumbling structure where the future business leaders of America were being educated. "They couldn't reach for their checkbooks fast enough," Parfet recalled.

But mostly Haenicke received pleasant surprises during his initial tours of the campus. After working at a huge Big 10 institution, he was delighted to discover "that the quality of undergraduate education is much more intense, more intimate, and more direct in a school like ours."

President Diether Haenicke posed with President Emeritus
John Bernhard, circa 1993.

Haenicke, who prided himself on being
"a man of the faculty," was also favorably
impressed with the quality of the teachers he
found. "I just simply enjoy the company of
faculty very much," he admitted. "I take a very
direct and genuine interest in the work. I read
what our faculty write ... I socialize with a very
large number of faculty. I continue to consider
the faculty the primary constituency with
which I have to interact and work."

Those statements pleased many faculty
members. Those who labored hard to produce
outside the classroom took heart with his
revelation: "I also am impressed with some of

the publications done by our faculty. We
have some departments with significant
intellectual impact on their field way
beyond this institution. And we have a
much larger number of very good researchers than I initially thought I would find."

Haenicke could praise those who
excelled but he was also very willing to
chide underachievers. Bob Beam, vice
president for business and finance since
1985, remembered during a 2003 interview, the day he listened to Haenicke scold
in his German accent a gathering of faculty
about their need to accomplish more and
better work. They accepted the criticism
meekly, something, Beam believed, "no
other president could have gotten away with."

But because change can be difficult and it
is often easier to continue unchallenged, not
all faculty and staff appreciated the president's
style of leadership. In a 1998 interview
Haenicke admitted: "I am very demanding. I
want excellent work. I want it fast. I don't want
people who sit around on their duff all the
time and procrastinate. I am really given to
action and don't mind if people make a
mistake once in a while. I'm known for that
myself, but at least I want to have motion and
have things happening. I tend to be very
impatient. I also take pride in
the fact that I work very hard
and I get most things accomplished. But I also take care of
people who work well here."

Haenicke firmly believed
that if the university accrued
academic excellence, economic
development would follow as a
byproduct. In pursuit of that
excellence, research, faculty soon
discovered, would be one of the
hallmarks of Haenicke's presidency. He inspired a campuswide crusade for research
support in August, 1985, when

Vice President for Research Donald Thompson (left) and Vice President for Finance
Robert Beam (right) chatted during a meeting with Representative Fred Upton, a
longtime friend of Western.

In 1985, Dr. Albert Castel, professor of history, received a distinguished faculty scholar award. Pictured, left to right are Trustee Maury E. Parfet, Mrs. Robert Russel, History Professor Emeritus Robert Russel, Dr. Albert Castel and President Diether Haenicke.

he said: "We must never lose sight of the fact that a university is a place of learning and inquiry, and not just for students. Scholarly research and teaching on the university level are critically interdependent."

One of his first steps was to bring Dr. Donald Thompson back to the campus where

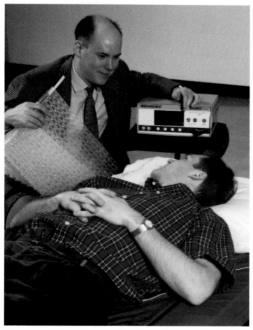

Members of the engineering faculty lay down on the job in 1998, while engaging in mattress research.

he had earned three academic degrees, as well as three varsity letters in wrestling, to serve as chief research officer. Four years later, Thompson filled the newly created position of vice president for research. He sought to match funding activities with the talents of faculty members. He acted as a facilitator, sometimes motivating less confident professors to start researching and publishing. He then helped them secure grants. "Tell me what you need to be successful," he encouraged more than one reluctant researcher.

In 1986, Haenicke challenged his faculty to double the annual outside support for research and sponsored programs to at least $7.8 million by the end of the 1990-91 academic year. Two years after he set that goal, the faculty responded by securing more than $8 million in external grants and contracts annually. In 1988-89, the research grants awarded Western soared to $9 million. The grants helped fund a diversity of research projects, ranging from preparing engineering students to deal with the ethical issues they faced in their careers, to evaluating the effectiveness of erosion control devices

The beauty of Coldsworth Valley was captured during the Celebration of the Arts Festival on October 10, 1998.

Western's band played for President Bill Clinton when he made a campaign stop in Comstock, Michigan, in August 1996.

installed on the shores of the Great Lakes, to reducing work-related injuries at large corporations, to designing tools to facilitate the cleanup of underground oil spills.

In 1990, Western's Evaluation Center received what was then the largest single grant in the University's history, when the U.S. Department of Education awarded it $5.2 million to establish a new national center to improve the performance of teachers and administrators in the country's school system. The ensuing center, called CREATE—the Center for Research on Educational Accountability and Teacher Evaluation—was developed over a five year period. It put Western in the forefront of a national movement to apply evaluation principles to improved teaching.

By the 1995-1996 fiscal year, Western was the recipient of more than $25 million in grants annually. Two years later, external sources supplied a record $31 million to cap a decade-long effort to expand Western's cadre of faculty researchers and improve the percentage of successful grant proposals. When interviewed in 1995 about the spectacular boom in research Haenicke replied, "Our faculty has far exceeded my expectations... I am not just speaking about faculty members who bring in grant dollars, an important component that can be measured. But we also have gone up significantly in the number of books and articles published by our faculty scholars, with a major impact on the intellectual life of their disciplines and on the university as a whole."

Hand in hand with the research emphasis came a push to regain some of the graduate programs lost in the early 1980s and to enhance Western's national reputation as a graduate college. In 1987, Haenicke summoned together the chairpersons of several key departments, including history, English, political science, economics and physics, to a meeting at the Oaklands. After they were comfortably seated, he "dropped a campus bombshell." He wanted to revolutionize their departments by creating doctoral programs!

Haenicke later recalled, "The reaction was stunned silence." When the naysayers began protesting that they didn't have the necessary resources, Haenicke told them "I've looked at the vitae of this faculty. You could do this..." By 1995, Western had doubled the number of its doctoral programs to 22 and increased its master's programs by nearly one-quarter to 60. And recognition of that rapid evolution came fast and furious. In early 1988, the Carnegie Foundation for the Advancement of Teaching designated Western as the only "Doctoral I" university in the state. Later that year, the Michigan legislature recognized Western, for the first time, as one of the state's "Big Five" graduate-intensive, public universities. More than just a pat on the back, that acknowledgement brought Western a three percent increase in appropriations.

Other kudos followed yearly. In September 1990, *Money* magazine rated Western 68th among the nation's top-100 "best buys," based on a computer analysis that weighed tuition against 17 measures of academic performance. The next month, *U.S. News & World Report* included Western among the best 204 national universities out of 1,374 institutions of higher learning surveyed. Western would be included in that prestigious grouping each following year, rising into the top-100 public universities in 1999.

Increased awareness of Western's renaissance came closer to home, as well. The Kalamazoo community woke up to realize that Western was no longer a teachers college on the hill but a university where serious academic work took place. What is more, the University was seen as an essential part of the county's economic structure. A study released in 1989 by the Department of Economics indicated that the University's impact on the county had climbed to more than $330 million a year. Its 2,800 employees made it second only to the Upjohn Company in payroll. If Western were to suddenly vanish, the county would lose 10,000 jobs and nearly 28,000 residents.

Buster Bronco posed with cheerleaders in 1996.

An enhanced image also paid off in attracting new students. In 1988, Western recorded an all-time record high of 24,852 students, counting both on-campus and off-campus continuing education enrollment. The numbers continued to climb yearly. In 1990, another record was smashed when a total of 26,995 students enrolled that fall. Nearly 24,000 students attended classes at the Kalamazoo campus, the largest number in the history of the university. Increasingly, families demonstrated loyalty to their alma mater by sending their offspring to the campus where they had been educated. Third-generation Western alumni became more and more common. In 1988, the Carpp family of Paw Paw cited with pride its four generations of Western students.

Another inducement that lured more new students to Western was its growing scholarship programs, a further indication of the university's commitment to quality. By 1987, the University dispensed $1 million in merit-based undergraduate scholarships annually. Scholarships available included Board of Trustees and Higher Education Incentive Scholarships worth $12,500 each, tuition scholarships worth $4,500, academic scholarships worth $3,000 and academic achievers awards valued at $500 per year.

Western's Medallion Scholarships, the concept of Trustee Emeritus J. Michael Kemp, who felt the university ought to offer something comparable to full-ride athletic scholarships to reward academic excellence, had emerged as the crown jewel of such awards. They were first awarded in 1984 via gifts from individuals, corporations, and foundations. Fifteen high school seniors competed for the initial six Medallion Scholarships worth

$20,000 over four years. Ten years later, nearly 1,000 cream-of-the-crop seniors from all over Michigan and ten other states were invited to campus in February to vie for the annual awards, which had grown to 21 worth $25,000 each. A selection committee evaluated grades, courses, test scores, and performance in the on-campus competition, as well as leadership, recommendations, and, in some cases, personal interviews to choose the winners. The Medallion Scholarships had become one of America's largest merit-based award programs in public higher education.

By the late 1980s and the 1990s, it was obvious to many university veterans that the students flocking to Western's campus had evolved into a different breed. Bob Beam, a 1965 graduate of Western who had parlayed a part-time job working for Vice President for Finance Robert Wetnight into an increasingly important position before succeeding Wetnight in 1985, remembered during a January 2003 interview how, as a student, he had waited in line in Vandercook Hall for his chance to use the sole phone installed there. He compared that experience with the myriad cell phones in the hands of current students. Students, Beam opined, had become more Republican, more conservative and more career focused. He remembered the time that, while standing with the president in the Gary Center parking lot one night, Haenicke had looked around the lot and said, "There's not a car in this lot I wouldn't be proud to take home." The era when students were lucky to drive "beaters" had given way to a time when possessing expensive automobiles had become a requisite of campus life. That may explain, in

By 1990, nearly 24,000 students attended classes at Western's Kalamazoo campuses.

Western's key administrators of the Haenicke years posed, circa 1996. Left to right are Vice President for Business and Finance Robert Beam, Vice President for Research Donald Thompson, Vice President for External Affairs Keith Pretty, President Diether Haenicke, Provost Timothy Light and Vice President for Student Affairs Theresa Powell.

part, why earning the traditional four-year bachelor's degree began to take five or six years.

Beam also recalled the day that, while traveling to Holland to visit alumnus Garrard Haworth, Haenicke remarked, "We're going to build for five years then stop." Such would not be the case. Throughout his tenure, Western's physical plant would grow at a pace commensurate with its enhanced prestige and booming enrollment, and Haenicke would become known as the "Building President."

In 1988, dignitaries gathered to dedicate the new $2.8 million Printing Management and Research Center named in honor of former state senator and long-time Western supporter, Robert A. Welborn, who died in 1985. Creating the 29,000 square feet of lecture, laboratory and seminar facilities entailed the renovation of the former Hardings Market on West Michigan Avenue and construction of a large addition. Outfitted with state-of-the-art equipment, the center allowed students and industry to experiment

with lithography, flexography and gravure printing techniques. Western became the only university in the nation to possess an operating pilot plant for printing as well as a similar facility for papermaking.

The following year, the university turned from celebrating the new to consideration of the old—its heritage buildings on the hill top. Haenicke appointed a study committee that recommended Western maintain rather than sell East Campus land and buildings, return the Davis Street hillside to its original design and house some offices in certain buildings, while employing a theme approach to utilize others. In 1990, landscapers began investigating the feasibility of restoring the Davis Street slope to the original Olmsted Brothers' design. That summer, trees were removed from a portion of the slope to offer a better view of the pillared portico of East Hall. Unfortunately, the project faltered and a few years later, part of the slope and tennis courts at the bottom fell victim to construction of a new

Originally constructed in 1938, Walwood Hall was renovated in 1992.

football practice field. By 1990, also, the University Archives and Regional History Collections had moved into the old Women's Gymnasium of crumbling East Hall. Other rooms in the dilapidated structure provided gallery space for art students. The following year, renovations of Spindler and Vandercook halls rendered them available for continued adaptive reuse by fraternities and offices.

In 1992, the WMU Foundation, the WMU Alumni Association and the offices of Alumni Relations, Development and External Affairs moved into the elegantly renovated Walwood Union. The similarly revamped Walwood Hall housed the Medieval Institute, Testing and Evaluation Services and the School of Public Affairs and Administration. Five years later, the

Faculty and staff celebrated the renovation of the Little Theatre in 1997.

opening of the Campus Cinema, a new theatre featuring foreign and independent films, marked the culmination of an arduous fund-raising campaign to renovate the 55-year-old Little Theatre.

For Haenicke, the fact that more of Western's heritage structures atop the hill had not been restored remains one of the disappointments of his presidency. During a January 2003 interview, he confided:

I always felt that old East Hall needed to be the next project. My idea was to raise the money to restore the building. But the first estimate was $18 million. We simply couldn't find a donor or donors interested enough. Nobody really wanted to take it on; I hope we don't lose the initiative. I hope one day it will be done.

There's so much history on that campus that the institution can never extend itself entirely from what is there and needs to be restored. I hope somebody will take it on as a project.

I always play the lottery when it's over $5 million. And I know exactly, with the way I live, I don't need $5 million. And I think, wouldn't it be wonderful to say to Carol, "Let's write this check that starts the East Hall renovations." I really mean it, that's where it would go. That's the only reason why I regret not being rich— that you can't do these wonderful things that the school needs, scholarships, faculty support, historic restoration.

Haenicke underscored the importance of donor support back in 1989, when he unveiled a six-year-long "Campaign for Excellence" fund drive. Its $55 million goal, with 40 percent of that already pledged, made it by far the largest fund-raising effort in the university's history. Haenicke articulated its theme and purpose as "to provide all the things the university needs to get over the threshold of being a fine, good institution to being an excellent one." Campaign objectives included $5.7 million for the annual fund, $10 million

By the 1990s, beautification of the campus had become a full-time job for numerous employees.

The stately pillars of East Hall have been a beacon of learning since 1905.

Dedicated in 1990, the Lee Honors College Building commemorates the generosity of donors Carl and Winifred Lee.

for endowment and scholarship funds and $15 million for certain priority projects such as the Mike Gary Athletic Fund and annual support for WMUK. But the largest and most visible objectives were brick and mortar, namely, new buildings for the College of Business and the Honors College, expansion of Waldo Library and an addition to Shaw Theatre.

The first fruit of the campaign came only one year later with the October 12, 1990, dedication of the Carl and Winifred Lee Honors College building. Fittingly, that date also marked the 50th wedding anniversary of the Lees, whose $500,000 gift helped finance the 8,400-square-foot structure costing $1.3 million. Lee joined John Fetzer's WKZO radio station in Kalamazoo in 1939 and worked his way up to become president, general manager and owner of Fetzer Broadcasting. He

and his wife gave the money because, "We have always been particularly impressed with the high quality of undergraduate instruction at Western." The Honors College, headed by Dean Faith Gabelnick after founder Samuel Clark retired in 1986, had grown to include 950 students and 60 faculty members. When

In 1998, Lee Honors College Dean Joe Reish conferred with students.

the highly selective college celebrated the tenth anniversary of the completion of the Lee Honors College building, it numbered nearly 1,200 students, with Dean Joseph Reish having succeeded Gabelnick.

The landscaping for the building featured a perennial garden provided by history professor John Houdek and his wife, Carolyn. That flowery oasis became part of Haenicke's ongoing campus beautification initiative. He felt that a scenic, well-maintained campus was important for the university's sense of self pride, as well as for projecting a positive image to prospective students and their parents. The program included the installation of brown and gold welcome banners; revitalization of the Fountain Plaza between Miller Auditorium and the Dalton Center; and the incorporation of more art into the landscape, such as the mammoth mural relief, composed of 182 handmade clay tiles, at the entrance to the Knauss Hall Space Gallery. The architectural gem of the West Campus, the Oaklands, underwent an extensive restoration in 1988, to emerge dressed in colors appropriate to its vintage Italianate style.

Meanwhile, Western's prestigious business college continued to struggle along in the deteriorating structures on the East Campus hilltop. Dr. Michael L. Moskovis, who started at Western as a business instructor in 1962, recalled some of his early experiences during a 2003 interview. His first office, which he occupied with two other faculty members, consisted of a former custodian's closet in East Hall. The entire department shared one telephone and a single typewriter on a stand with casters, which was wheeled back and forth as needed. Moskovis became one of numerous faculty members who went on to win promotions and become key administrators—a time honored Western tradition of drawing talent from the ranks. Ultimately, he would serve as vice president for academic

Composed of 182 handmade clay tiles, the mural relief at the entrance to the Knauss Hall Space Gallery was part of a campus beautification project.

affairs, vice president for institutional advancement, acting provost and acting president as well as in other important capacities.

In 1989, the Haworth family, proprietors of the Holland-based furniture manufacturing empire founded by Western graduate Gerrard Haworth, gave the University $5 million. Because family members preferred having their name associated with a living entity rather than bricks and mortar, the college was renamed the Haworth College of Business, in appreciation of their generosity. The Haworth donation helped a long-cherished dream of the business college become a reality in 1991 when it moved from the East Campus to its $20.1 million, 170,000-square-foot, teaching/

learning center. Dr. Darrell Jones, who succeeded Schnieder as dean of the college in 1974, led the campaign to secure the avant-garde building. The college's 150 faculty and staff members and 11,000 students had earned it a ranking among the nation's top business schools by the time of the move. The U-shaped building, faced with red brick similar to the Fetzer Center, houses behavioral laboratories, a student lounge and resources center, computer-based instructional facilities, an electronic classroom for satellite instruction, a 350-seat auditorium and a spectacular courtyard.

A diminishing pool of traditional students and anti-business reaction to the savings and loan scandals, bank failures, leveraged buy-outs and corporate layoffs of the 1980s brought shrinking enrollment to Western's and other business colleges across the nation. Yet, in 1994, the Haworth business college's 6,200 undergraduate students still made it the second largest such program in the nation. That year, the university named the Haworth College of Business building Schneider Hall, in honor of Dean Emeritus Arnold Schneider, who had been so instrumental in its development.

In 1991, the university community also breathed a collective sigh of relief when Waldo Library reopened in July. It had closed its doors in the spring of 1990 to expedite the major revamping taking place. The Bernhard Student Center's bowling alleys were converted into a makeshift library, and the main 800,000 volume collection was moved to a downtown warehouse dubbed "the annex." Researchers

The Oaklands received extensive renovations and a historically correct paint job in 1988.

Schneider Hall was opened in 1991.

filled out slips, then waited for retrieval from the annex. April 1992, brought dedication of the new Waldo Library. The $19.3 million project increased the facility from 145,000 square feet to 250,000 square feet and upped the seating capacity from 820 to 2,075. Set off by stunning heather and off-white glazed tile, the majestic structure, reminiscent of the Art Deco architecture of the 1930s, dominates the heart of the West Campus. Waldo Library had become one of the most architecturally pleasing, convenient and automated college libraries in the nation, a "building," as Haenicke put it, "you love to be in."

An automated computer network offered access to the library's growing collection of more than 2.8 million items. Added also was a rare book room, providing a protective environment for Western's numerous bibliographic treasures. A distinctive clock tower links the library with the $7.6 million University Computing Center, which features a second-floor classroom for hands-on training, a faculty resource center, a large open-access student laboratory and a secure first-floor

operations center that houses the computers that operate much of the university's network of services and functions. To the regret of generations of former music students, the construction project required the demolition of Harper Maybee Hall, the first named-structure on campus to be razed. Recognition of his many contributions to the development of Western continues in the renamed Maybee Music Library in the Dalton Center.

Also in 1992, the university embarked on an ambitious project to expand and renovate its athletic and recreational facilities. The $50 million endeavor included ten new tennis courts in Goldsworth Valley, new artificial turf for Waldo Stadium and improvements at Kanley Track. The major elements of the project, however, were the renovation and expansion of the Gary Center and Read Fieldhouse. Seemingly in response to this grand endorsement of athletics, Western's basketball team ended the 1991-92 season with its first winning record since 1982 and its highest Mid-American Conference finish since 1981. The Bronco hockey team finished its

It was standing room only during this Bronco game, around 1996.

seventh consecutive winning season and received a top-15 national ranking for most of the 1991-92 season.

In response to the high rating students of the 1990s gave to the need for a state-of-the-art workout center, August 1994 brought the unveiling of the new Student Recreation Center and Read Fieldhouse Complex. A 125,000-square-foot addition to the former Gary Center featured a large gymnasium; a weight/fitness room with everything from variable resistance machines and rowing machines to electronic bikes and cross-country ski machines; a glass enclosed pool; a climbing wall; and a jogging track cantilevered over the gymnasium. The attached Read Fieldhouse had been expanded by 70,000 square feet to create a 5,800-seat University Arena and practice space for varsity sports. The combined projects cost $32.9 million.

September 1994 witnessed the dedication of the University Medical and Health Sciences Center on the East Campus. A unique joint venture between the University, Borgess Medical Center, Bronson Methodist Hospital and the Michigan State University Center for Medical Studies, the $9 million project included renovation of an existing building and construction of an attached, four-story structure. The top two floors of the new building house several of the University's health and human services clinics.

Capping 1994's amazing string of dedications, in November, the Laura V. Shaw Theatre and the Zack L. York Arena Theatre were combined with a new $5.4 million educational wing and renamed the Irving S. Gilmore Theatre Complex, in honor of the Kalamazoo philanthropist who had created the foundation that contributed $2.4 million for the project. The 40,000-square-foot expansion features a unique 275-seat multiform theatre/classroom, an acting classroom, student design studio, administrative offices and a new street level entrance for patrons.

The new $32.9 million Student Recreation Center and Read Fieldhouse complex was completed in 1994.

Ground was broken for the thirteenth and final campus construction project of the Haenicke years in 1998. The new science research pavillon, part of a $44.4 million effort to provide enhanced facilities for science research and teaching, joined Rood Hall, Everett Tower and a completely renovated Wood Hall in a science quadrangle at the western periphery of the main campus. Completed the following year, Diether H. Haenicke Hall was named by a grateful Board of Trustees in recognition of the president's commitment to the fund raising that had made possible so many of the dazzling new structures that transformed the campus.

With the transfer of 120-acres and 20 buildings of the former Kalamazoo Psychiatric Hospital to Western in 1998, came the need for new terms to describe the burgeoning campus. The newly acquired land was named the Oakland Drive Campus. West

The Student Recreation Center, completed in 1994, featured a glass-enclosed pool and massive hot tub.

In 1992, the core of the university, the totally renovated Waldo Library, was dedicated.

The Irving S. Gilmore Theatre Complex was dedicated in 1994.

Campus remained the description for the major portion of the university, while the historic heart of Western, the 75-acres on both sides of Oakland Drive, encircled by Stadium Drive, Oliver, Austin and Davis streets, was defined as East Campus.

Naming and renaming structures, programs, scholarships and positions had also become a popular method to honor university supporters. In 1996, for example, the record $5.9 million bequest from the estate of Helen Stewart Frays, a 1934 Western graduate and longtime Kalamazoo teacher and social worker, occasioned the naming of the clock tower connecting Waldo Library and the University Computing Center as Stewart Tower, in memory of Frays' parents. Another portion of the Frays estate bequest went

toward the creation of a named professorship in her honor. Wendy L. Cornish became the first Helen Frays Professor of Dance. Part of a program implemented by Haenicke to recognize excellence in teaching and research, seven named professorships were created by the fall of 1997. Four additional named

President Haenicke, kneeling second from left, and wife, Carol, behind him, posed with some of Western's numerous international students, around 1996.

professorships, created in 1998, honor faculty members and donors.

The university's off-campus growth mirrored its Kalamazoo area boom of the Haenicke era. By 1990, Western's Division of Continuing Education had become Michigan's second largest off-campus education program. That year, the university dedicated a new $5.7 million, 40,000-square-foot, Grand Rapids Regional Center, located on the East Beltline.

While the university had been offering courses in Grand Rapids since 1909, the new structure's 21 classrooms, computer laboratory and facilities for teleconferencing allowed Western to consolidate its services to the state's second largest city. Western similarly enhanced its offerings in Battle Creek in 1993 with the ribbon cutting for its new downtown regional site, the Kendall Center, named after Battle Creek philanthropists Roy and Beulah I. Kendall.

A new continuing education program that did not require expenditures for bricks and mortar began in Muskegon in 1996. Offered at Muskegon Community College and jointly designed and implemented by that college, Western and Muskegon-area manufacturers, the manufacturing engineering degree program allowed students employed by Muskegon firms to move into the high-tech economy. By 2002, Western's newly renamed Extended University Programs (EUP) was providing more than 3,000 students with quality, extended-education programs at branch campus facilities in Grand Rapids,

The Waldo Library clock tower was named Stewart Tower in 1996 to honor the parents of donor Helen Stewart Frays.

Battle Creek, Holland, Lansing, Muskegon, St. Joseph/Benton Harbor, Traverse City and Kalamazoo.

Western also boosted its international presence when it pioneered a unique "twinning" program near the Malaysian capital of Kuala Lumpur in 1987. The twinning agreement allowed the newly created Sunway College to offer the first two years of Western's bachelor's degree programs, with courses, syllabi, texts, tests, and so forth, identical to those on campus. Students could then transfer

In 1998, the giant British Airways Concorde delivered a group of British students to begin their studies at Western's new International Pilot Training Centre at the W. K. Kellogg Airport Battle Creek, Michigan.

those credits to Western, where they completed their degrees. By 1992, enrollment in the Malaysian program had grown to 330.

Two years later came a second twinning program with Hong Kong Baptist University. The year 1997 brought another similar agreement with Christ College in Bangalore, India. That year, Western's enrollment included 667 Malaysian students, the most of any U.S. university. Two additional India-based twinning programs followed, and in 2000, the Office of International Affairs launched another twinning effort in Islamabad, Pakistan.

104 countries were enrolled at Western's Kalamazoo campus.

Another development with international implications came in 1998 when more than 40,000 spectators crowded the W.K. Kellogg

Airport in Battle Creek to witness the first southwestern Michigan landing of British Airways' Concorde. The giant aircraft delivered the first group of British Airways students to begin the 13-month course at Western's new International Pilot Training Centre. Four years before, Western had begun a dramatic $36.8 million expansion and relocation of its School of Aviation Sciences to the former Fort Custer Airport, thanks in part to support from Battle Creek Unlimited and the W.K. Kellogg Foundation. Additional training agreements with Arab, Irish, Dutch and U.S. aviation companies followed almost yearly. In 1999, the newly designated College of Aviation took over management, for a brief time, of the Romeo Airport in northwestern Macomb County.

The year that Western's aviation program began its expansion in Battle Creek, 1994, also brought the announcement of a new and much-needed bachelor's degree program in nursing. Capping a 30-month fund-raising effort, the innovative program featured a curriculum developed with the future of nursing education in mind. In validation of the College of Health and Human Services' nursing degree excellence, in 1998, it received national accreditation from a prestigious agency with unprecedented speed. The following year, the renamed WMU Bronson School of Nursing became the legal successor of that hospital's program, which had closed in 1998. The College of Health and Human Services' Department of Occupational Therapy also announced an innovation in 1997 when it established the world's first university-based program to certify health care professionals in the therapeutic use of horsemanship. Western's hippotherapy clinic at the Cheff Center for the Handicapped near Augusta opened in 1998.

Western's Department of Occupational Therapy pioneered in 1998 with its hippotherapy clinic at the Cheff Center for the Handicapped in Augusta, Michigan.

Costumed dancers offered an authentic taste of medieval culture at the 1999 version of the annual medieval congress.

The cast of Western's award-winning play, *Quilters,* posed in 1987.

From spurring a horse to spiking the ball, Western students made headlines in wide ranging and eclectic categories in the late 1980s and 1990s. Coach Rob Buck's volleyball squad won its seventh consecutive Mid-American Conference title and extended its MAC winning streak to 91 matches in 1988. Also that fall, the Bronco soccer team won the unofficial MAC championship by shutting out all four conference competitors. But the major sports highlight of the year came when Coach Al Molde's eleven captured sole possession of the MAC football crown for the first time. The team, along with more than 2,000 Western fans, traveled to Fresno to play in the post-season California Bowl, narrowly losing to Fresno State in one of the University's most exciting games.

In April 1988, a contingent of Western's theatre majors, accompanied by alumni and friends, journeyed to Washing-

ton, D.C.'s Kennedy Center to perform the play *Quilters.* Western's cast was one of only eight invited to perform during that year's American College Theatre Festival. In 2000, the Department of Theatre's presentation of *Native Son,* directed by Dr. Von Washington, became its fifth production to be sent to that

Left to right, theatre professor Lyda Stillwell, Department of Theatre Chairman D. Terry Williams, Eleanor York and Theatre Department Chairman Emeritus Zack York celebrated the 1988 performance of *Quilters* in Washington, D.C.

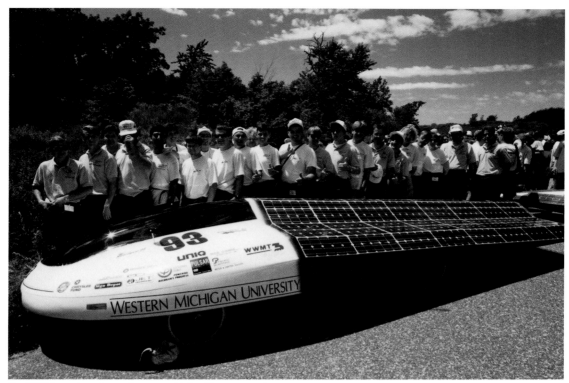

The 1993 Sunseeker solar car team posed before its cross-country race.

festival's regional competition, more than any other school in Michigan.

Western students received recognition in a different performance category in 1993 when they won honors in the Student Award Competition of the renowned jazz and blues publication, *Down Beat*. The university's Jazz Studies Program sent participants to the competition every year thereafter. By 1999, Western had won more *Down Beat* awards than any other college in the nation. When three additional students took *Down Beat's* top awards in 2001, Dr. Thomas Knific, head of the Jazz Studies Program, commented, "Our students are as good or better than any other students in the world!"

Students from practically every department in the College of Engineering and Applied Sciences shone in another competition in 1990 when they entered a national 1,800-mile solar-powered car race. Western's sleek Sunseeker, one of only 32 cars to be accepted in the challenge, took eighth place in the race from Orlando, Florida, to Warren, Michigan.

In 2001, the Sunseeker 295 sped 2,300 miles in 125 hours, powered only by the sun and batteries, to place fifth in the stock class in the American Solar Challenge Race. Western was one of only eight schools in the country to have competed in all six national collegiate races held since 1990.

Also in 2001, the College of Aviation's precision flight team, the Sky Broncos, took second place in the National Intercollegiate Flying Association championship. It was the 10th consecutive top-three national finish for the aviation student's club, which had been formed in 1946. In 1998, the Sky Broncos had soared to first place in the national championship contest. The following year, Western's 50-member sailing club earned a berth in *Sailing World's* list of top-20 collegiate sailing teams. Western was the sole Midwestern representative on the list and the only school without a varsity-coached program.

As might be expected, even as Western's students excelled in so many diverse endeavors, dissension periodically flared up. Approxi-

The Russell H. Seibert Administration Building was the scene of a 1990 student takeover.

mately 150 students took a page from the 1960s in April, 1990 when they seized control of the Seibert Administration Building and blocked access to its five entrances. Triggered by the alleged assault by two faculty members of a student who was taking a test, the demonstration focused on addressing minority student concerns on campus. After 24 hours and all-night negotiations by Haenicke and an administrative team, the student demonstrators vacated the building and the tense situation ended peacefully.

Two years later, it was the faculty and staff's turn to clash with the administration. The four unions on campus overwhelmingly rejected the pay concessions Haenicke had requested to stave off a projected budget deficit. That situation

A long-sought honor became a reality in 1998 when WMU became the home of the Theta of Michigan Chapter of the prestigious Phi Beta Kappa honor society. Dr. John Petro, left, posed with President Haenicke.

In 1997, President Haenicke appointed Kathy Beauregard as the first woman to be WMU's athletic director.

was ultimately resolved, and by 1994, faculty salaries had increased an average of 17.3 percent in just four years. It was the largest percentage increase among fifteen comparable universities.

At the same time, Haenicke worked hard to keep tuition at an affordable level. In 1995, he recommended only a 2.6 percent across-the-board increase in tuition, the lowest increase among the state's universities and Western's lowest in 10 years. The following year's 2.8 percent increase was also one of the lowest enacted by a Michigan university.

A major breakthrough in the University's ongoing campaign for gender equity came in

In 1991, Dr. Nancy S. Barrett was appointed as Western's first female provost.

1991, when Nancy S. Barrett was named to succeed George M. Dennison as provost and vice president for academic affairs. Barrett became the first woman to hold that vital position, second only to the president's.

Another important development came in 1995 when Haenicke unveiled a six-year plan to restructure the University's intercollegiate athletic programs to give women a better chance to play sports and win scholarships. Five women's sports were proposed, including swimming, badminton and fencing. As it turned out, scores of female athletes would be accommodated through the introduction of soccer in 1996 and synchronized skating in 1999.

By the summer of 1997, Haenicke had been Western's president for a dozen years. Counting his previous positions as provost at Ohio State and Wayne State universities, that made a quarter of a century of "really high pressure stuff." That June he announced his retirement, effective July 1, 1998. He cited

The Bill Brown Alumni Football Center was dedicated in 1998 with the help of, from left, President Haenicke, Coach Gary Darnell, Bill Brown, Athletic Director Kathy Beauregard and Trustee Emeritus James Brady.

"presidential fatigue," ongoing health problems and his desire "to have time left to do things that I do very well and that I really haven't had time to do much and that is writing and teaching." Like so many others who have moved to Kalamazoo with the intention of making it a stepping stone on their career quest, Haenicke and his wife Carol, had fallen in love with the vibrant community. Kalamazoo became their home and there they would stay.

In June 1998, President Haenicke presided over his last commencement before retirement.

Among Haenicke's final "class acts," performed in 1997 during his last year at the helm, was the appointment of Kathy Beauregard as the university's first woman athletic director. Born and raised in Kalamazoo, Beauregard had coached at Western for nearly two decades before being named to head its athletic endeavors.

Also in 1997, a campaign that had begun 28 years before under Dr. Russell Seibert finally reached fruition—the creation of a prestigious Phi Beta Kappa chapter on campus. Western became one of only 91 public universities in the nation to realize that honor. At the formal installation of the chapter on February 23, 1998, Haenicke proudly announced that the development would "stand as one of the greatest achievements in Western Michigan University's history."

Two final honors came to Haenicke in appreciation of the accomplishments he had overseen during his 13 years at the helm. On

More than 40 years of University leadership were represented when this group posed. From left, President Elson Floyd and Carmento Floyd; Carol Haenicke and President Diether Haenicke; Jane Miller, widow of President James Miller; Ramona Bernhard and President John Bernhard.

June 27, 1998, at his final commencement ceremony as president, he received an honorary doctor of humane letters degree from Western. At his last Board of Trustees meeting on July 24, the Diether Haenicke Center for International and Area Studies was created to coordinate intellectual and academic support for the many Western faculty members with international expertise.

In the meantime, a search committee composed of a wide range of campus constituents had spent 10 months narrowing down a field of presidential candidates. Five were brought to Kalamazoo for detailed interviews. One particularly articulate candidate stood head and shoulders above the others. He told the Board of Trustees:

> *I have, indeed, a very strong, very clear vision of where we should be as a university. I am absolutely convinced that we need to be a premier student—centered research university... The administration has one goal only—that is to make sure that we operate in an environment that will foster and promote teaching, research and service on behalf of the faculty. The administration itself should be as invisible as it possibly can in delivering the services that are absolutely paramount to move the university forward.*

President Elson Floyd took the podium on his first day at Western in 1998.

Engineering student Gurdeep Singh, left, developed Robo Bronco, a high-tech version of WMU's mascot that served as a symbol of President Floyd's support for technology.

Those words were spoken by Elson S. Floyd, and in April 1998, the Board of Trustees offered the presidency to the man they called "the best of the best." He took the reins, effective August 1. The 42-year-old Floyd was born and raised in Henderson, North Carolina, a small industrial town in the tobacco belt. His working-class parents, neither of whom had finished high school, knew well the American dream of a better life for their offspring, and they pushed Floyd and his three brothers to achieve. Ultimately, all four would graduate from college and pursue successful careers in diverse fields.

Floyd attended segregated public schools until the eighth grade, when integration finally came to North Carolina. He excelled in academics and sports in high school, winning a scholarship to finish his last two years at The Darlington School, a prep school for exceptional students in Rome, Georgia, where he became its first black graduate. Floyd then enrolled in the University of North Carolina at Chapel Hill, thanks to an academic scholarship. There, he earned a bachelor's degree in political science and speech and, with the assistance of additional scholarships, a master's in adult education and a doctorate in higher education. Floyd took a job as assistant dean for student life and judicial programs at his alma mater in 1978 and quickly advanced up the administrative hierarchy. Floyd, his wife, Carmento, and their children Kenny and Jessica, left in 1990 for Eastern Washington University, where Floyd served for five years as vice president and executive vice president. The year 1995 found him again in North Carolina, taking on the duties of chief administrative and operating officer at UNC's flagship campus.

A dynamic "workaholic" who sleeps only a few hours each night, Floyd spent part of his first day as head of Western conducting a live interactive television hook-up with alumni and friends in Kalamazoo, Chicago, Detroit and the university's numerous extended education facilities. Trustee Richard St. John never forgot Floyd's statement, "Our job as a university is to enhance the value of a degree." Among Floyd's primary missions to help achieve that task was

The starting line of the annual Campus Classic attracted more than 800 runners in October 1999.

President Floyd posed with members of the WMU Marching Band.

for the university to advance from Doctoral I to the Carnegie Foundation's next higher ranking, Research II, and he wasted little time in moving forward.

A $3 million "jump start" initiative to foster interdisciplinary work among departments had been announced by Haenicke the previous spring. The goal was to help push the university past the $15.5 million threshold in annual federal research awards required for the Research II designation. The initiative received continued support in the months after Floyd came and the funding was used to expand research in projects in such areas as school and mathematics reform, educational technology, the environment and non-wood fibers. It did not take long for results. Total grant support for the 1998-99 fiscal year reached a record-breaking $83 million. That and a growth in graduate programs resulted in a successful end to the decade-long quest to secure the placement of WMU in the Carnegie Foundation's highest classification. When the foundation's revised classification was announced, WMU was listed in the "Doctoral/Research Universities-Extensive category, along with just 101 other public higher education institutions.

Private gifts to the university increased as well. For the fiscal year 1998-99, support from alumni and faculty totaled a record $11 million, with another $15.2 pledged. Thanks largely to the efforts of the WMU Foundation that had been organized in 1976, private giving rose to $17.5 million in 1999-2000 and $18.4 million the following year.

In 2002, came announcement of the largest gift from a private donor in

Marci Meskin, an education junior from Bloomfield Hills, guided new students through orientation in 1998.

Western's history. Gwen Frostic, a celebrated poet, artist and publisher, left a bequest of more than $13 million. Unprecedented in another way, as well, Frostic's gift to the University, where she had taken classes but had not graduated, was totally unrestricted. Her generosity would help fund a new art facility and create numerous endowments, named-professorships, scholarships and other benefits to honor her name.

A unique venture that Floyd had envisioned with the support of State Senator Harry Gast became reality in October 2002. Western pioneered again in its outreach efforts with the dedication of a sleek $8.2 million facility on Lake Michigan College's Benton Harbor campus. Nationally praised as a model for university/community college cooperation, it became the first such structure to be constructed by a Michigan university on a community college campus. Designated WMU-Southwest, the 45,000-square-foot facility is equipped with state-of-the-art wireless technology, allowing interactive distance learning classes to be beamed to and

from any of the university's nine Kalamazoo or regional campus sites. WMU-Southwest was designed to offer a seamless transition from community college courses to completion of a WMU bachelor's or graduate degree without leaving the community.

As Western received increasing recognition for its status as one of America's finest universities, enrollment boomed to rarefied new heights at the dawning of the twenty-first century. In May 1999, having received more than 15,000 applications from prospective first-year students, the University closed freshman admissions for the first time in its history. The 5,779 first-year students admitted that fall marked the fifth consecutive record-breaking year. The fall of 2000 shattered all previous records, as total enrollment reached 28,657. The number of foreign students soared more than 15 percent from the previous year. Particularly satisfying was the fact that nearly half of beginning students were recipients of the state's new $2,500 Michigan Merit Awards. Western was surpassed by only two other Michigan universities as the destination of

Colorful Native American dancers performed at the 8th Annual Pow Wow, held at the University Arena in 1997.

choice for high school seniors whose academic achievements earned them the merit awards.

With total enrollment on an annual upswing, the number of minority students attending Western, unfortunately, was on a decrease. Over the period 1995 to 2001, enrollment of African Americans, Hispanic, Asian/Pacific Islanders and Native American students had dropped from 2,680 to 2,494. Part of the problem stemmed from the tightening of admission standards in order to boost Western's profile as a research university. Then, too, only 50 of the university's 952 faculty positions were held by blacks.

As the university struggled to reverse that troubling trend, some progress resulted. By 2002, the College of Education had hired six new black faculty members. The College of Education also received a $150,000 grant in 1999 to help it recruit and train more minority students in its teaching program. The following year saw the creation of the Greenleaf Asset Management Scholarships program to fund two, four-year, full ride

This jubilant Western graduate received her hard-earned diploma, around 1996.

President Floyd spoke at the groundbreaking of the Parkview Campus in 1999.

scholarships for minority students entering the field of finance. Another Haworth College of Business program, INROADS Inc., brought about 35 minority high school students to campus in the summer of 2000 to learn more about business and technology careers. The College of Aviation launched a similar program that summer through its week-long aviation camp that had a particular focus on increasing awareness of aviation careers among underrepresented groups such as minorities and women.

In 1999, the Haworth College of Business launched the Women's Business Development Center, designed to assist women business owners through low-cost training, consultation and support group assistance. The center soon joined forces with WESTOPS (the University's Office of Business Development Services) and a new Professional Education Program. Relocated to the Kalamazoo Chamber of Commerce Building, it provided "one stop shopping" for service to businesswomen and other members of the business community.

In 1999, excavation began on the first stage of the sprawling new engineering complex. Haenicke had faced stiff opposition from some elements of the Kalamazoo community over his efforts to establish a business technology and research development on the 268-acre Lee Baker Farm, located at the southwest corner of Parkview Avenue and Drake Road. In a January 2003, interview he recalled with humor how he watched his successor grapple with the problem:

He played the local situation and the historical event to its fullest. If you don't want to go with us, we have plans to build the engineering college in Grand Rapids or Battle Creek or maybe here if the conditions are right [he said]. I think he never really thought that. I thought it was so bold. I said, "Elson you are going to fall flat on your face. Nobody will ever believe this bs story that you are selling." He said, "You wait." And he was right. People fell for it. It was a bluff. It was a poker game and he played and the others folded. I thought it would never work and it worked. I was just pleased as punch that it worked—all the blood, sweat and tears that had already gone into it. I'm mainly thinking here of Dick Burke, who fought for it like a lion. And now it's there and so all good things happen in time if the right people are there at the right time to say, "This is the moment."

Floyd also shrewdly merged the much-needed expansion of Western's College of Engineering and Applied Sciences with the private research park, largely to quell citizen concerns. The following year, roadwork, sidewalks and curbs had been installed and construction began on the college's Paper and Printing Science Pilot Plant. In 2001, the University broke ground for a new $70 million, 300,000-square-foot facility to house the college. When completed, the entire Parkview Campus would provide a nucleus "of engineering education and collaborative research and economic development." An

adjunct of the development, the Business Technology and Research Park, was designated a Michigan "SmartZone," a special tax district favorable to start-up businesses. Plans also called for moving Western's Southwest Michigan Innovation Center, then housed in McCracken Hall, to a new $12 million structure at the park.

Cooperative ventures between the university and the local business community helped win support for further brick-and-mortar growth in late 1999, when Michigan Governor John Engler approved a capital outlay bill providing partial funding for Western's new $45 million College of Health and Human Services Building to be located on the Oakland Drive Campus. Engler backed the project, in part, because of the potential it had to enhance existing collaboration with the Pharmacia Corporation (into which the Kalamazoo-based Upjohn Company had merged). The college's numerous programs, five of which were ranked among the best in the nation, were then housed in eight far-flung campus locations.

Provost Daniel Litynski, second from left; President Floyd; and Kalamazoo Mayor Robert Jones, far right, were among those who did the honors at a "paper-tearing" ceremony to open the Paper Coating Pilot Plant in October 2002.

Thrills and spills at Western's Homecoming soapbox derby

In the spring of 2001, work began on an impressive new indoor athletic practice field, named in honor of longtime Western supporter and founder of the Seelye Ford Dealership, Donald J Seelye. Seelye had played football and baseball for State High before leaving at the start of WW II to join the marines. The Seelye structure was planned to complement the 55,000-square-foot addition to Waldo Stadium, completed at a cost of $8.2 million in 1998. Named the Bill Brown Alumni Football Center, it recognized the many contributions of the former Bronco football star and longtime WMU supporter who co-chaired the fund-raising campaign for the facility. Brown had gotten involved in the campaign when he realized Western's varsity team was using the same run-down facility, with only four working shower heads, that he had used when he played in the early 1950s under Coach John Gill. Workers battered down all but the front facade of historic Oakland Gym, which was preserved to

form an entry to the 112,000-square-foot structure. Completed in 2003, at a cost of $25 million, with $8 million of that coming from a special fund-raising drive, the dazzling concrete and glass structure provides a multiple sport practice field under a 70-foot high ceiling.

The drive that made possible the Bill Brown Center was precursor to the "most

The Knollwood Tavern, a gathering spot familiar to Western students for many decades, vanished in 1999.

ambitious fund raising effort in university history" announced by Floyd on August 30, 2001. "Partnering for Success: The Centennial Campaign for Western Michigan University" set a goal of $125 million, of which sixty percent had already been raised according to William Upjohn Parfet, chairman of the campaign. A local businessman, who had also led the Campaign for Excellence that surpassed its goal of $55 million in 1992 by $7 million, Parfet had agreed to devote his time and energy to doubling that earlier achievement because he was "convinced that an investment in this university will pay solid dividends to our community, state and nation." A successful campaign promised enhanced support for practically every aspect of Western's future. More than $52 million would go for three major new structures already begun, as well as a projected building for the Department of Art. Students would garner $14 million in scholarships, fellowships and internships. Faculty programs to attract and retain the best teachers would get $13 million. The remainder of the $125 million would fund specialized equipment needs, visiting artists and scholars programs and other initiatives.

Dale Pattison, a State High graduate and retired WMU history professor, promoted an unrelated fund-raising drive in 2001 as well. The Fund for the Preservation of East Campus sought enough financial backing to make possible the preservation and adaptive reuse of the historic structures on the University's "Heritage Hill." The 150-member Friends of Historic East Campus, initially headed by Pattison, suggested possible uses for the inspiring Greek-revival buildings, including renovation of North Hall as a home for the Archives and Regional History Collections and reutilization of East Hall for administrative functions.

The Campus Master Plan, also released in 2001, corroborated the importance of the historic campus and its potential for ongoing reuse. It also cited the need for a pedestrian

bridge for safer crossing of Oakland Drive. The plan also proposed a similar bridge across Stadium Drive and development of a pedestrian mall and bicycle lanes on the West Campus. The newly acquired 176-acre Oakland Drive Campus would be used primarily for recreational and athletic fields and academic, research, clinical and residential structures. The recommendations included preservation of the main Kalamazoo Psychiatric Hospital Quadrangle, slated to be eventually vacated. Preservation also was recommended for the adjacent monumental, red-brick water tower that had been saved from the wrecking ball in the 1970s by a community wide drive headed by Alexis Praus, longtime director of the Kalamazoo Public Museum.

A common thread running through the master plan was that future growth, no matter how unlimited, ought to incorporate the best of what had been built in the past. And contemplation of the past became imperative as the University moved toward the dawning of its second century. In May 2001, Floyd named Edward and Ruth Heinig to head the Centennial Celebration Committee, which would plan and coordinate the University's 100th birthday observance in 2003. The husband-and-wife team had both retired in 1992 after distinguished teaching careers of nearly 30 years at Western—he in education, she in communication. They also shared a passionate loyalty to Western.

Building on the groundwork previously laid by an *ad hoc* committee composed of Professors Emeriti John T. Houdek and Charles F. Heller, Director of the WMU Archives and Regional History Collections Sharon Carlson and former Vice President for Student Services Thomas E. Coyne, the Heinigs rolled up their sleeves. From their headquarters in Walwood Hall, they began rounding up volunteers and gearing up for the "Celebration of the Century."

Amidst these plans, a worrisome era grew worse. It had not been an easy transition into a

The ornate cupola of East Hall has become a symbol of Western's heritage.

The Bronco Bash of 2000 offered a gala celebration for thousands.

The University and community bade President Floyd goodbye at his last commencement.

new millennium. Millions stockpiled food and water in fear of the Y2-K bug that fortunately proved a false alarm. Then came a divisive, disputed presidential election and financial evisceration—the bursting of the dot-com bubble, the bear market, shameful disclosures by Enron, Worldcom and other gilt-edged firms. Out of the blue of a beautiful September morning came the horrors of 9/11. Like hundreds of millions of other Americans, the WMU campus shared the shock, anger and grief of that day. As they learned of friends and relatives senselessly murdered, students and faculty held candlelight vigils, collected funds for the Red Cross and gave blood. A nation that had forever changed endured war in Afghanistan and a looming attack on Iraq. Frightening scenarios for the future abounded, but no one seemed able to accurately predict what would happen next.

Kalamazooans also worried about the future of their local economy. The turn of the millennium had brought major plant closings,

mergers of dominant firms and removal of headquarters to other states. Yet, as has been Kalamazoo's fate repeatedly in the past, changing times brought economic evolution. When segments of the economy faltered, something else emerged to take up the slack. It became more and more apparent to many that Western Michigan University would fill that role. Richard St. John, a 16-year member of the WMU Board of Trustees, proclaimed in a 2003 interview: "Western has emerged as the leading economic development in Kalamazoo, the crown jewel of southwest Michigan."

Haenicke echoed these sentiments:

> The community, over time, has begun to respond to the institution. They really see that we are the one. We're not going to merge. We're going to be here and we are going to be big, big, big! Already we are among the major employers of the area and we love it here. We'll be here forever. We're one of

A winter snowstorm left a mantle of distinctive beauty on the WMU campus.

Sprau Tower, seen here in 1991, is symbolic of the architectural elegance of the West Campus.

*the things that is not going to disappear.
And if any institution has the potential
of really doing major things for the
region, it is this university. The better
we become academically, the more
prominent, the more attractive, the
better for this community.*

In November 2002, the University and
the Kalamazoo community were saddened by
the announcement that Floyd would be
resigning effective January 5, 2003, to accept
the presidency of the 60,000-student University of Missouri system. In an interview with
Heidi Kobler, news editor of the *Western
Herald,* Floyd confided:

> *This was the most difficult decision
> because it was so emotionally charged
> for me. It had to do with the nature of
> the relationships we have established at
> the university and community. This was
> the most emotionally wrenching part of
> it for me. I have a wonderful group of
> students I work with and faculty and
> staff. It's virtually like leaving a family.*

Floyd left a campus considerably enriched
through his efforts. Jamie Jeremy, executive
director of alumni relations, outlined what
may be his most significant long-term accomplishments—all pioneering efforts in the state
or nation. They were, she said, "the appointment of the first information technology vice
president, insistence that all graduates be
computer literate and the completion of a
totally wireless and ubiquitous computing
campus."

WMU Board of Trustees Chairman
Richard St. John assured the University
community that an interim president would
soon be appointed and a successor to Floyd,
the first Western president to leave prior to
retirement would be in place by the fall
semester of 2003. In December 2002,
Provost and Vice President for Academic
Affairs Dr. Daniel M. Litynski, a retired
brigadier general and former dean of WMU's
College of Engineering and Applied Sciences,
was named interim president.

When asked what kind of president the
Board of Trustees was looking for, St. John

Cast by artist Veryl Goodnight, the majestic bronze bronco was unveiled in April 1997.

replied, "God on a good day." The University has been fortunate throughout its first century in having at the helm a series of presidents with quite different backgrounds, philosophies and leadership styles. But each proved himself very much the right man for the times.

The 14-member Presidential Search Advisory Committee representing the spectrum of Western's interests moved decisively and on May 1, 2003 announced its choice. Western's seventh president would be the right *woman* for the changing times. Judith Bailey, president of Northern Michigan University, officially took over Western's helm on June 9, 2003. There seemed a pleasant symmetry to the realization that precisely a century before Dwight Waldo had made the same journey from Marquette to Kalamazoo to found Western.

A native of Winston-Salem, N.C., Bailey embraced a career in higher education as her life's work in order, as she told *Kalamazoo Gazette* reporter Ed Finnerty, "to be involved with the adult learner and the life of the mind, to experience that culture that allows us to develop as educators, citizens, intellectual leaders, researchers, scientists, artists, creative performers, and that nurtures that interest and excitement in our learners."

Western's first female president had pioneered in breaking gender barriers before. She served as the first woman director of cooperative extension at the University of Maine for example, as well as Northern's first woman president. Highlights of her tenure at Northern included an over-the-top fund raising drive, campus brick and mortar accomplishments and a technology initiative that required all students to possess lap top computers.

The warm welcome she received at the Fetzer Center on June 9, as she held audience for hundreds of campus constituents who queued up in long lines to meet her may perhaps have masked the daunting challenges she and her colleagues in education faced as Michigan again girded to make the best of bleak economic times.

Yet, if the past is any guide for the future some things seem certain: the University will expand and contract, programs will come and go in tune with evolving times, exuberant students will sometimes clash with overreactive police and demographics and economics will ebb and flow.

When Western was but a gleam in the eyes of legislators in 1903, Kalamazoo was home to a vast celery growing operation, the world's largest corset factory and sprawling industries producing stoves, buggies and windmills. It was papermaker to the nation. The Kalamazoo State Hospital was a small city in itself with more than 3,000 patients. One hundred years later, those and many other once thriving enterprises are gone or but a mere fragment of what they once were. But Western Michigan University—a vital pillar of the area's economy, world-class educational institution, with dynamic and breathtaking campuses—is here to stay. Happy Birthday Western, my alma mater.

Western's seventh president, Judith Bailey

Appendix
The Relative Value of the Dollar based on the Consumer Price Index

Year	Value	Year	Value	Year	Value
1903	$0.96	1942	$1.64	1981	$9.18
1904	$1.00	1943	$1.81	1982	$10.13
1905	$1.00	1944	$1.92	1983	$10.75
1906	$1.00	1945	$1.96	1984	$11.10
1907	$1.00	1946	$2.00	1985	$11.58
1908	$1.04	1947	$2.17	1986	$11.99
1909	$1.00	1948	$2.48	1987	$12.22
1910	$1.00	1949	$2.68	1988	$12.66
1911	$1.04	1950	$2.65	1989	$13.18
1912	$1.04	1951	$2.68	1990	$13.81
1913	$1.07	1952	$2.89	1991	$14.56
1914	$1.10	1953	$2.95	1992	$15.17
1915	$1.12	1954	$2.98	1993	$15.62
1916	$1.13	1955	$2.99	1994	$16.09
1917	$1.21	1956	$2.98	1995	$16.51
1918	$1.42	1957	$3.02	1996	$16.92
1919	$1.67	1958	$3.13	1997	$17.43
1920	$1.92	1959	$3.22	1998	$18.20
1921	$2.22	1960	$3.24	1999	$18.60
1922	$1.98	1961	$3.29	2000	$19.20
1923	$1.86	1962	$3.33	2001	$19.80
1924	$1.89	1963	$3.36	2002	$20.10
1925	$1.90	1964	$3.40		
1926	$1.94	1965	$3.45		
1927	$1.96	1966	$3.51		
1928	$1.93	1967	$3.61		
1929	$1.90	1968	$3.71		
1930	$1.90	1969	$3.87		
1931	$1.85	1970	$4.08		
1932	$1.69	1971	$4.32		
1933	$1.52	1972	$4.50		
1934	$1.44	1973	$4.65		
1935	$1.49	1974	$4.94		
1936	$1.53	1975	$5.48		
1937	$1.54	1976	$5.98		
1938	$1.56	1977	$6.33		
1939	$1.57	1978	$6.74		
1940	$1.54	1979	$7.25		
1941	$1.56	1980	$8.09		

To convert a cost to a specific year, multiply the cost by the given figure.

For example, a 1904 (BASE YEAR) dollar costs $1.00 times 20.10 (INDEX VALUE) for 2002 (COST YEAR) = $20.10

What you could buy in 1904 for $1.00 would cost $20.10 in 2002.

Sources Consulted

Allegan Gazette. September 5, 1903.

Allegan Press. September 4, 1903.

Annual Report of the Superintendent of Public Instruction... Michigan...Lansing, 1905, 1906, 1910.

Barron's Profiles of American Colleges. "An In-Depth Study. Western Michigan University." Woodbury, New York, 1974.

Betz, Robert and Betz, Diane Tanas. *Emergence of a University Department. Fifty Years of Counselor Education and Counseling Psychology at Western Michigan University*. Kalamazoo, 1986.

Bigelow, Martha. "Michigan, Pioneer in Education." *Michigan Historical Collections Bulletin No. 7*. June, 1955.

Brown and Gold Yearbooks. 1906-1985.

[Burnell, Shari L.]. *Racism and Discrimination. Are We to Blame?* [Kalamazoo, 1986].

Campus Life at Western State Normal School. Vol. 22. No. 2. Fall Quarter, 1926.

Case, Herbert S., ed. *The Official Who's Who in Michigan*. [Munising], 1936.

de Figueroa, Michelle Martin and Miquel A. Ramirez. *La Raza: The Legacy Continues. Hispanic Students at Western Michigan University*. Kalamazoo, [1994].

Dedicatory Program Walwood Hall. [Kalamazoo], 1938.

Dedication Ceremony for the New Building Housing Waldo Library and the University Computing Center. [Kalamazoo]. 1992.

Dedication of John P. Everett Office Tower and Paul Rood Hall for Mathematics and Physical Science. October 25, 1970.

Dedication of Lavina Spindler Hall for Women. [Kalamazoo], 1940.

Dedication The Liberal Arts Complex May 4, 1968. [Kalamazoo, 1968].

Definite Educational Advantages; Western State Teachers College. [Kalamazoo, 1930].

Denenfeld, Philip. "Western Michigan University. Faculty Participation in the Government of the University: The Faculty Senate." *AAUP Bulletin*. Winter 1966.

Dooley, Howard, "Chronology/History of International Education Programs at Western Michigan University." Unpublished Typescript. August 20, 2002.

Dunbar, Willis F. *Kalamazoo and How it Grew...and Grew*. Kalamazoo, 1969.

_____. *The Michigan Record in Higher Education*. Detroit. 1963.

_____. Revised edition by George May. *Michigan, A History of the Wolverine State*. Grand Rapids, [1980].

Education for Democracy Western Michigan College. [Kalamazoo, ca. 1946].

Educational Record. Vol. 75 No. 4 (Fall 1994) Special Issue: The GI Bill's Lasting Legacy.

Educators of Michigan. Biographical. Chicago, 1900.

Encore Magazine. 1972-2002.

Ferraro, Charlotte A., ed. *Alpha Beta Epsilon Alumni Sorority. "Fifty Years of Service" to Our Alma Mater*. Kalamazoo, 1988.

For Women Only. Western Michigan College. n.p., [ca. 1955].

"Forty-Five Years of Men's Faculty Science Club History From Its Beginning in 1918 to 1963." Unpublished Typescript.

Gagie, Martin R. Joe, ed. *Seventy-five Years of Growth: Western Michigan University, A Pictorial History*. [Kalamazoo, 1978].

Gekas, George. *The Life and Times of George Gipp*. South Bend, Indiana, [1987].

Gernant, Leonard. "Peace Corps and Teacher Education." Unpublished Paper Presented at American Association of Colleges for Teacher Education Meeting at Chicago on February 18, 1966.

Golden Anniversary Highlights Campus School of Western Michigan College. [Kalamazoo], 1953.

Sources Consulted

Graduate Education at Western Michigan University: A Report by the All-University Committee on Graduate and Professional Education. [Kalamazoo], 1976.

Grand Opening Festival University Auditorium 1968. [Kalamazoo], 1968.

Greenberg, Milton. *The GI Bill: The Law That Changed America.* [New York, 1997].

_____. "WMU's First Department Chairman," Unpublished Typescript. 2002.

Hilton, Miriam. *Northern Michigan University: The First 75 Years.* Marquette, [1975].

History of the Chemistry Department Western Michigan University. [Kalamazoo], 1968.

"History of the Physics Department." Unpublished Typescript. [1972].

Hollinshead, Ann. *Eminent and Interesting Albionians.* Vol 1. Albion, [1955].

International Teacher Development Program. [Kalamazoo, 1962].

International Teacher Development Program Coordinator's Report. [Kalamazoo], 1963.

Jones, James Earl and Penelope Niven. *Voices and Silences.* New York, 1993.

Kalamazoo Centennial Program and Historical Review 1829-1929. Kalamazoo, 1929.

Kalamazoo Gazette. 1903-2002.

The Kalamazoo Normal Record. Vol. 1, No. 1-Vol.7, No. 2. (May 1910-January 1917).

Kercher, Leonard. "Western in the Eye of the Great Depression." Unpublished Typescript. 1975.

Knauss, James O. *A History of Western State Teachers College, 1904-1929.* Kalamazoo, 1929.

_____. *The First Fifty Years: A History of Western Michigan College of Education, 1903-1953.* Kalamazoo, 1953.

Kohrman, George E. *Final Report Western Michigan University Aid Program Ibadan Technical College. Ibadan, Nigeria.* Kalamazoo, [1968].

Mallinson, Jacqueline, "Graduate Studies at Western Michigan University: An Informal, Behind-the-Scenes View of the Growth and Development of the Graduate College." Unpublished Typescript, 1995.

The Martin Luther King Students at Western Michigan University. [Kalamazoo, 1969].

Massie, Larry B. "The Acropolis of Kalamazoo: The Birth of a Campus" in *Michigan Memories.* Allegan, 1994.

_____. *Heritage of Helping: The First 75 Years of Western Michigan University's Department of Occupational Therapy.* Allegan, 1997.

_____. and Peter J. Schmitt. *Kalamazoo, The Place Behind the Product.* Sun Valley, California, 1998.

Michigan Biographies. 2 Vols. Lansing, 1924.

Michigan Official Directory and Legislative Manual. [Lansing], 1933.

Miller, James. *Report of the President. 1961-1965.*

_____. *Report of the President 1961-1973.*

_____. *Report of the President 1966-1967.*

_____. *Report of the President 1961-1970. Portrait of a Decade.*

Milton, Melissa S. "East Hall: Center of Collective Memory," History 519 Paper. 2000.

Musser, Necia. "Historical Survey" [of Western's Library]. Unpublished Typescript. 1981.

A Pageant of the Progress of Education in Michigan. [Kalamazoo]. 1919.

Portage Public Schools. 75 Years of Shaping the Future. [Kalamazoo, 1997].

The Power of Faith: A Pageant. [Kalamazoo], 1921.

Progress Report on the Bicentennial Celebration at Western Michigan University. June, 1975.

Program Western State Normal. January 27, 1914.

Psycho-Educational Clinic 1932-1957 "Twenty-Five Years." [Kalamazoo], 1957.

*Public Acts of the Legislature of the State of Michigan...*Lansing, 1907.

Reading Center and Clinic 1932-1982 Golden Anniversary. [Kalamazoo], 1982.

Redpath Chautauqua Program Deluxe Season 1916. n.p., 1916.

Report of the Ad Hoc Committee on Liberal Education at Western Michigan University. May 1978.

Russell, Robert R. "Some Recollections of Western Michigan University." Unpublished Typescript. 1976.

Sangren, Paul V. *1935-1960 at Western Michigan University.* [Kalamazoo, 1960].

[Schmitt, Peter]. *Preservation and Progress: Historic Homes of Western Michigan University.* [Kalamazoo], n.d.

Sebaly, Avis Leo. *Michigan State Normal Schools and Teachers Colleges in Transition, With Special Reference to Western Michigan College of Education.* Ph.D. Dissertation. University of Michigan. 1950.

Seibert, Eloise. "A Little History and Memories of W.M.U. Dames." Unpublished Typescript. 1975.

Seibert, Russell. "Recollections of WMU." Unpublished Typescript. 1974.

Shriekers Prevailable Western State Abnormal School. [Kalamazoo, 1925].

Silver Anniversary Souvenir Western State Teachers College. [Kalamazoo], 1929.

Slaughter, Thomas C. and edited by Harold L. Ray. *Go Broncos!: The History of Western Michigan University's Athletics. Men's Athletics Football and Basketball.* Volume One. [Kalamazoo, 1996].

_____. "Go Broncos!: The 20th Century History of Western Michigan University's Men's Athletics..." Volume Two. Unpublished Typescript. 2000.

Songs W. Kalamazoo, 1921.

Speakers Available. Western State Normal School Bulletin. Winter Quarter, 1925. Vol. 20, No. 3.

"Speech Pathology and Audiology at Western: A Brief History." Unpublished Typescript. [ca. 1976].

Stine, Leo C. *Western—A Twentieth Century University.* Kalamazoo, [1980].

Tripp, Beatrice, compiler. *Songs of Western State Teachers College.* [Cincinnati], 1930.

Twenty Years, 1904-1924. Western State Normal School. [Kalamazoo, 1924].

Valley, Richard B. "Thirty Years of Industry—University Cooperation An Overview." Unpublished Paper Presented at Nineteenth Annual Meeting of the Paper Technology Foundation, Inc. on October 26, 1978.

Vision Unfolding: A Pageant. [Kalamazoo, 1929].

Warren, Francis H., compiler. *Michigan Manual of Freedmen's Progress.* Detroit, 1915.

The Western Herald (title varies) 1916-2002.

Western Michigan College News Magazine. (title varies) 1942-2003

Western Michigan University [Kalamazoo, 1956].

Western Michigan University Affirmative Action Plan. [Kalamazoo], 1974.

Western Michigan University Dedicates Willis F. Dunbar Hall, Robert Friedmann Hall & James O. Knauss Hall. May 13, 1972.

Western Michigan University Role and Mission: A Response to the Recommendation of the Governor's Commission on Higher Education. April 1985.

The Westerner (title varies) 1980-2002.

Wheat Substitutes. Recipes Tested by Students of Cookery Department Western State Normal. Kalamazoo, [1919].

Women's Coalition. Report on Women's Programs at Western. September, 1985.

Your Future in Teaching. Western Michigan College. [Kalamazoo, 1955].

Oral History Sources

Beagle, Kenneth. Interviewed by James Louis. November 23, 1993.

Beam, Robert. Interviewed by Larry B. Massie. January 27, 2003.

Blair, Harold. Interviewed by James O. Knauss. March 18, 1958.

Botan, Carl. Interviewed by Thomas E. Coyne. January 17, 1990.

Brawer, Milt. Interviewed by Lewis Carlson. November 17, 1989.

Brisco, Tom. Interviewed by Lewis Carlson. 1989. (month and day not recorded).

Brown, Charles Bassett. Interviewed by Lewis Carlson. August 22, 1989.

Brown, William. Interviewed by James O. Knauss. April 24, 1958.

Burke, Richard. Interviewed by Lewis Carlson. December 7, 1993.

Carr, Thomas. Interviewed by Lewis Carlson. December 6, 1996.

Chandler, Robert. Interviewed by Lewis Carlson. n.d.

Chormann, Richard F. Interviewed by Karen L. Miller. December 13, 1993.

Combs, William. Interviewed by Lewis Carlson. November 17, 1989.

Coyne, Tom. Interviewed by Alan Brown. May 31, 1989 and June 2, 1989.

Denenfeld, Phil. Interviewed by Thomas Coyne. March 2, 1995.

Doolittle, Bill. Interviewed by Lewis Carlson. August 2, 1989.

Dunlap, Samuel. Interviewed by James O. Knauss. April 28, 1958.

Ensfield, Mary. Interviewed by Alan S. Brown. July 31, 1963.

Everett, John. Interviewed by James O. Knauss. n.d.

Franks, Julius. Interviewed by Lewis Carlson. August 10, 1989.

Gabier, Russell. Interviewed by Lewis Carlson. November 8, 1990.

Gernant, Len. Interviewed by Lewis Carlson. July 25, 1989.

Gill, John. Interviewed by James O. Knauss. May 7, 1958.

Haenicke, Diether. Interviewed by Larry B. Massie. January 31, 2003.

Harrison, Lucia. Interviewed by James O. Knauss. March 13, 1958.

Haworth, Garrard, Interviewed by Tom Coyne and Alan Brown. n.d.

Houston, Guy V. Interviewed by Nathaniel Jackson, Jr. October 23, 1971.

Jackson, Josephine Wing. Interviewed by James O. Knauss. February 26, 1958.

Jeremy, Jamie. Interviewed by Larry B. Massie. January 29, 2003.

Jesson, Lloyd. Interviewed by Alan S. Brown. February 20, 1964.

_____. Interviewed by Lewis Carlson. August 23, 1989.

Kohrman, George. Interviewed by Lynn Houghton. February 5, 1990.

Kowalski, William. Interviewed by Robert N. Karrer. December 9, 1993.

MacDonald, Cornelius B. Interviewed by Alan S. Brown. August 8, 1963.

_____. Interviewed by Lewis Carlson. September 4, 1989.

MacLeod, Garrard. Interviewed by John Provancher. March 8, 1990.

MacMillan, Margaret. Interviewed by James O. Knauss. April 9, 1958.

_____. Interviewed by Alfred Camp. May 29, 1968.

Mallard, Louis. Interviewed by Lewis Carlson. May 24, 1989.

McQuigg, Elizabeth. Unknown Interviewer. November 15, 1993.

Miller, Phil. Interviewed by Lewis Carlson. August 13, 1991.

Moore, Floyd. Interviewed by James O. Knauss. April 15, 1958.

Moskovis, Mike. Interviewed by Larry B. Massie. February 6, 2003.

Murchison, Ira. Interviewed by Lewis Carlson. December 1986.

Nobbs, Lucille. Interviewed by Charles Smith. May 20, 1965.

Norris, Budd. Interviewed by John R. G. Barrett, Jr. December 6, 1994.

Osborn, Dorothy. Interviewed by Alan S. Brown. October 27, 1989.

Phelan, Michael. Interviewed by Lewis Carlson. November 3, 1989.

Phillips, Claude. Interviewed by Lewis Carlson. May 4, 1990.

Polley, Mrs. Archibald. Interviewed by James O. Knauss. March, 1958.

Ralston, Ralph. Interviewed by Alan S. Brown. July 17, 1963.

Ray, Leroi. Interviewed by Tom Coyne. January 9, 1985.

Redmond, Leo. Interviewed by Lewis Carlson. May 6, 1989.

Robinson, William McKinley. Interviewed by Alan S. Brown. August 2, 1963.

_____. Interviewed by Alfred Camp. May 22, 1968.

Read, Herbert W. Interviewed by James O. Knauss. March 24, 1958.

Rossi, Francine Zeidman. Interviewed by Thomas E. Coyne. October 20, 1989.

Russell, Lawrence. Interviewed by Lewis Carlson. October 17, 1989.

St. John, Richard. Interviewed by Larry B. Massie January 22, 2003.

Saye, Hazel Cleveland. Interviewed by Kara L. Pedersen. November 20, 1993.

Schneider, Arnold. Interviewed by Thomas E. Coyne. October 12, 1990.

Scott, Don. Interviewed by Lewis Carlson. July 27, 1989.

Seibert, Russell. Interviewed by Alan Brown. November 23, 1988.

Sherwood, Marion. Interviewed by Alan S. Brown. July 24, 1963.

Smith, J. Towner. Interviewed by Lewis Carlson. May 5, 1989.

Stapler, Dorothy Waldo. Interviewed by Lewis Carlson. 1989.

Starring, Charles. Interviewed by Alan S. Brown. May 24, 1960.

Streidl, Jack and Phyllis. Interviewed by Abraham Hohnke. February 6, 1998.

Strong, Dana Sleeman. Interviewed by Russell Strong. March, 1963.

Tashjian, Janette Teitler. Interviewed by James O. Knauss. March 5, 1958.

Thompson, Don. Interviewed by Lewis Carlson. November 2, 1989.

Thurn, Elizabeth Waldo. Interviewed by Lewis Carlson. November 18, 1989.

Van Hoeven, Don. Interviewed by Thomas E. Coyne. September 25, 1991.

Virgo, Betty Jane Schultz. Interviewed by JoAnne Thomas. October 28, 1993 and November 24, 1993.

Waszkiewicz, Carol. Interviewed by Lewis Carlson. July 23, 1989.

Wolpe, Howard. Unknown interviewer. November 16, 1993.

Woods, John. Interviewed by Donna Rosu. December 2, 1993.

York, Zack. Interviewed by John Provancher. September 18, 1989.

_____. Interviewed by Robert C. Meyers. November 10, 1993.

Index

Index

Index

Index

Index

Index

Index

About the Author

Larry B. Massie is a Michigan product and proud of it. Born in Grand Rapids, he grew up in Allegan. Following a tour in Vietnam as a U.S. Army paratrooper, he worked as a telephone lineman, construction laborer, bartender and as a pickle meister before earning three degrees in history from Western Michigan University.

After honing his research skills during an eight year position with the WMU Archives and Regional History Collections, he launched a career as a self-employed Michigan historian in 1983.

Massie's activities include research and writing, old book appraisals, museum consultations and Michigan history storytelling. He travels both peninsulas of his beloved state to share his enthusiasm for Michigan's colorful heritage with conferences, school assemblies, libraries, community groups and other audiences.

Brown and Golden Memories is his seventeenth book about Michigan history.

An avid book collector, he lives with his wife and workmate Priscilla, their daughters Maureen and Autumn, as well as their 35,000 volume reference library, in a rambling old school house nestled in the Allegan State Forest.

Colophon

Printed by Rogers Printing Incorporated, Ravenna, Michigan
Paper is White Influence Matte 80 lb. text weight, 84 Brightness and 95 Opacity,
with a spot varnish on all photos
Jacket is White Mirage Gloss 80 lb. text weight, 88 Brightness and 95 Opacity,
with a film laminate

Principal type faces used were Adobe Garamond Regular, Adobe Garamond Italic,
Sanvito Roman ODS, TradeGothic Condensed, and TradeGothic Condensed Oblique

Hardware used was a Macintosh G4
Software used was Photoshop 7.0, Microsoft Word Office X for Mac and PageMaker 7.0

High resolution color photo scanning by Superior Imaging Services, Kalamazoo, Michigan
Black and white scans made by an Epson Expression 1640XL Scanner

Bound by Dekker Bookbinding, Grand Rapids, Michigan
88 lb. cover board
Cover fabric is Arrestox 39500 (v), French Roast
Cover printing is Lustrofoil #B-24 on front cover and spine only
End paper is 80 lb. Rainbow Oatmeal A, with an Antique finish
Head band is solid brown

Known contributing photographers:
Western Michigan University Archives and Regional History Collections
John Gilroy, John Lacko, Michael Lanka, Larry Massie, Mike McNun, Neil Rankin
and Norman Russell

Team Mandy!!
I will miss working
with you and plotting
at the front desk! I'm
glad we've gotten so close!
I love you baby girl! ♥ Kerstan

Mandy,
You always make
me smile/laugh. Thank
you for your impact on the
SAP office. Best of luck in
all you do!
~Jill~

Mandy Pandy!
It's been so wonderful
to work w/you and be
you friend ♡ I'm so glad
you will still be here next
year! Good luck!
♡ Liz T.

Good luck
I know you will
be doing great things
-Josh Kannert